To David,

without whom all this would not have been possible.

Richard. 9/1/96

Export Finance

Risks, Structures and Documentation

Export Finance

Risks, Structures and Documentation

Richard Willsher

MACMILLAN

First published in the United Kingdom by
MACMILLAN PRESS LTD, 1995
Companies and representatives throughout the world.

Distributed by Macmillan Direct
Brunel Road, Houndmills,
Basingstoke, Hants RG21 6XS.

ISBN 0-333-65391-2

A catalogue record for this book is available
from the British Library.

10   9   8   7   6   5   4   3   2   1
04   03   02   01   00   99   98   97   96   95

While every care has been taken in compiling the information
contained in this publication, the publishers and editors accept
no resposibilty for any errors or omissions.

Printed in Great Britain by Antony Rowe Ltd, Chippenham.

Contents

Introduction

World trade was expected to grow by US$755bn as a result of the Uruguay Round of negotiations of the General Agreement on Tariffs and Trade (GATT). During 1994 the worldwide trade in goods had already increased by 9 per cent. The World Trade Organisation which took over from GATT is continuing with the work of liberalising trade between nations, removing barriers to the free movement of goods.

Of course every piece of merchandise sold worldwide needs paying for just as it has since trade first began. Because trade is increasing at such a rate, issues of payment and credit finance are becoming the concern of many more people than before. They are important to everyone involved in international sales and cannot be considered an esoteric subject understood only by the trade financing departments of international banks.

The purpose of this book is to explain how payment is made and how credit is extended to buyers of goods. Part I, 'Structures, Instruments and Pricing', is designed to be a reference for the main techniques currently used. But they are only techniques and, like a pianist's scales, they are merely academic until harnessed for a greater purpose of performance.

'Performance' in the context of export financing means facilitating and perhaps funding a purchase and sale of goods. The commercial transaction and the payment mechanism bring with them a number of risk considerations which are examined in Part II, 'Analysing and Assessing Credit Risk'.

The effort to secure transactions against the risks involved means not only using the right structure but also employing formal written documentation as evidence that the transaction took place. Documentation becomes convenient for counterparties to handle as proxy for goods themselves. International trade and finance are heavy on paperwork – many would say dogged and weighed down by it. That is why the documentation is examined in detail in Part III.

Part IV is about harnessing some of the techniques, bearing in mind the specifics of the underlying commercial trade in goods and applying a hefty dose of common sense about what to do. The case studies are our pianist's dress rehearsal before a live performance.

I have added a glossary section because I often wish I could have had one to hand when I needed it myself. I'd like to think that when you reach for this section you'll find the word that's been bugging you, explained simply and adequately. However complete the glossary is I am bound to have missed something but I reckon to have captured the majority of commonly used jargon and technical terms.

This book is not intended as a legal reference work. There are learned legal tomes which fulfil that purpose and no shortage of lawyers who can opine on specific points of law and draw up documentation to support transactions. In my experience many transactions are carried our despite legal advice which is often based on caution, safety and precedent. But that is often why we use lawyers, to cover the downsides. If we want to develop international trade we have to make commercial judgements, ensure that we know our counterparties and get on with the deal.

In this book I am powerless to deal with the most important factor of all in the business of financing international trade, that is the specific circumstances of particular real life sales transactions. That's what it's all about in the end and we shouldn't forget that without two counterparties coming to terms over the exchange of goods for payment there'd be no international trade and we'd all be out of a job.

Part I
Structures, Instruments
and Pricing

1: Introduction

Text books tend to present the instruments and structures used to finance international trade as standard-sized building blocks. All you have to do is to choose the one whose measurements fit the gap, slot it into place and the job is done. But this is far from the case.

That is very much the way bankers would like it to be, however, because then it could be fitted into a bank's system and turned into a standardised, volume banking product. Consequently training given to trade finance bankers tends to run along the lines of: 'This is a letter of credit. This is how it works. Customers have to make their transactions fit this form or they won't get paid.'

This approach, however, only works up to a certain point. Large volumes of small transactions are now carried out electronically, in standard forms, but banks increasingly offer what they term 'structured trade finance'. This is a response to the fact that rarely do any two transactions turn out the same by the very nature of the differences in price, size of shipments, terms of supply contract and the many other ingredients which make up international sales of goods and services.

For this reason no trade finance transactions are quoted on bank dealing room screens and traded in the same way as financial instruments such as eurobonds, equities, eurocurrency deposits or foreign exchange. Even the market in forfaited paper, perhaps the nearest we get to securitised trade finance, is a long way from being standardised.

There are some common features to trade financing techniques, tools and documentation which will be explained below. However, these have been arrived at as much by trial and error as anything else and are still evolving. The important thing is to see them as clues to solving a puzzle.

Every requirement to finance international sales presents a new set of commercial realities and risks. The object of the exercise is to arrange transactions which will achieve the required goals as far as is reasonable while making, and not losing, money. The goal posts in the finance of international trade really are set that far apart.

2: Money Transfer

Transferring funds is not a financing structure in itself but it plays a part at one time or another in all international sales.

PAPER PAYMENT METHODS

Some smaller sums can be paid by cheque, although this does involve presenting the cheque at your own bank and waiting for it to clear, just as with a domestic cheque. The reason this method can be so long-winded and therefore should be avoided is that clearing the cheque means passing it back to the bank on which it is drawn, probably by post, and waiting for the sum to be credited to your bank from the paying bank.

A better way, if paper has to be used, is to use a banker's draft made payable to the exporter by the importer's bank. A draft can be requested from the payer's bank in local or foreign currency and debited to the payer's account. In this case it is usually drawn on a bank in the exporter's country. A payment, for example, in New Zealand Dollars, payable to a New Zealand exporter would be drawn on the New Zealand correspondent bank of the payer's bank. The draft can be paid into the exporter's bank account in the normal way.

ELECTRONIC PAYMENT

Electronic payments are preferable even for modest amounts. Many post offices are members of the international giro payment system which is cheap, efficient and easy to use. Larger amounts can also be transferred this way, although many firms choose to use their own banks for reasons of convenience.

The Payment Chain

The way banks transfer money internationally is remarkably efficient, considering the number of transactions which are carried out and the number of counterparties involved. The London foreign exchange market alone carries out US$1,000bn of business per day, much of which is settled through the interbank payment chain. This chain is best explained using a typical trade transaction:

Eastern Imports, an importer based in Hong Kong, is buying a shipment of machinery from Schmidt, a German company based in Cologne. Payment is being made on open account to Schmidt in US Dollars.

Eastern Imports instructs its local bank to make the payment, via its bank's New York correspondent to Schmidt's bank via its New York correspondent. The chain of payment will look like this:

Eastern Imports

♦

Eastern Imports' bank

♦

Eastern Imports' bank's New York correspondent bank

♦

Schmidt's bank's New York correspondent bank

♦

Schmidt's bank

♦

Schmidt

The bulk of world trade is denominated in US Dollars but we could have drawn a similar payment chain for payments in any of the major financing currencies such as Deutschmarks, Swiss Francs and so on. The correspondent/clearing bank will be based in the financial centre of the currency, for instance Frankfurt or Zurich. Larger international banks which are members of the clearing system in more than one centre will use their own branches or subsidiaries as their clearing bank.

Book entries and reconciliations
Despite there being so many counterparties in the payment chain it is not as cumbersome a system as it might at first appear, because most of the funds are not actually moving. In making payments in foreign currencies banks merely make book entries between themselves. A New York clearing or 'money centre' bank may make hundreds of payments to a particular

correspondent bank, say Schmidt's bank, every day. It may also receive hundreds of instructions from Schmidt's bank to make payments on their behalf. It makes sense if the two banks periodically settle any outstanding balance in favour of one or other.

Entries across this clearing account held with the correspondent, in our example based in New York, are reconciled regularly. Depending on the traffic of payments, reconciliations may be carried out more or less frequently. Because of the likely time difference between a bank and its correspondent, reconciliation may, for example, take place twice a day, at the close of business in each location. Thus Schmidt's bank may prefer to square its books at close of business in Germany and may well receive a computerised statement from New York overnight so as to be able to check its position at its opening next day.

To ensure that Schmidt's bank had sufficient funds to cover any payments it needed to make, the New York bank would probably allow it a certain overdraft limit so that an actual transfer of funds between the banks would be unlikely to be necessary. Likewise any credit balance would be held on deposit. The size of such bank-to-bank overdrafts is likely to be substantial, perhaps running to several millions or tens of millions of dollars. This is not surprising considering the amount of payments which may be involved within the space of a single day and that the account is reconciled twice each day.

Electronic instructions
The instructions by Schmidt's bank to its New York correspondent to make the book entries would typically be given by one of two methods, tested telex or SWIFT. The telex sent to the New York bank describes the payment to be made, the currency and amount, the beneficiary, the name of the bank or banks through which the payment is to be made, the value date of the payment and the details of the account to be debited. It also lists a code or 'test key' which takes the form of a series of numbers or letters known only to the two banks. The New York bank verifies the code, checking that it matches the payment's position in a sequence of similar instructions which have previously passed between the banks. If the 'test agrees' the payment is released.

Tested telex has been superseded to a large extent by the second and increasingly common method of making interbank payments, SWIFT. This is the acronym for Society for Worldwide Interbank Financial Telecommunications. As for tested telex instructions, full details of the transaction are listed and the payments secured through an authentication protocol which is electronically managed and therefore requires little human intervention.

Payments are now made quite rapidly. This is as a result of the sheer volume of international payments of this sort now flowing through international banks every day which need to be digested quickly. There has also been considerable demand from beneficiary banks, firms and individuals for more speedy crediting of proceeds to beneficiaries.

Same day value, spot and business days
Same day payment is now expected where it is denominated in US Dollars. In the example shown, the time zoning of the parties should make this easy to achieve as the instructing bank is located in an earlier time zone than both Schmidt and the New York clearing banks in the chain. Practically speaking the payment instructions and advices to beneficiary can be given by the close of business in Hong Kong well before opening in New York.

In most other major currencies two working days in the country of the currency concerned would be referred to as 'spot' – the quickest that can be arranged. Thus payments in Deutschmarks, Swiss Francs and so on would be made in two working days from the date payment instructions were issued.

It is important to check on public holidays however. Taking Easter 1994 as a case in point, a payment to be made spot in Sterling against instructions given in the morning of Thursday 31 March would not have been credited to the beneficiary's account until Tuesday 5 April. Both Friday and Monday were bank holidays in the market of the currency, London. This would have meant a minimum of five days' loss of value for the payee. Delay of a large payment could be costly. As a rough rule of thumb, interest on US$10,000,000 at 5 per cent per annum would cost US$1,388 per day or US$6,944 for the five days over Easter 1994.

Another potentially delaying factor to take into account is so-called 'cut-off time'. Banks may stipulate that only payment instructions received before the cut-off time can be processed during that working day. As a safe guide, instructions relating to payments to be actioned that day should be received by the bank before midday. Of course if the centre through which payment is to be made is already closed for that day it will slip into the next day.

The system for moving money electronically between the banks is on the whole astonishingly efficient, although errors and omissions do sometimes occur. The reason often lies in human interference and inefficiency. Wherever someone physically gives, receives or processes payment instructions there is scope for delay.

It may also be noted that it is not in a bank's interest to move money any quicker than it has to, especially if a beneficiary is inclined to accept the excuse that payments can be subject to 'administrative delays in the system'.

This is much less likely to wash when payments are between banks, especially where the funds are in settlement of trades such as foreign exchange, deposit or bond dealing. Where large sums of money are late paid, banks will usually correct the value date applied to the payments unless there is a dispute. The value date correction or backdating the date on which the funds could have been used is deemed to have the same effect as paying delay interest. Where delays are more than a day or two then delay interest is generally paid as value dating is usually impractical.

The following tips may help to tighten up on paying and receiving money:

- If paying, give instructions to bankers clearly in writing including the name, address and account number of the payee and the name, address and correspondent bank details of the payee's bank.
- A payee should make sure that the payer has his or her full details including account number, banker's name and address and the details of the banker's correspondent where the money is to be paid. The payee should ask the payer to fax a copy of the instruction given to the bank so that the payment can be tracked and any delay pinpointed. The payee should ask the bankers to advise him or her as soon as the payment arrives.
- Chase banks at either end of the payment chain by phone if you suspect they are not carrying out your payment instructions in a timely manner, making sure you have written confirmation from the payee that the payment has been made.
- Use SWIFT payment wherever possible.
- In advance of arranging payments check the public holidays and cut-off times in the places where the payment is coming from, going to and in the banking centre in the country of the currency where the payment is to be made (such as New York for US dollars). Try and time payments to allow for lost days.

3: Letters of Credit

Because letters of credit have evolved for the benefit of parties involved in international trade the following discussion centres upon their interests.

Of course a bank involved in letter of credit operations will have its own security interest and role to play. But very often banks seem to take the view that letters of credit have evolved for their benefit merely as a banking product, when clearly without the demands of a trade transaction they would not be required.

DEFINITION

In essence a letter of credit ('L/C' or 'credit') is a list of documents. Also known as a 'documentary credit' it represents a secure compromise between a buyer and seller of goods. A letter of credit gives the seller the security of knowing that payment can be collected once the goods have been shipped. It gives the buyer the comfort of knowing that shipment of the goods has taken place before payment has to be made.

Conventional L/Cs are written undertakings, issued by a bank at the request of a customer or a buyer of goods. The bank commits to pay up to a certain amount of money to a named beneficiary within a defined period of time if it receives the documents listed in the L/C, provided they conform to its terms.

There are several essential points to bear in mind:

- L/Cs are entirely separate from any underlying commercial agreement or contract of sale.
- Banks are not bound by any commercial contractual relationship or terms of the commercial contract to which the L/C relates.
- Banks handling L/Cs are concerned with documents not with goods.
- Documents presented under an L/C must be correct in every detail.

L/Cs should be issued subject to *Uniform Customs and Practice for Documentary Credits*. This is a booklet issued by the Paris-based International

9

Chamber of Commerce. The current version of it is ICC publication 500, 1993 revision in force as at 1 January 1994. It is generally referred to as 'UCP 500'. It sets out the ground rules governing the issuance and handling of L/Cs and related documentation and those contemplating becoming involved with L/Cs in any way should read it.

STRUCTURE AND TERMINOLOGY

The basic structure of an L/C is shown in Figure 3.1. There is a variety of names given to the parties to an L/C. The precise name will depend on their function in the purchase/sale, shipment/delivery, payment chain. These terms can sometimes be used interchangeably but not necessarily. The buyer *may* be the importer, applicant, account party and the consignee but each could be someone other than the buyer depending on the specifics of the transaction.

Having agreed the terms of sale for goods and that payment will be made by L/C the buyer applies to his or her bank to open or establish the L/C on the buyer's behalf in favour of the *beneficiary*, who will be the seller or the seller's nominated agent. The *opening bank* instructs either another of its branches or a different bank, usually located near to or in the same country as the beneficiary to *advise* the beneficiary that the L/C has been

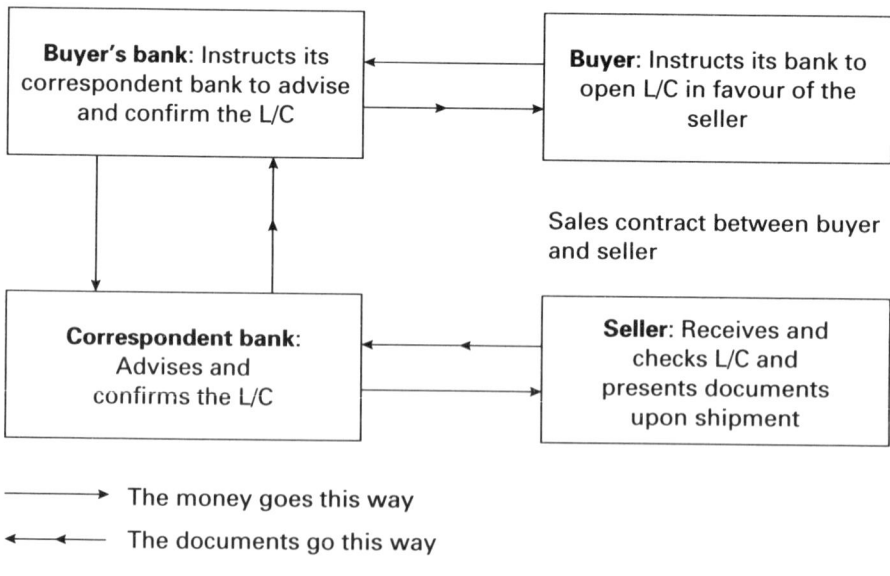

Figure 3.1: Basic structure of a letter of credit

Table 3.1: Terms used for parties to a letter of credit

Buyer	Buyer's bank	Buyer's correspondent bank	Seller
Importer: Not necessarily the buyer	*Opening bank:* (Not necessarily the buyer's regular bank)	*Advising bank:* If its function is to advise the beneficiary	*Exporter:* (Not necessarily the seller)
Applicant: The party who applies to the bank to open a letter of credit (not necessarily the buyer)		*Confirming bank:* If its function is to add its confirmation to the credit	*Beneficiary:* (Not necessarily the seller)
Account party: The party to whose account the funds will be debited by the opening bank (not necessarily the buyer)		*Negotiating bank:* If it examines documents and purchases drafts. Has recourse to the beneficiary unless confirming a credit on behalf of the opening bank	*Shipper:* (Not necessarily the seller)
Consignee: The party to whom the goods will be shipped (not necessarily the buyer)			*Consignee:* (Not necessarily the seller)

opened in his or her favour. The advising bank forwards a copy of the L/C to the beneficiary.

The *advising bank* may also *confirm* the L/C. This means that the documents will need to be presented at its counters and that it has been empowered by the opening bank to inspect the documents and make payment against the *drafts* or *bills of exchange* when they are presented to it. As an L/C is merely a list of documents, not a document of payment itself, a draft will usually be required to be presented under it, in order to facilitate payment, in addition to the other documents which it calls for. Where a bank adds its confirmation the L/C is said to be a *confirmed* L/C.

The beneficiary, stated on the L/C, will then read the L/C and ensure that he or she can meet its terms. We will look at the sort of issues which may arise at this stage a little later. An essential feature of the L/C is that it should specifically state that it is *irrevocable*. This means that it cannot be rescinded, cancelled or *revoked* by the buyer of the goods without the beneficiary agreeing to it. If it is not designated as 'irrevocable' then it is assumed to be so under UCP. If it is revocable the risk that the buyer may revoke it is a real one and the beneficiary should seriously consider whether the risk is worth accepting. In addition to revoking the L/C the buyer may also refuse to pay. The beneficiary should probably reject the L/C and insist on it being both irrevocable and confirmed. Indeed if a revocable credit is an acceptable risk to the seller one might well ask why have an L/C at all as the agreed method of payment because it gives little, if any, of the security which L/Cs are designed to provide. A *documentary collection* (see below) or *open account* may be more appropriate if the beneficiary is content with the risk of the buyer not paying under a revocable instrument.

BENEFICIARY REVIEW OF CREDIT DETAILS

On being advised of the confirmed, irrevocable L/C drawn under UCP 500 and opened in favour of the beneficiary, he or she needs to review it immediately and make sure that its terms can be met. These are points to look out for:

1   *Is payment under the credit to be made when and where agreed?*
    Payment will be due on acceptance of the documents by the confirming bank if payment is to be made *at sight*. Payments under credits can also be made at a later date against accepted documents under a *usance* L/C. In this case the credit would stipulate when payment would be made. The beneficiary needs to check that the date of payment is that agreed with the payer.

    Likewise the place of payment needs to be as agreed. Most desirable from the beneficiary's point of view is that funds will be payable in the beneficiary's own country, at his or her own bank. If it is anywhere else the beneficiary should consider whether this is desirable and acceptable.

2   *Is the payment to be made under the credit correct in size and currency?*
    The amount for which the credit is opened should allow for the full agreed price. This might for example include insurance and freight under

a CIF delivery contract. Does the amount allow for contractually agreed price increases or tolerances in the amount of goods shipped. The beneficiary should ensure that all amounts due to be paid will be covered by the credit.

3   *Are the terms of shipment mentioned in the credit those which have been agreed?*
    These include FOB, CIF and so on. (See shipping terms in Part II.)

4   *Are the names and addresses of both the beneficiary and buyer correct?*
    When submitting an invoice as part of the required documentation the beneficiary's details will need to match those given for the beneficiary on the credit itself. A bank may refuse to make payment if they do not.
    If the buyer's name is incorrect it is important the name appears consistently on all documents submitted by the beneficiary. This will be necessary to ensure payment. It may, however, create technical difficulties to the buyer when goods are collected or documents taken up. It is advisable to have the matter clarified straight away.

5   *Are partial shipments permitted?*
    If the terms of the sales contract permit or require shipment to be made by stages then this should be allowed for in the credit. Under UCP 500 Article 40a they are permitted unless the credit states otherwise.

6   *Can the beneficiary present documents within the expiry date of the credit?*
    This may mean that the beneficiary has to have completed all production, packing, delivery and document collation tasks to be able to present documents arising from those activities by the expiry date. In any case chamber of commerce documents and inspection certificates need to be presented within 21 days of the shipment date shown on the shipping documents. If this is likely to be impossible then the credit should be drawn to allow a longer period for documents to be presented.

7   *Where goods are described in the credit are they described accurately and are the details correct?*
    Again details of goods and packing mentioned in the credit will need to be matched by details given in documents presented. Therefore the beneficiary needs to ensure that this will be achievable.

8   *Can the documents called for in the credit be provided?*
    The beneficiary should not agree to present a document which may be impossible to obtain. Likewise if the credit calls for originals rather than

13

copies or specifically excludes or includes copies, faxes or telex messages the beneficiary needs to be confident of being able to present them in accordance with the credit.

9 *If insurance cover and an insurance certificate are required can these be obtained for the risks stipulated in the credit?*
If for example the shipment route were to be to or through or over a war zone, insurance cover for war risks would be difficult to arrange.

10 *Are charges and commissions listed as payable as agreed?*
The opener or the beneficiary will pay the banks' commissions for operating the credit. Sometimes these are shared, sometimes one or other party pays them all. These should be agreed prior to opening the credit. (See section below on Reward.)

11 *Are there any other aspects of the credit which are mistaken, unclear or in any way at odds with the beneficiary's understanding of the transaction and related payment arrangements?*
A credit should be amended, corrected or clarified at an early stage either by direct discussion between the buyer and the beneficiary or by communicating through the chain of banks which are party to it. It is common for amendments to be made and for difficulties to be ironed out early on. The result is a formal amendment to the credit issued by the opening bank and advised through the advising bank. The amendment then becomes an integral part of the original credit which all parties have agreed to and which is correctly documented.

An agreement between counterparties over the telephone or by fax to accept a document which differs in any way from the terms of the credit should not to be relied upon. Should the person with whom the beneficiary agreed the change leave the buyer's firm there may be no formal record of what was said. More importantly, unless the bank handling the documents has been specifically authorised to accept changes to the documentary requirements stipulated in the credit it *must not* accept them. Were a bank to do otherwise it would weaken the security which parties seek when using the banking chain to process documents and payments through the use of letters of credit.

PRESENTATION OF DOCUMENTS

Once the beneficiary has reviewed the credit, arranged for it to be amended if necessary and is confident that its terms can be met he or she is in a position to accept it. The next stage will be the presentation of documents.

It is unlikely that any two letters of credit will be the same. Documents are likely to differ depending on the goods, destination, transport, inspection arrangements and so forth. Part III of this book gives examples of some of the documents which are typically called for, but there are some important considerations which will apply to just about every documentary presentation:

1   *The documents presented must match the credit*
    While this may appear to be obvious it remains the case that more than 50 per cent of documents presented under L/Cs are *discrepant*, that is, do not match the terms of the credit.

2   *Under UCP a bank is obliged to accept documents which appear on their face to match the terms of the credit*
    Documents should also be consistent one with another. If they are not consistent they will be treated by the bank as not being in accordance with the credit.

3   *Cross check documents against one another*
    Invoices, bills of lading, packing lists and so on should show similar details such as descriptions, weights, measures and number of packages. The job of the bank inspecting the documents is to pick up any discrepancies of this sort.

4   *Double and triple check all documents thoroughly before presenting them to the bank*
    In many organisations a junior person is given the task of collating and checking documents. As failure to get it right will cost the company money it is reasonable and prudent that a junior's work is double checked by an experienced person who points out mistakes or oversights so that the junior can learn about what is quite a complex set of requirements.

5   *Assemble the documents in the right number*
    Some credits require extraordinary numbers of documents or copies of them. This usually has to do with local customs or other government requirements in the importer's country. If for example six copies of a 50-page packing list are required then anything less will not be accepted

15

by the bank even if, to the beneficiary, this seems unduly bureaucratic. The importer may have no choice in the matter and the bank *must* adhere to its instructions. If originals, copies, confirmed copies or authenticated copies are called for, again the beneficiary must ensure that the precise requirements are met.

6   *The particular definitions of each document must be met*
    If the credit specifies that invoices must be made out to include partic-
    ular information this must be done even if it differs from the way the
    beneficiary normally raises invoices.

7   *The beneficiary must present documents within the expiry date of the*
    credit and within the 21 days from shipment normally allowed for
    transport documents, unless the credit allows otherwise
    If documents arrive late they will be declared *stale* and the bank must
    not accept them unless it is permitted to do so under the credit – and
    it would be unusual if it were.

DISCREPANCIES

Even the most careful collation and double checking cannot eradicate all discrepancies. The inexperienced beneficiary does admittedly have a disadvantage in presenting documents to banks whose business is handling huge volumes of documents.

The bank may have dozens of eagle-eyed staff waiting to pounce on every minor error or omission. The beneficiary sometimes needs to have patience – this is after all what the documentary credit clerk is paid to do. If he or she gets it wrong the bank may face at best a dispute over why it paid out against discrepant documents or at worst a lengthy and expensive legal wrangle which results in a loss for the bank.

A discrepancy in presented documents is not the end of the world, however. There are several remedies:

1   *Correcting documents*
    The documents can be retrieved, the alterations made and re-presented
    to the bank. This needs to be done within the expiry date of the credit
    and within the transport document time.

2   *'Permission to pay'*
    The bank inspecting the documents can contact the opening bank or
    branch or the beneficiary himself for permission to pay despite the
    discrepancy. This is usually done telegraphically, perhaps by telex or

authenticated SWIFT message (see Chapter 2). It may, however, take time and the beneficiary is in the hands of the customer.

It is in the customer's interest to delay because as the goods are being transported he or she can gain a few extra days credit before paying. Sooner or later the importer is likely to need the shipping documents to collect the goods. As these will be with the confirming bank, the process cannot be delayed indefinitely. In some territories it is not unknown for goods to be spirited into to the importer's possession even without, say, bills of lading (although it must be said that it is uncommon).

3   *Payment under indemnity*
Payment may be made by the bank if it is prepared to accept a written indemnity from the beneficiary that the funds will be repaid should the documents not eventually be taken up by the customer. This will depend on the beneficiary's credibility with the bank and whether the nature of the documentary discrepancy is so minor as to pose little risk of documents not being taken up. The beneficiary does, however, have a contingent risk of having to repay the funds until the bank finally releases the indemnity.

4   *Payment under reserve*
Similar in effect to payment under indemnity, the bank will make payment to the beneficiary with the reservation that it must be repaid if the documents are not taken up. Interest will be charged by the bank, if the money is clawed back, for the period during which the beneficiary had use of it. Payment under reserve has the advantage of not requiring a written indemnity to be issued.

5   *Documents on collection*
The discrepant shipping documents are sent to the issuing bank with the instruction that they will only be released to the importer against payment. The importer may have the opportunity to inspect the documents at the issuing bank's premises and as for 'telex to pay' above, he or she can delay until the last moment before paying.

But, worse, the importer can reject the documents. As the beneficiary has not conformed to the terms of the credit the option is entirely with the importer as to whether the documents are accepted. If the goods are no longer wanted the documents may be rejected. Although it is more likely that the importer will need the documents to take delivery of the goods.

The beneficiary will still have control over the goods. He or she will not have been paid, however, and by the time payment comes through quite some time may have elapsed since shipment.

PAYMENT INSTRUCTIONS

Assuming that documents do conform to the credit's terms, payment should then be forthcoming. As mentioned above, payment under a sight letter of credit would be made once the documents had been accepted by the bank. Under a usance or term credit payment is made either on a fixed date or a date so many days after the date of shipment as evidenced by the shipping documents. Clear payment instructions should be given in either case.

As far as the beneficiary is concerned it is important that the bank knows to which account at which bank to pay the proceeds and in which currency. Failure to provide this information will inevitably result in delayed payment.

For a bank confirming a letter of credit and taking on the responsibility of paying the beneficiary against correct presentation of documents it is important to know how to *reimburse* itself. Thus if a bank in Hong Kong opens the credit in favour of a German exporter denominated in US dollars and confirmed by a German bank, instructions received by the German bank will be to reimburse itself from the Hong Kong bank's US dollar clearing account with a bank in New York. The German bank will then request the funds to be paid to its US dollar clearing account. Such reimbursement instructions will form an integral part of the opening bank's instructions to the confirming bank when the credit is established.

PARTIAL DRAWINGS

Where a number of shipments are contemplated in the context of one order, partial shipments and partial drawings may be permitted under the credit. Under UCP they are allowed unless expressly prohibited in the credit.

An example of where partial shipments and drawings would be useful is where a contract to supply, say, US$100 million worth of crude oil has been negotiated and a credit for that amount established. If a typical tanker shipment is valued at around US$20 million then clearly several shipments would be needed to fulfil the contract. As these would be shipped in separate vessels, separate sets of shipping documents would have to be presented. It may be that the supply is due to take place over several weeks or months and therefore partial shipments/drawings would be allowable under the credit.

Partial drawings under a credit must be made within the expiry date for the credit and the shipping documents' time limit. They must not exceed the total value of the credit. It is conventional for partial drawings to be noted on the back of the original L/C to record how much of the credit has been drawn and that the total has not been reached. Whether written on the credit document itself or not, banks, suppliers and buyers should all keep records of how much of the credit has been drawn and when.

BANK'S SECURITY ARRANGEMENTS

The establishment of a credit on behalf of a buyer or account party hinges initially on the opening bank's view that it is prepared to pay on the account party's behalf when documents are presented. This view will be based on a credit risk judgement made by the opening bank.

Corporate Risk

The opening bank may take the view that the importer or the customer on whose behalf the credit is being established is of sufficient strength to make payment to the bank when required. If the customer has a good track record with the opening bank the chances are that the bank will continue to be prepared to issue credits on its corporate name.

Collateralised L/Cs

Where a customer is not of sufficient standing the opening bank will seek other security. One obvious way would be to take a pledge over the account party's assets, real property, stock in warehouse and so on. Another would be to take security over the goods being financed. In this case the goods may be consigned to the bank which will only release documents (and therefore the goods themselves) to the customer against payment.

Avoiding Risk Aggregation

Where a large corporate customer has a number of different strands to its relationship with a bank, the bank may establish an overall limit to the customer to cover all exposures. There may be short-term overdraft arrangements, foreign exchange settlement facilities, medium-term lending and letter of credit issuance facilities. In a large bank these different exposures may be utilised by different parts of the organisation such as corporate lending, foreign exchange and trade finance departments.

19

To avoid over-exposure to one risk the bank will wish to establish strict control and monitoring of its various exposures. These will need to link with centralised credit review procedures to ensure that if the credit standing of the customer weakens the risk is managed prudently and if it improves more, new business can be developed with the customer.

Term Exposure to Account Parties

L/Cs may be established many months before shipments are made. In addition, especially under usance L/Cs, drawings may, perhaps, not be made until a long time after shipment. Meanwhile the exposure of the issuing bank to the account party on whose behalf the credit has been issued continues and, from beginning to end, this can be a long time. The issuing bank needs to take into account this time consideration, bearing in mind that the credit is likely to be *irrevocable*.

Inter-bank Risk

A *confirming bank* will also have to arrive at a credit risk judgement about its exposure to the issuing bank. Its confirmation and agreement to inspect documents and make payment carries with it the risk that the issuing bank may not reimburse. Most international banks establish limits to cover these and other risks to banks, such as foreign exchange and deposit dealing risks and payment settlement risks.

The sensitivity of these risk limits has become more significant as accidents have occurred. In practice formal reschedulings of commercial bank debt where a debt crisis has occurred usually exclude short-term trade-related exposures. This is one reason why banks have regarded trade finance as inherently safer to engage in. Practically speaking, if trade debts were rescheduled or defaulted upon the support from international banks for imports would quickly evaporate. However, banks have sharpened their bank line review procedures following the collapse of the Bank for Credit and Commerce International, the disappearance of Barings, problems with Iranian trade-related credits and the collapse of various banks in Latin America, Africa and the countries of the former eastern bloc. Establishing and reviewing lines can be difficult, especially considering the length of exposures where usance credits are involved. If there is an intervening political risk to take into consideration then the job is even more difficult (see Part II).

Use of Capital – Confirming Bank

It is important for all those involved with trade finance services to be aware of the risks and judgements which form the basis for L/C issuance and confirmation. They should also bear in mind the capital employed in taking the risks of running a book of L/C assets.

The rules governing capital adequacy and apportionment of capital to particular classes of risk asset are constantly evolving. Central banks will normally follow the Bank for International Settlements' guidelines as to how to regulate their national banks. Letters of credit which are short-term, self-liquidating trade-related items, collateralised by underlying shipments, currently comport a 20 per cent risk asset weighting. Otherwise they are 100 per cent weighted.

In addition to risk/asset weighting central banks may require country risk guidelines to be adhered to. This can mean that provisions may need to be made against exposures to some countries. This will differ from country to country and allows for the prospect of default on due date. The effect of this is that there are many banks which are keen to work with short-term L/Cs with low risk countries but once the term extends beyond one year, or the risk is on difficult markets, the number of interested banks decreases significantly.

Use of Capital – Issuing Bank

The issuing bank's capital requirement will depend on the degree of security provided by the customer to the bank to underpin the credit issued on its behalf. In the best case, there may be a zero weighting if the credit is collateralised against cash held by the bank. In the worst case 100 per cent capital to loan ratio may be required if the exposure is purely to the corporate risk of the customer. The important considerations are:

- what is the risk/security position?
- what are the local risk-asset weighting requirements for the class of risk?
- is the return on capital and on the assets adequate to compensate for the risk taken?

Reward

Having considered the risks involved in L/C issuance and confirmation and the use of capital employed, pricing has to be set. There are several types of commission which trade financing banks charge for handling letters of

Table 3.2: Commissions and interest for handling letters of credit

Name of commission	Description
Opening or issuing commission	Charged by the opening bank for opening the credit. Likely to be calculated as a fixed percentage on the value of the credit. There is likely to be a minimum commission.
Advising commission	Charged by the advising bank for advising the beneficiary of receipt of the credit. Minimum charge likely.
Confirmation commission	Charged by the confirming bank for adding its confirmation to the credit.
Commitment commission	Charged on a time basis by the opening bank for its commitment to issue the credit on the opener's behalf.
Payment commission	Charged by the paying bank for making the payment to the beneficiary. Minimum charge likely.

credit. These can vary widely depending on the risks involved and therefore specific pricing levels are not listed. A similar commission may also be called by a different name by different banks. The party responsible for paying the fees will be defined in the credit opening form addressed to the opening bank. Typical wordings can be:

- 'all charges for the account of the beneficiary';
- 'all charges for the account of the opener';
- 'all charges outside of the beneficiary's country are for the account of the opener'; or
- 'all charges outside of the opener's country are for the account of the beneficiary'.

STRUCTURES INVOLVING LETTERS OF CREDIT

The basic L/C instrument and its operation have been described above. L/Cs are, however, used in a number of structures which are based on similar principals and which have evolved for certain specific purposes.

Confirmation of Payment

A simplified form of L/C arrangement can be used for making payments where the payee is seeking additional assurance that they will be forthcoming when due. Examples of such payments might be monthly retainers, insurance premiums and stage payments for work completed. The L/C would merely require presentation to a nominated bank of the supplier's invoice, progress certificate or a straightforward request for money made by letter, fax or telex.

The bank's instruction from the payer would be to debit the funds to the payer's account upon receipt of the specified document. Sometimes funds will actually be deposited in an *escrow account* where funds are held for the specific purpose of making such payments. The 'beneficiary' will have the security of knowing that the funds have been deposited with a bank for the purpose intended and can be drawn once they are due. The payer knows that the funds will only be paid out once certain proof that they are payable is presented.

There can be any number of ways in which such a mechanism can be put to use. To the extent that payment is triggered by presentation of documents to a bank it can still be regarded as a rudimentary form of documentary credit which uses the banking system to provide security to the counterparties.

Standby Letters of Credit

The term 'standby L/C' is used to cover a variety of instruments, some of which are effectively guarantees and others more like the conventional L/Cs explained above. The 'standby' aspect implies a contingency that something has to have happened – or in the case of payment guarantees, failed to happen – before a drawing can be made.

Standby L/Cs are a form of demand guarantee and therefore reference should be made to the International Chamber of Commerce booklet *ICC Uniform Rules for Contract Guarantees* (ICC Publication no. 325) before agreeing to the terms of a guarantee or issuing one.

Performance bonds
In the United States standbys may take the form of financial guarantees. Indeed they evolved in the US to replace *performance bonds*, although they have a wide variety of applications these days. Performance bonds will not be dealt with here because this area is not necessarily concerned with financing international trade. It is also fraught with complications and on some occasions the guarantee which appears to be on offer is not all it seems.

23

Standby L/C obligations are widely offered to and by banks and other financial institutions. They should be carefully checked out and legal opinions called for if the terms under which they can be exercised are unclear or are effective in a foreign jurisdiction.

Trade related standbys

Where a standby relates to a specific trade transaction it is often a secondary guarantee to underpin particular payment obligations. This could, for example, apply in the context of a forfaiting transaction. If the primary obligor fails to pay, the payee can draw under the standby if it can meet its documentary requirements.

As a guarantee the standby should be subject to the following considerations:

- The issuer of the standby should be creditworthy.
- The standby should include clear reference to the underlying trade transaction and the guarantee it provides should be unequivocal.
- Express declarations:

  - The guarantee offered by the standby must be irrevocable otherwise it could be unilaterally cancelled by the issuer.
  - It should also be unconditional beyond its basic documentary conditions.
  - If it is intended to support a transaction which can be sold or traded on, such as in a forfaiting transaction, then its obligation to pay should be transferable by endorsement.

- The total guaranteed amount should be stated. In order that the beneficiary knows the full scope of the guarantee offered, the standby should state the total sum which can be drawn.
- Amounts and maturities of individual obligations:

  - If it is intended to cover principal and interest then the amounts covered should be itemised or able to be calculated by reference to its terms. Interest covered should be either listed as exact amounts due or calculated by reference to a given interest rate or margin over a funding rate.
  - Particularly where a series of future payments are guaranteed the actual sums due should be listed alongside their respective due dates.

- The period during which drawings can be made under the standby should begin well before the first payment which it guarantees and extend well beyond the last. This needs to tie in with the practicality of making a drawing. If, for example, documents need to be presented under the standby a certain number of days after a default by a primary obligor, enough time must be allowed for the documents to be collated and presented.

- For the beneficiary of the standby the circumstances in which drawings can be made should preferably be as user-friendly as possible, such as in the beneficiary's own town or City, at the counters of his or her own bank, and within a long time frame.
- The signatories to the standby on behalf of the issuer should be empowered to give such an undertaking. This should be evidenced by a board resolution of the issuer, by power of attorney or by a standard signature protocol. Signatures should be in right number and valid at the time the undertaking is given. Satisfactory evidence should be sought by the beneficiary before the standby is accepted.

It goes without saying that if a beneficiary accepts a standby he or she should be wholly confident of being able to meet its terms if and when it becomes necessary to make a drawing.

From the guarantor bank's point of view recourse will normally be taken to the party on whose behalf the standby is being issued. This can take the form of a counter-indemnity or other security such as mortgage over property.

Reducing balance guarantee
The obligation of the issuing bank will probably continue throughout the full term of the transaction guaranteed, which could be several years in the case of medium-term standby. The terms of the guarantee offered may be

Table 3.3: Reducing balance guarantee schedule

	Due date	Principal due	*Interest due @ 10%	Total due	*Guarantee fee @ 1%
1	01/01/96	100,000.00	50,000.00	150,000.00	6,375.00
2	01/07/96	100,000.00	45,000.00	145,000.00	5,625.00
3	01/01/97	100,000.00	40,000.00	140,000.00	4,900.00
4	01/07/97	100,000.00	35,000.00	135,000.00	4,200.00
5	01/01/98	100,000.00	30,000.00	130,000.00	3,525.00
6	01/07/98	100,000.00	25,000.00	125,000.00	2,875.00
7	01/01/99	100,000.00	20,000.00	120,000.00	2,250.00
8	01/07/99	100,000.00	15,000.00	115,000.00	1,650.00
9	01/01/2000	100,000.00	10,000.00	110,000.00	1,075.00
10	01/07/2000	100,000.00	5,000.00	105,000.00	525.00
Total		1,000,000.00	275,000.00	1,275,000.00	33,000.00

* For the purposes of illustration it has been assumed that there are 180 days between each of the due dates.

such that a single payment or a series of such payments can be claimed from the standby. Pricing would therefore be calculated with reference to the nature of the outstanding guaranteed obligations.

Table 3.3 sets out a schedule of payments covered under a reducing balance guarantee standby. The amounts covered represent principal and interest due over five years. For the purposes of illustration the fee payable to the bank by the party on whose behalf it is issued is 1 per cent per annum. It is calculated on the total outstanding unexpired balance of the guarantee.

Exactly when the bank will collect its guarantee fee will be agreed between the bank and its customer. Conventionally the fee will be taken up front, at the signature of the guarantee or periodically throughout its life.

Balance sheet considerations
As far as the issuing bank's balance sheet is concerned an outstanding, unexpired standby represents a contingent liability. It should be accounted for accordingly, in line with local accounting practice and bank regulations in force in the territory of the bank's domicile.

The extent to which capital will need to be set against this contingent risk will also be determined by the degree of security held by the bank. Thus a cash collateralised standby would consume no capital while one based purely on the corporate risk of the customer would be likely to require full capital weighting.

Pre-financing, green clause and red clause letters of credit

The essence of pre-financing or pre-export financing is that funds are made available in advance of goods and cargoes being shipped. This gives the exporter a cashflow advantage in manufacturing or processing goods or otherwise financing the business.

A bank advances the funds to the exporter rather in the manner of a secured loan but the related security package conventionally includes an L/C. There are many forms which this can take, depending on the trade in question and the available security. The following case study illustrates a possible structure:

Acme Metals, a firm producing steel billets, used a pre-export finance facility from Export Bank to raise money using both a letter of credit from its customer XYZ in Japan and billets held in storage pending shipment.

Delivery is due to take place in three months' time, FOB at a port near to Acme's works. The billets will in fact take only one month to produce and will be held in a warehouse until delivery.

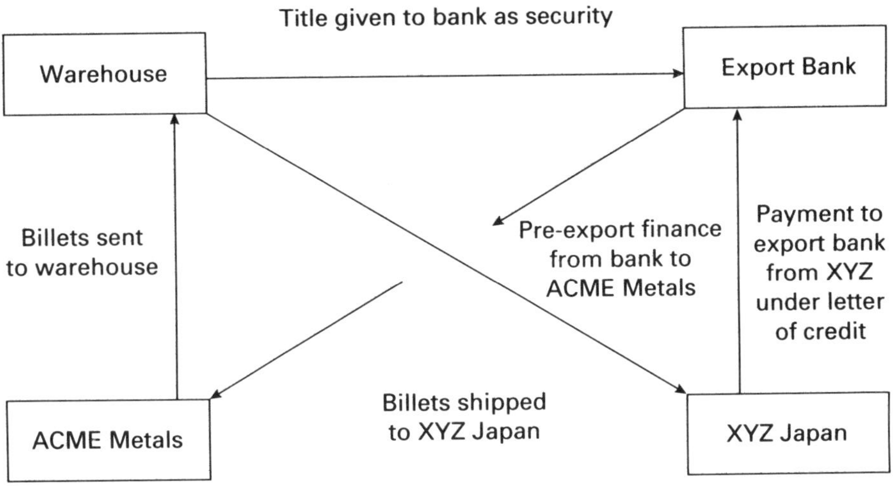

Figure 3.2: A pre-export finance structure

Export Bank is holding a confirmed irrevocable sight L/C issued by XYZ in favour of Acme under which payment will be made straight away upon shipment following presentation of complying documents.

Acme agrees an arrangement with Export Bank that it:

1 signs over ('endorses') to the bank its rights to payment under the L/C when it is due to be made in three months' time, upon shipment;
2 gives an undertaking to the bank that it will deliver the billets to the warehouse in one month as agreed and will provide documentation to the bank evidencing delivery, such as warehouse receipts;
3 provides the bank with security over the billets while held in the warehouse pending shipment;
4 insures the billets while they are warehoused and assigns the proceeds of any claim paid under the insurance policy to the bank as 'loss payee'. In the event of a claim the bank will receive a sum equal to or greater than the money it will advance to Acme plus interest on the advance;
5 gives an undertaking to the bank that it will repay the advance, if for any reason the billets are not placed in the warehouse and/or sale of the billets does not go ahead, plus any interest which accrues while Acme has the use of the advanced funds;
6 Acme is being asked to give the bank security over its new production equipment to protect the bank if Acme fails to pay back the advance to the bank. But Acme resists this.

In consideration of this package of documentation and security the bank is prepared to advance 85 per cent of the value of the billets to Acme for the three months up until shipment takes place.

This is a rough outline of how the deal might work. It is usually the case that the bank will only advance a proportion of the value of a pre-export financed cargo to ensure that it is covered in the event of complete collapse of the transaction. Then it would look to sell the cargo to recover its advance.

Pre-export financing is often used to provide funding to traders with high turnover levels but small balance sheets to assist them to increase their ability to trade more goods. It is commonly employed in respect of traded commodities where the world market value can be verified, such as oil and soft commodities. By reference to these values a bank can easily calculate the value of its security.

Acme's transaction had a happy ending. Everything went according to plan:

- Export Bank advanced 85 per cent of the value of the billets to Acme.
- The billets were manufactured and delivered to the warehouse within one month.
- All security documentation was passed to the bank.
- The billets were shipped.
- Acme presented shipping documents to the bank.
- The bank was repaid together with interest from the proceeds of the L/C.
- Remaining funds paid under the L/C were paid to Acme.

In another variation of pre-export financing permission to advance funds under the L/C can be given by the opener of the L/C. In our example this would be given to Export Bank by XYZ in respect of the L/C which it opens in Acme's favour. In other words the buyer of the goods is taking a view on the creditworthiness and performance capability of the supplier.

Where the L/C incorporates language allowing this to happen it is called a *red clause* credit because the instruction was traditionally written in red to draw the attention of the confirming bank (Export Bank in this case). The confirming bank is advised that it may advance the funds to the exporter up to the full amount of the credit against the opening bank's undertaking that it will reimburse it if documents are not subsequently presented by the exporter. The exporter will pay interest on the advance at local rates.

Within the definition of red clause L/Cs there are two variations. An unsecured or clean red clause L/C requires an undertaking to be issued by the exporter that he or she will use the funds advanced for a defined purpose. Secondly, a secured or documentary red clause L/C will provide for the advance to be made to the exporter against warehouse receipts or other similar documents. The exporter retains title, however, in order to enable the goods to be shipped. Once shipment has been made the proceeds of the L/C are used to repay the pre-shipment advance as in our case study above.

A further variation is the *green clause* L/C. The basic structure remains the same as for a red clause but goods in storage are held in the name of the issuing bank as an additional security feature.

Back-to-back letters of credit

Where someone (a 'merchant') is buying goods from a supplier and selling them on, simultaneously, to customers at a higher price, a back-to-back L/C can be used.

The ultimate buyer opens an L/C in favour of the merchant while the merchant in turn opens an L/C in favour of the supplier. The effect is that both payments, from the ultimate buyer to the merchant and from the merchant to the supplier, can be made securely for both beneficiaries. As both payments involve the same goods some of the same documentation can be used to present under both of these credits. Banks handling such arrangements will insist that both credits are opened through them so that they have control of the issuance and confirmation of both credits. They will also have control of the documentary chain once shipment has been made.

The supplier will make shipment and present documents ('documents 1' in Figure 3.3) under the L/C issued by the merchant in order to claim the funds. In all probability the documents will be presented at the counters of the branch of the bank in the exporter's territory.

Once the documents have been found to be in order the bank will pay out in the normal way, confident that it has the shipping documents in its hands, that they are in order and that a larger amount will be payable by the ultimate buyer of the goods. The bank will already have satisfied itself that the credit risk on the ultimate buyer is adequate as a basis for the entire transaction.

The bank will receive additional documents such as the merchant's invoices which it substitutes for those of the original supplier. The bank effectively presents documents itself under the second L/C ('documents 2' in Figure 3.3).

This structure often provides merchants, wholesalers or traders with the funding for such purchase and sale operations. Working purely on the margin between buying and selling prices they might not otherwise have the substance to sustain L/C issuance in their own name. Where the goods are being supplied to much larger firms such as supermarkets, department stores and large manufacturers it is *their* standing which enables the operation to be carried out.

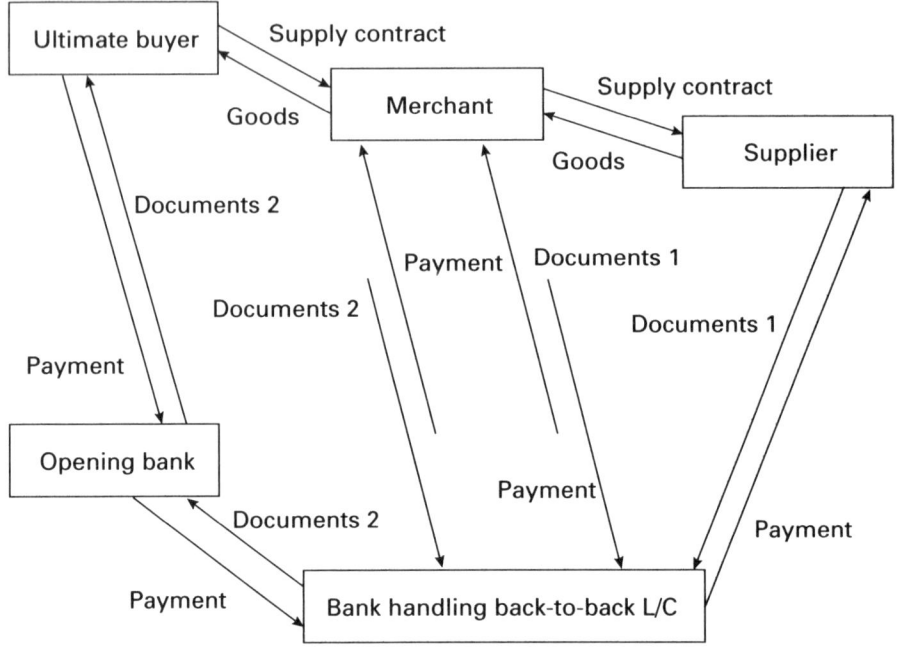

Figure 3.3: Back-to-back letters of credit

Revolving letters of credit

This is a structure which can be used where there are successive shipments and payments passing between the same counterparties.

The credit is issued in favour of the supplier for a particular sum. The supplier ships and presents the documents to the bank in the normal way. Once this has occurred and the funds have been paid out the credit is immediately reinstated to allow for further drawings up to the same amount. If shipment does not take place or there are other difficulties in supply the arrangement may be cancelled and the credit will not revolve. Where there is ongoing repeat business the buyer is able to avoid the administration involved in establishing a new credit for each shipment by simply revolving the existing arrangement. The supplier has a clear idea of what needs to be done to get paid and merely has to repeat what he or she did successfully last time around.

From the issuing bank's point of view the risk on the applicant/buyer remains the same because the credit issued on the buyer's behalf is re-established. Usually the buyer will be charged a commission by the bank for its

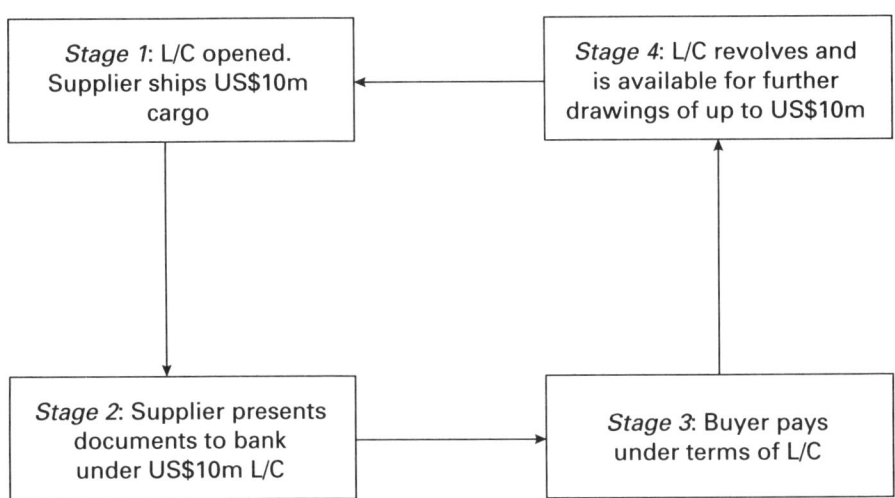

Figure 3.4: Revolving letter of credit

ongoing commitment to maintain the revolving facility. This will be calculated on the basis of a percentage of that commitment for days elapsed and
payable monthly or quarterly in arrears.

In order to protect itself from any weakening in the opener's credit
standing the bank should review the credit risk regularly. It can happen that
the trade finance area of the bank continues revolving the credit in favour
of the supplier unaware that the customer has run into problems. This risk
is particularly common where a relationship manager, credit approvals
department and trade finance operations of the bank are not well enough
co-ordinated.

The confirming bank will follow the procedure for confirming a credit
as per the conventional structure set out above. Its risk remains that of
the issuing bank fulfilling its obligations and its own care in inspecting
documents.

Referring back the contract to supply US$100 million worth of crude oil
mentioned above, the revolving credit structure could be used to make
payment if it was decided that partial drawings under a single, global credit
were not appropriate. After each cargo of oil was shipped the credit would
be reinstated to make way for the next shipment.

Revolving credits can revolve by time as well as by amount. If a monthly
delivery programme has been agreed between a supplier and a buyer,
perhaps for manufactured goods or components, deliveries could take
place and drawings be limited to, say, one per month for all shipments or
deliveries made during that month.

Another limitation to revolving credits can be the total number of revolutions which the credit can make. Wording in the credit might, for example, read 'this credit may revolve three times only'. In this case four drawings are permitted because there will be the initial drawing followed by three revolutions re-establishing the credit for three further drawings.

Lastly, a cap may be placed on the total amount of funds which may be drawn under the credit. Thus for our US$100 million worth of oil deliveries, successive drawings may be made until the US$100 million has been fully drawn. Further deliveries would require an amendment/extension to the value of the credit or a new L/C would need to be opened. Banks, suppliers and buyers involved in using revolving credits should keep a close watch on drawings, amounts, time limits and expiry dates. It is easy to lose track of what is going on, especially if there are numerous shipments and drawings.

Letter of credit issuance facility

Where a number of separate letters of credit need to be opened by a customer in favour of several beneficiaries, a bank may establish an L/C issuance facility. The L/Cs can be quite standard, other than referring to the particulars of each payment and delivery. As far as the applicant is concerned an established facility with the bank to open credits on its behalf can be particularly useful if time is of the essence.

A trader in a highly competitive commodity market might need to open credits at a moment's notice in order to secure contracts. If the facility is already established then the bank will not need to go through an approvals procedure before opening the credits which can save valuable time. If the credits are issued electronically, perhaps through an on-line computer link between the trader and the opening bank, a protocol can be established between the bank and the customer enabling L/Cs to be issued virtually instantaneously. Banks operating credit issuance facilities of this nature will base them on credit judgements made through credit approval procedures established by the bank and reviewed regularly for any change in circumstances.

Transferable Letters of Credit and Assignment of Proceeds

Letters of credit are not negotiable instruments, like bills of exchange and promissory notes. They cannot be transferred by endorsement to another beneficiary, nor by being physically passed to another holder or bearer. However, the beneficiary under a credit may wish to allow the credit to be available to another or second beneficiary. In this case the second beneficiary would be able to present documents and draw funds provided the L/C specifically permits this. Such a credit is termed a transferable credit.

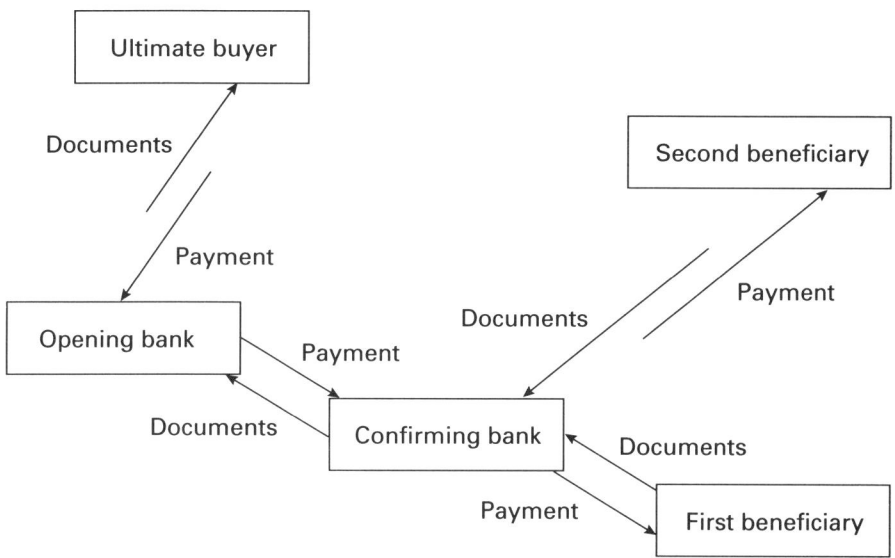

Figure 3.5: Transferable letter of credit

A merchant, trader or other intermediary may be the first beneficiary, as for a back-to-back L/C. He or she may wish to pass the credit through to the original supplier of goods. In this case the first beneficiary would retain the right to submit invoices and draw drafts under the credit, drawing funds from the transaction. The original supplier would submit documents to draw what was due to him or her. Such transfers are covered by article 48 of UCP. Unless expressly stated to the contrary in the credit, transferable L/Cs can only be transferred once.

Assigning the proceeds of a letter of credit is, however, quite different from a transferable credit. Where a credit is not transferable the beneficiary simply instructs the paying bank to credit the funds to another party due as a result of a successful documentary presentation.

The assignee of the funds does risk the beneficiary (or assignor) not fulfilling his or her obligations under the credit. The assignee may be involved in entirely separate business activities with the assignor and the function of the assignment is to earmark the particular funds for the assignee's account. If, for example, the assignor had cashflow constraints and wished to assure the assignee that funds owing would be paid he or she could use such an assignment of proceeds under an L/C. In start up or work-out situations, for example, such an assignment could be of value to creditors.

Article 49 was inserted in the latest revision of UCP to cover assignments of proceeds. It draws a clear distinction between transferring the rights to the proceeds and the rights to perform in accordance with the terms of the credit. The beneficiary's rights to perform under the credit can only be transferred if the credit is specifically designated as being transferable.

Silent Confirmations

If a beneficiary cannot obtain a satisfactory conventional confirmation of an L/C he or she may seek a silent confirmation from a bank. This may occur where the issuing bank does not wish its credit to be confirmed or feels that to add confirmation casts aspersions on its creditworthiness. In recent times beneficiaries of credits issued by Iranian banks have often sought silent confirmations.

The bank providing silent confirmation will agree to pay the beneficiary if the documents are accepted by the issuing/paying bank as being in accordance with the terms of the L/C. In such cases the bank giving the silent confirmation may have no direct, contractual relationship to the bank issuing the credit. In a conventional confirmed credit the bank's confirmation would be added at the opening/paying bank's request and such a relationship would exist. Silent confirmations are not covered by UCP and are merely an agreement between the confirming bank and the beneficiary. The confirming bank will therefore enter into a legally binding agreement with the beneficiary which is likely to include provisions that:

- if discount of a usance L/C has taken place the beneficiary will assign proceeds payable under the credit to the confirming bank when the issuing/paying bank disburses funds;
- the confirming bank checks the documents prior to formal presentation under the credit, in order to ensure that they conform to the terms of the credit and contain nothing which might be grounds for the issuing/paying bank to withhold payment;
- the beneficiary acts on the confirming bank's behalf in the event of legal action becoming necessary.

In recent times silent confirmations have often been given in tandem with discount of deferred payment credits. Here the credit would typically allow for payment to be made 180 or 360 days after shipment or presentation of documents. The bank silently confirming the credit would not only guarantee payment but would also pay the beneficiary a discounted amount in relation to the value of the documents upon their acceptance. The discount applied would reflect the cost of funding until maturity of the usance period and the risk of non-payment under the credit. In this case the beneficiary assigns to the bank the proceeds of the credit at maturity.

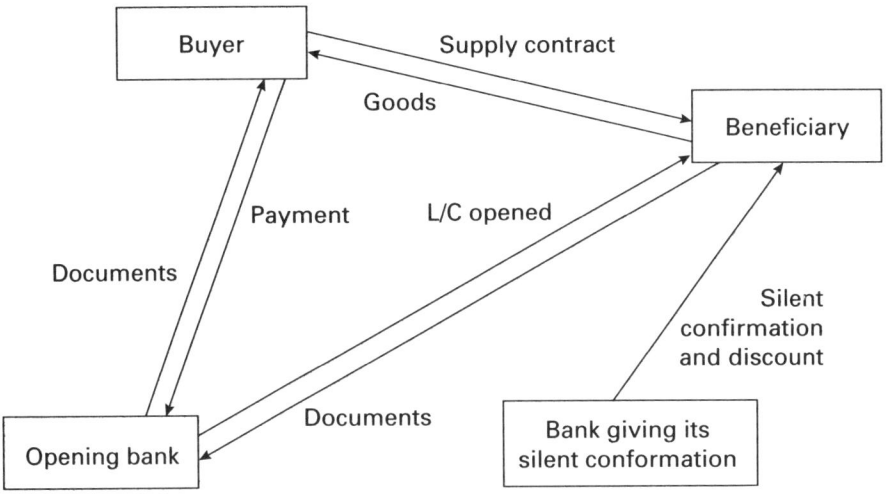

Figure 3.6: Silent confirmation structure

The risks to banks giving silent confirmations are threefold:

- that the banks directly involved in the transaction may reject the documents or subsequent documentary problems may arise. Banks giving silent confirmation cannot be directly involved in sorting out such matters although they can steer the action via the beneficiary;
- that of the credit risk of the issuing/paying banks directly involved in the L/C. A silent confirmation would be unlikely to be sought in the first place if the L/C did not involve a significant credit risk. An international bank may be in a better position than a beneficiary to evaluate the credit risk on another, probably foreign, bank although failures to pay have been common in the recent past;
- that of the political risk of the country of origin of the issuing and/or paying banks. Where a deferred payment L/C is involved the silently confirming bank will be open to changing political circumstances in that country over the term of the L/C. For this reason it is not unusual to find that banks issuing silent confirmations often have their base in the same country as the perceived political risk in the transaction. By virtue of their origin, they may be immune to such risk.

Electronic Letters of Credit
A number of international banks specialising in financing overseas trade have developed their own proprietary electronic L/C issuing systems. This often

involves the applicant having a computer link with the bank and effectively filling in an application form on screen.

The advantages for the opener are that it has easy access to the bank, the process is quick, it does not need to send its application by post or courier, it gets to know the bank's standard form and therefore is less likely to make mistakes.

The bank has a more or less captive client which is obliged to adopt a standardised format which makes data handling and credit management much more administratively efficient. Shipping and other documents called for under the credit continue to be presented in their original state and not electronically. Standardised documents are however widespread, based upon UN recommendations. Examples of these are shown in Part III.

Once approved by the bank the credit can then be issued via its branch network in the beneficiary's country. A printout is effectively given to the beneficiary who examines the credit and meets its terms as per a regular paper L/C.

Each bank operating such a system will effectively have its own configuration, although they are similar. For speed, efficiency and security electronic L/Cs are certainly the way forward where large volumes of similar instruments are involved.

4: Factoring

HISTORY

Factoring is often assumed to mean purely the discounting of invoices. But there is more to it today and it deserves consideration as one of the range of financing techniques which trade financiers can make available to exporters.

Factoring originated in the United States where 'factors', who were responsible for distributing goods about the country, would sometimes pay suppliers before having themselves received payment from the customer. As the logistics of delivery of goods across the United States became less arduous the factors focused on the financial aspects of their business and eventually became engaged in discounting invoices on a much larger scale.

It is still the case today that much factoring work concerns the discounting of trade receivables in the domestic market of the seller. This involves the factoring house assessing the credit risk of the party owing the debt and paying the seller a proportion of the value of the sum owed immediately upon invoicing. The debtor will, all being well, pay on due date and the factor will be repaid. However, the nature of the 'domestic market' is changing.

Firstly, new trading blocks are developing, foremost among them the Single European Market and the North American Free Trade Area. There is a general increase in free trade between nations which is being actively encouraged, fostered and monitored by the World Trade Organisation and other multilateral bodies. Access to credit and other financial information is becoming increasingly rapid. For all these reasons it is likely that international factoring will be carried out on a much larger scale, worldwide, in the future.

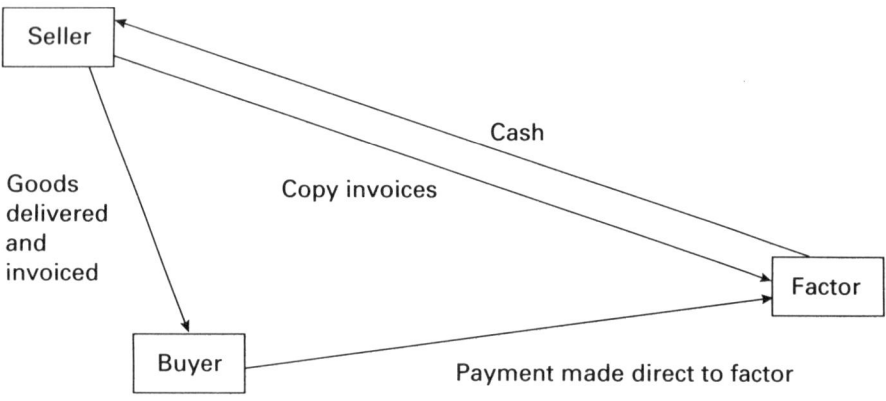

Figure 4.1: Basic factoring structure

FORMS OF FACTORING

Evidence of a Trade Transaction

Invoices are the principal form of evidence of the existence of a trade debt. Where regular orders are processed, ledger entries (perhaps electronically registered) could be another. Letters of credit, bills of exchange and promissory notes would also be adequate evidence for the factor to consider discounting.

Partial Discount

Factoring of trade receivables, unlike forfaiting, is partial and does not cover the entire invoice value. Some 80–90 per cent of the invoice value may be advanced, the balance being at the exporter's risk rather in the manner that insurance will usually carry an insured's risk portion.

With Recourse Discounting

Further risk will be shouldered by the seller if the discounting is 'with recourse'. In this case the factor will advance funds but if, at the end of the credit period, the customer does not pay, the factor will go to the seller for reimbursement.

Without Recourse Discounting

'Without recourse' factoring is also frequently available. Here the factor takes over the full credit risk of the customer not paying. If the customer does not indeed pay, the factor will, in principal, shoulder the loss. 'In principal' because a factor will usually make an extra charge for without recourse factoring which will be used to take out credit insurance. Therefore upon default the factor will make a claim under its insurance policy.

In any case the seller is well advised to credit insure sales which are discounted without recourse, thus having the protection for the factor's request for reimbursement should the customer not pay.

Discount of Entire Receivables Book and Full Service Factoring

In order to spread their risk factoring firms will normally insist on discounting the seller's entire book of trade receivables, subject of course to careful examination of the customers and their credit standing. Factors do say that they will carry out discounts of individual invoices but in practice this is not their preference. Discounting the full receivables book does not necessarily inhibit the seller's choice of customer if the factor does not rate the seller's customer sufficiently creditworthy. The seller continues to carry through the sale but it may be excluded from those items included in the factoring service.

In addition to invoice discounting a full service factoring may be offered where the factor will not only buy the whole receivables book but take over the running of the entire invoicing and collection administration of the seller. This brings savings to the seller who does not become involved in the administration of the sales ledger nor need to pay staff to run it. It also gives the factoring house full control of their factored material which it can monitor closely for changes in payment efficiency and enables it to keep a watch on the seller so as to know how the business is progressing.

Disclosed and Undisclosed Factoring

A factor may offer a 'disclosed' or 'undisclosed' service. If the seller is content for the factor to collect receivables directly from the buyer the factor's involvement will be disclosed. Payments from the buyer of the goods will be made to the factoring company as illustrated in Figure 4.1 opposite.

If, however, the seller feels that the involvement of the factor may create a negative impression with the customer, that the business is short of cash for example, the factor's service will be undisclosed. The factor will still discount receivables but the seller will receive payments directly from the buyer who will be completely unaware that the supplier makes use of factoring.

Short Term Versus Medium Term

Typically factoring will provide short-term credit on the basis of discounting future cashflows from trade receivables. Maximum terms are unlikely to exceed 360 days with 90 to 180 days being the norm. In contrast forfaiting (see Chapter 5) tends to be concerned with longer, medium-term credit periods extending in some cases to seven years or more. There is some overlap in credit period between long-term factoring and short-term forfaiting but the documentation is likely to be quite different.

Finally, it is noteworthy that the factor may work according to minimum turnover levels requiring a consistent level of business throughput from a seller to make the costs of administrating a factoring facility worthwhile.

THE BENEFITS OF FACTORING

1   Factoring brings several advantages to the seller: the main one being cash-flow. The seller can offer credit to the customer, within the terms approved by the factor, and yet receive prompt payment as soon as, or shortly after invoicing is carried out. This may be cheaper than financing by means of bank overdraft which many smaller companies use to cover their working capital needs.

2   The debt management service which factors provide relieves the seller of the burden of administration and saves on staff and office space costs. In other words it enables the seller to concentrate on developing his business.

3   The debt management service may include formal or informal advice on credit standing. Factors hold large amounts of information about the trading histories of commercial firms. This can be valuable to those using factoring who can avoid doing business with customers with poor payment records.

4   Where the factor is providing without recourse discounting the seller will have the advantage of repositioning the risk of customers not paying their bills. This will, as we have said, cost more than with recourse factoring but allows the seller to escape the potentially dire consequences of customers not paying.

PRICING

Charges for factoring services will vary according to the type of services provided and the competition between companies in the factoring market. The structure of pricing is likely to be as follows (all levels shown are purely indicative):

- *Interest:* As long as funds are outstanding interest will be charged at a floating rate. This will normally be in the region of 3 per cent over base lending rate.
- *Finance charges:* These depend on the amount advanced by the factoring company and how long it is likely to be outstanding. They are likely to range from 0.25 to 0.75 per cent assuming the seller is handling his or her own credit control. Where a complete sales ledger management service is provided this charge is more likely to fall in the range 0.75 to 2.75 per cent.
- *Credit insurance:* Non-recourse factoring will cost in the region of 0.2 to 1 per cent in addition to the level of the finance charge to cover the cost of the factor's additional credit protection. This can be higher if the factored receivables are in respect of exports to uncreditworthy countries where the cost of credit insurance is higher.

5: Forfaiting

DEFINITION

Forfaiting in essence is the forfeiting of the right to future payment through discounting future cashflows. It is also referred to by the French term *à forfait*. Convention has now evolved both the word and the practice to mean the discounting or forfaiting of future trade-related receivables under credits made available by suppliers to their customers. While it is possible to discount purely financial receivables these may be shunned by some market practitioners as being more akin to working capital funding.

HISTORY

The discounting of future cash flows has been carried out for many centuries but the forfaiting market as we know it today is a mid-twentieth century phenomenon.

The need for credit to support the rebuilding of the industrial base of central and eastern Europe in the wake of World War Two gave rise to the practice of suppliers of capital goods and equipment agreeing to accept payment from their customers over terms longer than they would normally have conceded. In order to strengthen the increased credit risk of such payment arrangements they would firstly seek bills of exchange or promissory notes as evidence of the debt, both for the principal sum involved and the interest payable on the credit. Secondly, they would ask for a bank guarantee or aval so that if the buyer of the goods did not pay on due date then the guarantor bank would do so.

Because the risk associated with bills or notes had been enhanced by the bank aval it was possible for the seller not only to discount them with other banks and so improve their cash flow but to do so *without recourse*. This meant that the discounting bank would not have the right to ask the supplier of goods for reimbursement should either the original customer or the guaranteeing bank fail to pay on due date.

Table 5.1: Comparison of paper markets

	Forfaiting	Factoring	Commercial paper	Bonds	Letters of credit
Corporate risk	Rarely	Mostly	Mostly	Yes	For opening bank
Bank risk	Yes	Rarely	Rarely	Yes	Yes
Sovereign risk	Yes	Unlikely	Unlikely	Yes	Possible
Screen traded	No	No	Yes	Yes	No
Recourse	Usually not	Usually yes	Yes	Yes	Yes for opening bank
Rated	No	No	Yes	Yes	No
Documentation	Case by case	Case by case	Standard	Standard	Case by case
Interest rate: variable/fixed	Fixed or variable	Fixed or variable	Fixed	Fixed	Fixed or variable
Liquidity high/low	Relatively low	Not liquid	High	High	Low
Term: short/ medium / long	Medium	Short	Short	Medium to long	Short

THE FORFAITING MARKET

The forfaiting market is smaller and more specialised than many of the other corporate funding and credit markets. This stems from the fact that transactions are often small, less than US$5 million in size, and only rarely are two supplies of goods likely to be the same.

Transactions differ from one to another in many respects; size, the type of goods financed, the documentation evidencing the trade in goods, the term of credit and the identity of counterparties and guarantors. This makes forfaiting paper difficult to 'package' in the standard way in which bonds and commercial paper conventionally are. Hence forfaited paper is on the whole less liquid. The discrete nature of the forfaiting market can be illustrated by Table 5.1 above which compares forfaiting and other comparable paper markets.

Typical forfaiting transactions which are dealt with by the market are:

- trade-related;
- the result of suppliers' credits;
- evidenced by bills of exchange or promissory notes;
- bank guaranteed;
- discounted without recourse;
- supported by original or copy shipping documents;
- bearing verifiable signatures of the parties to the transaction;
- freely transferable by endorsement.

Country	Maximum Final Maturity (Yrs)	Country	Maximum Final Maturity (Yrs)	Country	Maximum Final Maturity (Yrs)
Eastern Europe and C.I.S.		Hong Kong	5	Oman	5
Belarus	*	India	7	Qatar	5
Croatia	1	Indonesia	5	Saudi Arabia	5
Czech Republic	5	Malaysia	7	South Africa	7
Estonia	*	Myanmar	1	Syria	1
Hungary	5	Nepal	1	Tunisia	5
Kazakhstan	*	Pakistan	5	Turkey	3
Latvia	*	Philippines	5	Zimbabwe	2
Lithuania	*	Singapore	7		
Poland	5	South Korea	7	*Latin America*	
Romania	5	Sri Lanka	2	Argentina	3
Russia	2	Taiwan	7	Bahamas	1
Slovak Republic	5	Thailand	7	Bermuda	5
Slovenia	5	Vietnam	5	Bolivia	1
				Brazil	5
		Middle East and Africa		Chile	7
Europe		Abu Dhabi	5	Colombia	5
Cyprus	5	Bahrain	5	Costa Rica	1
Greece	5	Botswana	1	Ecuador	5
Iceland	5	Dubai	5	El Salvador	1
Malta	5	Egypt	5	Guatemala	1
Norway	7	Ghana	1	Honduras	1
Portugal	7	Jordan	5	Mexico	*
		Kuwait	5	Paraguay	1
		Lebanon	3	Peru	5
Far East		Mauritius	1	Puerto Rico	1
Bangladesh	1	Morocco	5	Uruguay	5
China	5	Namibia	1	Venezuela	*

Figure 5.1: Example of forfaiter's country list
Courtesy of West Merchant Bank

FORFAITING, POLITICAL RISK AND EMERGING MARKETS

Forfaiters often circulate lists of markets they 'may' cover. See Figure 5.1 opposite for an example.

This demonstrates the ever-increasing spread of political risks which the forfaiting market can cover. To a degree this reflects the impact of what we might call 'the emerging market mind-set'.

Latin America and 'Bradyisation'

Latin American markets and some far eastern countries did not figure in forfaiters' lists until de facto rescheduling initiatives brought markets such as Mexico back to the capital markets. 'Brady plans', involving the issuing of partially-secured bonds maturing over long terms, brought liquidity to the petrified debt burden which many banks and their developing country borrowers had been locked into. This enabled banks to trade away their formerly impaired debts in a new market which grew for the purpose. It also led to privatisation-related issues of equity, the consequent growth of emerging stock markets and the issue of fresh debt in the new issue bond markets for the former delinquent debtors.

The effect on the forfaiting market was twofold. Firstly, new economic growth in the emerging markets fuelled increased imports of capital goods and equipment. This led to a greater need for importer credit which was provided by their suppliers. Forfaiting, the discounting of a supplier's credit cashflows, was one of the key methods of providing such credit along with traditional state-supported export credits, letters of credit and one or two other instruments. Secondly, forfaiters were able to place forfait paper more easily with their counterparty banks who had been able to free up their country limits, having sold off their holdings of third world debt.

'Liquidity' became a key concept in dealing in any form of emerging market's debt, of which trade-related forfait paper was one. The effect of Brady in bringing about the trading of third world debt in its various forms led banks to avoid being locked into such debt positions in the future. The markets became a largely profitable game of musical chairs – of buying and selling paper and making sure you were not holding it if prices dropped. While there are winners and losers, in an emerging or growth scenario, the number of winners should exceed the number of those who lose out. So those who actively traded paper stood a good chance of making money if they read the market correctly. We are in a similar position today with liquidity being as crucial to a healthy forfaiting market as to any other form of emerging market's debt trading.

In dealing in forfaiting paper, or as exporters in understanding what a forfaiter is about, it is important to recognise the 'emerging market mindset' which focuses on this liquidity of debt and the ability to 'buy low' in price terms. The importance of the saleability of the paper you are intending to sell must be appreciated if disappointment and delay are to be avoided.

MARKET PARTICIPANTS

The principal forfaiting centre is London. This is due to several factors:

- the presence of 500 or so banks from all parts of the world;
- availability of staff with forfaiting and trade finance skills;
- London's tradition as a centre for financing international trade.

Many foreign and domestic banks take part in the forfaiting market as buyers of sellers of paper, usually buying when the risk is in their own country or selling if they are handling paper from their exporting clients where the risks fall outside their own territory.

There are, however, forfaiting houses, either independent or owned by banking groups, which make a two-way market in a forfait paper. They buy and sell bills or notes, running a book which they aim to turn over regularly. Their aim is to make their profit on the trading margin between buying and selling prices, not solely from a lending margin on paper held in portfolio as banking assets.

The principal players in the market are:

- London Forfaiting Company PLC;
- Morgan Grenfell Trade Finance Limited;
- West Merchant Bank Limited;
- Hungarian International Bank; and
- Midland Bank Aval;

There are a number of others, including the various international banks who may hold portfolios more diverse than merely their own country risk.

Other financial centres such as New York, Paris, Zurich, Frankfurt, Vienna, Milan and Hong Kong are increasingly homes to forfaiters. In fact, apart from their traditional activity in the London market, forfaiters have established offshoots to expand their capability of placing paper with local banks. In many cases it was necessary to place staff from London in those centres because local forfaiting skills were not available.

PRIMARY AND SECONDARY TRANSACTIONS

When a bank or forfaiting house buys bills or notes directly from the exporter this is termed a 'primary transaction'. The primary forfaiter helps the exporter through the transaction with a view to discounting the paper. The primary forfaiter's interest is to try and configure the paper so that it can be held for his or her own portfolio or sold to another bank or forfaiter.

Because of the extra burden of structuring the transaction the primary forfaiter will expect to enjoy a better income. For this reason primary deals are much sought after with banks and forfaiters bidding against each other for the exporter's business. The primary forfaiter may take a commitment fee for committing to buy the paper several weeks or months before it is ready for discount. He or she may also charge an arrangement or manage-ment fee for work done in setting up the deal. In addition the primary forfaiter will either earn a margin for funding the transaction payable over the life of the transaction or, if he or she chooses to sell the paper, will profit from the difference between buying and selling prices.

When a bank or forfaiting house on-sells the paper to another bank or forfaiter it becomes a 'secondary market transaction'. It is still termed a secondary market transaction regardless of how many times it has changed hands.

For the secondary market forfaiter there may be the possibility of earning a commitment fee if there is a need to commit to purchase the paper well in advance of discount. But principally the secondary market buyer will either hold the transaction as a lender/investor or sell the paper again when he or

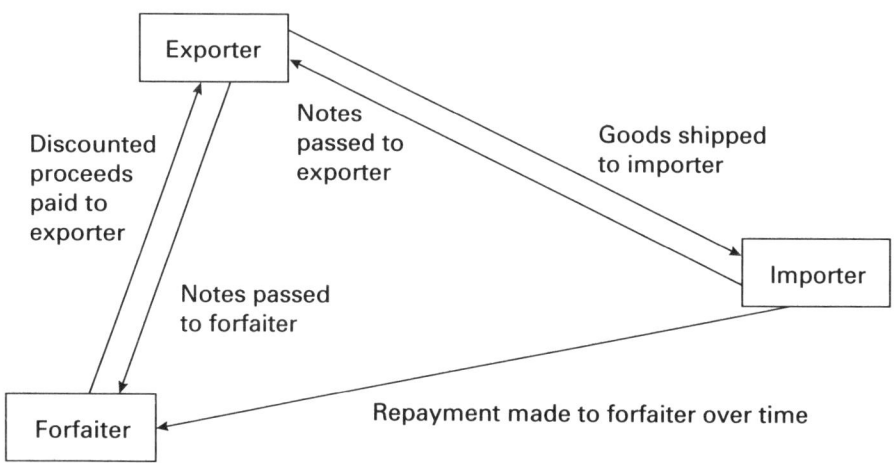

Figure 5.2: Primary market transaction structure

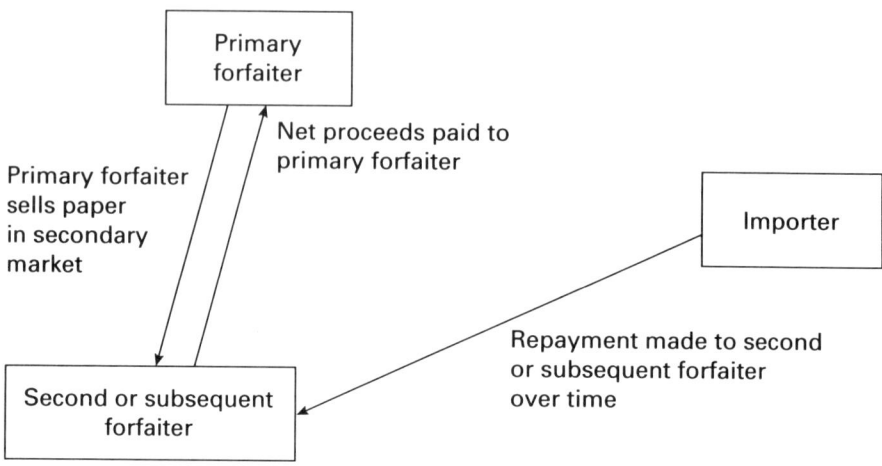

Figure 5.3: Secondary market transaction structure

she is ready. Clearly the scope for profit is less in a secondary market transaction.

EXPORTER AND IMPORTER

The further the transaction develops from its origins in financing international trade the easier it is to forget that the disembodied notes or bills
relate to the sale and purchase of real goods. Therefore, before we look at
the technicalities of discounting we should look at why exporters and
importers might use forfaiting as their preferred credit finance technique.
Table 5.2 compares benefits and disadvantages of forfaiting.

SOFTWARE

Banks and forfaiting houses involved in transactions on a regular basis use
specifically dedicated software to carry out discount calculations, monitor
currency, interest rates and portfolio management arithmetic.

The Rohirst Forfait Management System is the market standard. It enables
the time-consuming number crunching to be carried out very quickly indeed.
It is used in keeping records of deals bought and sold, adjusting pricing and
checking profitability, recording interest rate changes and making summary
reports of the forfaiter's portfolio categorised by country, risk name and
currency. For the exporter, a basic calculation package from Rohirst enables

Table 5.2: Benefits and disadvantages of forfaiting

	Buyer	**Seller**
Benefits of forfaiting	100% credit possible for purchase of goods	Can use credit as a selling tool to sell goods
	Gains medium-term credit	Can offer credit without taking the risk
	Fixed or floating interest rate	Can offer fixed or floating interest rate
	Low interest rate possible	Can offer cheap credit
	Simple, cheap documentation, easy to execute	Simple, cheap documentation, easy to execute
	Cashflow benefit	Cashflow benefit
	Origin of goods unimportant	Origin of goods unimportant
	Can eradicate currency risk	Can eradicate currency risk
	Hidden cost of credit can be tax beneficial	Can hide cost of credit
		Eradicates risk of non-payment
		Eradicates transfer risk
		Without recourse
Disadvantages of forfaiting	May retain currency risk	May retain currency risk
	Hidden cost of credit	May suffer cost of credit
	Aval/guarantee expense	Commitment commission expense
	Exposure to banking sector delays	Exposure to banking sector delays
		Difficult to off-load without bank Aval/guarantee

not only quick calculation but also checking and matching the forfaiter's numbers.

The calculation schedules in the following pages have been made using Rohirst and are a useful tool for dissecting a transaction into its detailed parts.

DISCOUNT CALCULATIONS

STRAIGHT DISCOUNT

$$\text{Net} = \text{Face Value} \times (1 - \frac{\%}{100} \times \frac{\text{Total Days}}{360})$$

SIMPLE YIELD

$$\text{Net} = \frac{\text{Face Value}}{1 + \frac{\%}{100} \times \frac{\text{Total Days}}{360}}$$

SEMI-ANNUAL YIELD

Split total days into   N1 × 183 days plus
                                N2 × 182 days plus
                                Odd days

$$\text{Net} = \frac{\text{Face Value}}{(1 + \frac{\%}{100} \times \frac{183}{360})^{N1} \times (1 + \frac{\%}{100} \times \frac{182}{360})^{N2} \times (1 + \frac{\%}{100} \times \frac{\text{Odd Days}}{360})}$$

ANNUAL YIELD

Split total days into   N1 × 365 days plus
                                Odd days

$$\text{Net} = \frac{\text{Face Value}}{(1 + \frac{\%}{100} \times \frac{365}{360})^{N1} \times (1 + \frac{\%}{100} \times \frac{\text{Odd Days}}{360})}$$

Figure 5.4: Formulae for manual discounts

```
ROHIRST DEMONSTRATION SYSTEM                    12:25     21/2/1990

                EXPORT CALCULATION Ref: DEMO/1

        From:          EXPORTER NAME              Ref:
        Importer:      IMPORTER NAME
        Guarantor:     GUARANTOR NAME
        Details 1:     ADDITIONAL INFORMATION

                    BASIS OF CALCULATION

        Interest/Shipment Date                            1/7/90
        Currency                                        STERLING
        Required Amount                           1,000/000.00
        Down Payment %                                        10
        Number of Bills                                      10
        Interest Paid By Importer % p.a.                      5
        Method of Interest Calculation                  365/365
        Commitment Date                                  9/10/89
        Commitment Fee % p.a.                                  1
        Days of Grace                                         3
        Notes Available on                               23/7/90
        Method of Discounting            STRAIGHT DISCOUNT
        Discount Rate % p.a.                             9.9/16

                   SUMMARY OF CALCULATION

        Contract Value (Multiplier = 1.1629)     1,162,900.60
        Down Payment                               116,290.06
        Principal                                1,046,610.50
        Interest                                   144,116.89
        Total Face Value                         1,190,727.39
        Discounted Value                           893,072.66
        Total Proceeds To Exporter               1,009,362.72
        Commitment Fee (287 days)                    9,362.71
        Final Proceeds
1,000,000.01

                        BILL DETAILS

No  MATURITY      PRINCIPAL       INTEREST    FACE VALUE     NET VALUE
 1   1/1/91      104,661.05     26,380.32    131,041.37    125,342.42
 2   1/7/91      104,661.05     23,355.19    128,016.24    116,411.92
 3   1/1/92      104,661.05     21,104.27    125,765.32    108,269.51
 4   1/7/92      104,661.05     18,265.51    122,926.56     99,996.55
 5   1/1/93      104,661.05     15,828.20    120,489.25     92,110.94
 6   1/7/93      104,661.05     12,975.10    117,636.15     84,444.02
 7   1/1/94      104,661.05     10,552.13    115,213.18     77,060.26
 8   1/7/94      104,661.05      7,785.07    112,446.12     69,965.75
 9   1/1/95      104,661.05      5,276.07    109,937.12     63,047.43
10   1/7/95      104,661.05      2,595.03    107,256.08     56,423.86
             1,046,610.50    144,116.89   1,190,727.39   893,072.66

ROHIRST DEMONSTRATION SYSTEM 21/2/90        12:25
```

Figure 5.5: Export calculation

Forfaiting discounts are normally expressed either in terms of a fixed rate, for example 10 per cent per annum or a floating rate such as LIBOR plus a margin of 1 per cent. The method of discount will involve compounding either quarterly, semi-annually or annually and will be calculated as a 'straight discount' or a 'discount to yield'. The following are the formulae for manual calculation.

Export Quotations (Primary Transactions)

An exporter intending to extend credit to a customer will want to know the costs involved as soon as possible as this will affect the pricing of the goods. The exporter may therefore request quotations of terms and conditions from one or more banks or forfaiters who will produce an 'export calculation' (see Figure 5.5).

We will examine the elements of the export calculation one by one:

Lines 1–4   Names of the counterparties.

Basis of calculation

Interest/shipment date Date from which the supplier's credit is assumed to have started and from which interest is calculated. This is often the shipment date but need not necessarily be.

Currency   The currency in which the bills or notes are denominated. The vast majority of forfaited paper is denominated in US Dollars, Deutschmarks or Swiss Francs. In practice the principal restriction on the choice of currency is the liquidity of the paper. If the currency is too exotic the forfaiter will take the view that it will deter future counterparties from buying the paper.

Required amount   The total income which the exporter wishes to receive after discount. This will be the full contract value if the exporter is uplifting the price of the goods to include the total cost of credit.

Downpayment   The percentage amount of the contract paid 'up front', that is with order, at shipment or under a letter of credit.

Number of bills   Effectively the number of payments evidenced by bills or notes over the life of the transaction. The figure '10' in the example represents ten semi-annual instalments of principal and interest over this five-year transaction.

Interest paid by importer	This is the rate of interest on the bills or notes themselves. It is not the discount rate. It is often the consensus rate (especially under Italian trans-actions supported by Mediocredito Centrale – see below). It is whatever interest rate has been agreed between the buyer and the seller under the sales contract. It is visible to the buyer of the goods/the issuer of the notes or bills, whereas the discount rate will not be.
Method of calculation	Number of days elapsing/in a year of days. Trans-actions denominated in US Dollars and most other major currencies use 365/360 – 365 days elapsed in a year of 360 days. Sterling and Canadian Dollar interest are usually calculated on a 365/365 basis. Some transactions may be calculated on a 360/360 so-called 'bond basis'.
Commitment date	The date from which the bank or forfaiter commits to buy the paper. This may be some months in advance of shipment to give the exporter the confidence of knowing that the paper can be sold as soon as it is available for discount. This is therefore the date from which the discounting bank or forfaiter will charge its commitment fee.
Commitment fee	The rate at which the commitment fee will be charged on the face value of the paper.
Days of grace	An extra number of days included in the credit period, per maturity of each bill or note, to allow for administration delays in the country where the buyer is based.
	The worse the political risk and/or more inefficient the banking system is perceived to be the greater will be the number of grace days. Effectively this is an entirely negotiable aspect of the transaction.
	The effect of adding for example 7 days' grace to the present transaction is to add 70 days' interest cost to the transaction (7×10 bills or notes) making it more profitable to the forfaiter and more costly to the seller.
Notes available	The date on which the paper will be ready for discount. In practice it is usually fixed as a reason-able time after shipment, say two weeks, by which time any shipping documents required to support the paper will also be available.

53

Method of discount	Will usually be either 'straight discount' or 'discount to yield'. Which is chosen is not important provided both counterparties understand which they are using.
Discount rate	The rate which the forfaiter will use in calculating the amount he or she will pay of the paper.

Summary of calculation

Contract multiplier	The amount by which the original costing of contract value or 'required amount' given above needs to be uplifted in order to absorb the costs of the discount and the commitment fee in producing the 'required amount'.
Downpayment	The amount in money of the 'Downpayment %' listed above. It is calculated as a proportion of the 'revised contract value' in the preceding line.
Principal	The new principal value of all of the bills.
Interest	The interest on the principal amount over the life of the transaction calculated at the rate entered into the line 'Interest payable by importer % p.a.' above.
Total face value	This is the total of the principal and interest in the two previous lines. Note: the term 'Face Value' means total principal and interest due under the notes or bills over the life of the transaction.
Discounted value	The discounted amount which the exporter is paid by the forfaiter of the bills or notes, the total face value of which is given in the previous line. This is distinct from any downpayment.
Total proceeds to exporter	The total of the downpayment and the discounted value before deduction of the forfaiter's commitment fee.
Commitment fee	The commitment fee payable to the forfaiter. It is calculated on the number of days between the 'Commitment date' and the 'Notes availability on' date listed above. The percentage rate used is given at 'commitment fee' above.
Final proceeds	The final net amount which the exporter will receive for selling the paper to the forfaiter after the cost of discount and commitment fee are taken into account. This is the same as 'Required amount' given above.
Bill details	This section tabulates the values of the bills or notes in the forfaited package. The principal, interest and

```
        EXPORT DATA (No adjustment)

Interest/Shipment Date          1/7/90
First Maturity                  1/1/91
Required                  1,000,000.00
Down Payment                       10%
Interest                            5%
    Basis                      365/365
    Compound                 0 monthly
Method                 REDUCING BALANCE
                         NO ADJUSTMENT
Multiplier                     1.0000
Contract                 1,000,000.00
Down Payment               100,000.00
Bill Proceeds              768,506.82
Less: Fees                   8,051.17
Final Proceeds             860,455.65


        EXPORT DATA (With adjustment)

Interest/Shipment Date          1/7/90
First Maturity                  1/1/91
Required                  1,000,000.00
Down Payment                       10%
Interest                            5%
    Basis                      365/365
    Compound                 0 monthly
Method                 REDUCING BALANCE
                   ADJUST CONTRACT VALUE
Multiplier                     1.1622
Contract                 1,162.174.95
Down Payment               116,217.49
Bill Proceeds              893,139.39
Less: Fees                   9,356.86
Final Proceeds           1,000,000.02
```

Figure 5.6: Export calculation with and without adjustment

face amounts reflect the total amounts given in the 'Summary of calculation' section. They are what the importer will draw his or her bills or notes for.

The net value column shows what the exporter will receive for each of the bills in the series when they are sold to the forfaiter.

12:25   21/2/1990

VALUATION REPORT Ref: DEMO/1 (Not held)

From: EXPORTER NAME   Ref:
Importer: IMPORTER NAME
Guarantor: GUARANTOR NAME
Details 1:   ADDITIONAL INFORMATION

				Annual	Semi-Ann	Straight
Number of Bills	10	PRIMARY	INVESTMENT			(Matched)
Currency	STERLING	Days Grace Notes	LIBOR 3	Cost of Funds 11.084059	10.824553	
Commitment Date	9/10/89	Basis 365/365	365/365	Margin 1.082302	1.031074	1.033941
Disbursement Date	23/7/90	LIBOR Compound	6 monthly	Yield 12.163361	11.855627	13.867888
Commit Fee %	1(6)	Cost of Carry %	0	Discount		9.9/16
Commit Fee GBP	9,362.71	Average Life (Yrs) 2.61		A/c Yield		11.896670

				FACE	SEMI-ANNUAL COMPOUND			STRAIGHT DISCOUNT		
No	MATURITY DATE	LIFE DAYS	LIBOR %	VALUES	NET VALUE	DISCOUNT	STR DISC	NET VALUE	DISCOUNT	SEM YIELD
1	1/1/91+1	166	10.5/16	131,041.37	124,337.26	6,704.11	11.249092	125,342.42	5,698.95	9.997272
2	1/7/91	346	10.9/16	128,016.24	114,758.03	13,258.21	10.925381	116,411.92	11,604.32	10.266756
3	1/1/92+1	531	10.5/8	125,765.32	106,349.09	19,416.23	10.612125	108,269.51	17,495.81	10.558470
4	1/7/92	712	10.11/16	122,926.56	98,177.01	24,749.55	10.321301	99,996.55	22,930.01	10.861984
5	1/1/93+3	899	10.3/4	120,489.25	90,719.32	29,769.93	10.031426	92,110.94	28,378.31	11.202418
6	1/7/93	1077	10.13/16	117,636.15	83,730.73	33,905.42	9.767906	84,444.02	33,192.13	11.551570
7	1/1/94+3	1264	10.7/8	115,213.18	77,309.64	37,903.54	9.499995	77,060.26	38,152.92	11.954425
8	1/7/94	1442	10.15/16	112,446.12	71,329.39	41,116.73	9.255539	69,965.75	42,480.37	12.373479
9	1/1/95+2	1628	10.15/16	109,937.12	65,764.21	44,172.91	9.008451	63,047.43	46,889.69	12.859459
10	1/7/95+2	1809	11	107,256.08	60,597.98	46,658.10	8.777269	56,423.86	50,832.22	13.385774
				1,190,727.39	893,072.66			893,072.66		

Equivalent rates INCLUDE days of grace

DATE	COMMITMENT FEE		FIXED FEES		TOTAL FEES
	DAYS	AMOUNT	DAYS	AMOUNT	
9/10/89	182	5,937.33			
9/4/90	105	3,425.38			
Totals		9,362.71			

ROHIRST DEMONSTRATION SYSTEM 21/2/90   12:26

Figure 5.7: Valuation report

Alternative Calculation

If the exporter agrees to shoulder the cost of the discount and commitment fee the same 'basis of calculation' information can be input and the calculation adjusted to show what the bills or notes should now be drawn for. Thus for the same underlying transaction the adjusted export calculation shown in Figure 5.6 will result.

Secondary Market Transactions

Where a forfaiter is already holding a transaction and wishes to on-sell it, a similar calculation can be carried out which leaves aside the specifics of the export such as shipment, interest rate on the notes and payable by the importer, required amount and downpayment.

Once the transaction has been discounted the export itself becomes less and less important in trading the paper. It is sufficient to prove that the export in fact took place using copy shipping documents passed along with the notes to the next holder.

This typical 'Valuation report' would be used for the above transaction in a secondary market transaction already held in a forfaiter's portfolio (see Figure 5.7). Additional data will probably have been added by the forfaiter wishing to re-sell the transaction. This would usually include a new discount date and rate of discount. If the period over which the discount is calculated is shorter and/or the rate of discount less than the terms at which the deal was purchased the seller will make a profit.

Rates of discount can be applied to transactions very easily as they are offered to counterparties who may make a counter bid. A price is arrived at virtually simultaneously which enables trading to take place efficiently, assuming all supporting documentation is acceptable to the new purchaser.

OTHER FACTORS AFFECTING A FORFAITING TRANSACTION

Term

In principle the forfaiting market should be able to cover credit terms of almost any length. There are, however, several practical restrictions which limit the credit periods which banks and forfaiters will cover.

Unless the credit term is at least a few months there may not be time to profit from a transaction as the discount unwinds. This can be tempered by the size of a transaction. The larger it is the more interest will accrue and the more worthwhile it will be.

Political Risk

At the longer end of the spectrum political or country risk becomes a factor which forfaiters have to consider at an early stage. Where they accept a bank aval or guarantee as their ultimate risk the avalising bank may be based in a country where changes in political regime may affect their ability to meet their obligations. Most forfaiters will have arrived at a view as to how long they can comfortably see into the future and have established country limits accordingly.

Liquidity

Liquidity is also a factor taken into account in setting limits. At any given time the forfaiter's entire portfolio needs to be able to be sold off if necessary. It is therefore unlikely that any one forfaiting house will offer credit significantly longer than the others, otherwise they would not have the confidence of knowing that they could place a deal in the market if need be.

Some more adventurous forfaiters might buy paper at a very deep discount if they feel that, as the term of the deal shortens, buyers will become more numerous. This is especially true of emerging markets where perceptions of rapidly improving credit standing can encourage banks to be more open to taking on their risk.

Interest Rate Risk

Funding is an important issue. Forfaiters will usually try to arrange funding to ensure that any rise in interest rate over the credit period does not eat into their profit margin. This can be illustrated by the following example:

A five-year transaction, made up of ten notes payable semi-annually, is purchased from the exporter at a price of 10 per cent discount to yield. The price is made up of two elements: i) a funding rate for the currency of the transaction of 9 per cent which the forfaiter has had to pay to bankers to borrow the money to buy the transaction and ii) a margin of 1 per cent, representing the forfaiter's risk premium and profit on the lending.

The forfaiter may obtain five-year fixed rate funding for the entire term of the transaction and can therefore rely on a profit of 1 per cent per annum throughout its life. This is referred to as 'match funding'.

But if the forfaiter prefers to fund from short-term borrowings, say on overdraft, and there is a 1 per cent rise in the cost of this funding then the additional cost will wipe out the profit margin.

Conversely, of course, should there be a 1 per cent fall in funding costs for a transaction purchased at a fixed rate but funded on a short-term basis, the forfaiter's profit margin will increase by that proportion. His or her judgement to fund short-term would certainly be vindicated.

Thus if a transaction cannot be match funded to its final maturity or successfully hedged in the funding of the book of forfait paper it is unlikely that the forfaiter will buy it – unless it is going to be sold straight away to another firm which can obtain the funding.

Where the transaction is being sold to a bank which accounts in the currency of the transaction, for example a Peseta-denominated transaction is sold to a Spanish bank, then the purchasing bank may be prepared to take a more lenient view of the interest rate risk. The Spanish bank in this example will still be vulnerable to a Peseta interest rate rise, of course, but may have a cheap deposit base among its domestic customers.

An exporter wishing to sell paper to a forfaiter should bear these funding considerations in mind because they will be on the forfaiter's agenda when appraising and pricing a transaction.

Transaction Size

In principle any size of transaction should be able to be handled by the forfaiter. In practice this is not the case. The forfaiter may argue that a transaction which is too small may be difficult to fund, especially if it is over a longish term. A transaction of US$100,000 repayable by ten semi-annual instalments will involve funding ten amounts of US$10,000 each to their respective maturities. The argument is that the bank supplying funding to the forfaiter will charge a premium over its normal LIBOR rate. In practice both the forfaiter and bank will probably have pigeon-holed the transaction as 'too much aggravation' considering the profit to be made over the transaction's life. Remember for the banker and the forfaiter the administration cost of a transaction of US$10,000 is much the same as that for one of US$10,000,000, but the profit available for the latter is much greater.

At the top end of the size scale, transactions which are larger than $10m are difficult to place. This can be either because of restricted risk limits which the forfaiter may have for particular names, banks or country risks or a general policy that no one transaction held in portfolio may exceed a certain figure. More enterprising forfaiters may be able to share or 'syndicate' a larger transaction with other forfaiters in the same way as large loans are syndicated or bond issues are underwritten by a group of banks.

The exporter needs to appreciate the forfaiter's agenda. If term or size criteria are out of kilter the forfaiter may recommend using another payment method to finance the export sales transaction.

The Italian Factor

For a number of years, until quite recently, the forfaiting market was dominated by the trade in paper relating to underlying exports of Italian goods. Local differences among exporting countries would not, on the face of it, seem worthwhile treating in a volume of this sort; however, Italy's involvement in forfaiting is wholly disproportionate. Some banks' portfolios of paper derive entirely from trade in Italian goods.

The government of Italy, through its state-owned medium-term lending institution, Istituto Centrale per il Credito a Medio Termine, commonly referred to as 'Mediocredito', pays a subsidy to exporters to make up for the discount suffered in the forfaiting process. The amount of the subsidy is roughly equal to the difference between the fixed 'consensus' interest rate applying to the political risk of the market concerned and the actual cost of the discount, being a total of the average cost of funding the transaction for its full term plus the risk margin charged by the forfaiter.

The subsidy allows Italian exporters to offer credit to importing customers overseas and to sell the resulting bills or notes at a price which is sufficiently interesting to attract the forfaiter to buy it. If and when this subsidy is phased out altogether, and it inevitably will be if only through the sheer cost to the Italian state, the forfaiting market is bound to change in character. It is difficult to predict whether this will result in a decrease in trading volumes or in an increase as exporters from other countries will be able to compete for export contracts on equal terms.

BILLS OF EXCHANGE, PROMISORY NOTES AND AVALS

Forfaiters will often refer to bills or notes in 'international form'. There is no real standard, however, rather a set of conventions which have evolved over time.

Both bills of exchange and promissory notes are unconditional undertakings to pay sums of money at a later date. Bills of exchange are drawn by the person owed the money (*the drawer*) on the person owing it (*the drawee*). The person owing *accepts* the obligation to pay by signing the bill as *acceptor*. We might refer to a bill of exchange as a 'you owe me'.

The promissory note is simpler and is a promise to pay issued by the person owing money (*the obligor*) to the person owed it. There is no acceptance applied to promissory notes. They are in essence 'IOUs'.

Promissory note

At/on. [*date*] .... for value received, we promise to pay against this promissory note to the order of [*exporter*] .... the sum of [*in figures and words*] ....
effective payment to be made in [*currency*] ...., without deduction for and free of any taxes, impost, levies or duties present or future of any nature.
This promissory note is payable at [*name of bank and place and branch where sum is payable*]

[*Name and address of importer/obligor*]

[*Signature of importer/obligor*]

Per Aval: [*Name and address of avalising bank*]

[*Signatures of empowered officers of avalising bank*]

Figure 5.8: Form of promissory note

Bill of exchange

At/on. [*date*] .... for value received, pay against this bill of exchange to the order of [*the drawer/exporter*]......................... the sum of [*in figures and words*] .... effective payment to be made in [*currency*] ...., without deduction for and free of any taxes, impost, levies or duties present or future of any nature.
This bill of exchange is payable at [*name of bank and place and branch where sum is payable*]

Drawn on: [*Name and address of drawee/importer*]

For Acceptance: [*Signature of drawee/importer*]

Per Aval for the account of the drawee: [*Name and address of avalising bank*]

[*Signatures of empowered officers of avalising bank*]

Figure 5.9: Form of a bill of exchange

The forms of bills and notes vary. They are usually obtained from commercial stationers. Banks and large companies may use their own standard forms which are printed and bound in the same manner as domestic cheque books. Figures 5.8 and 5.9 are examples of a bill of exchange and promissory note. Bills or notes can be payable at sight or on a particular date, which is expressly stated or can be determined with reference to a particular point in time, such as a date in the past. The forfaiting market is only concerned with term instruments.

Central to the forfaiting process is the fact that bills or notes can be endorsed in favour of other holders to whom the debt becomes payable. However, the obligor cannot pass on his or her obligation to make payment.

Avals

Bills and notes preferably carry an additional guarantee, usually that of a bank. Such a guarantee either takes the form of a separate guarantee in letter form or of an 'aval' which appears on the instrument itself. An aval is an unconditional guarantee on the part of the 'avalisor' or guarantor to meet the obligations set out on the instrument should the obligor fail to do so.

The Law Affecting Bills of Exchange and Promissory Notes

The law of several jurisdictions may affect transactions documented by bills or notes depending on the location of the parties involved, the importer, the exporter, the avalisor, the holders and future endorsers. There are, however, two principal sets of rules by which most transactions are governed, English law and the Geneva Convention.

English law
In English law the Bills of Exchange Act 1882 defines a bill of exchange as:

> an unconditional order in writing, addressed by one person to another, signed by the person giving it, requiring the person to whom it is addressed to pay on demand or at a fixed or determinable future time a sum certain in money to the order of a specified person or bearer

Promissory notes are generally treated as a sub-set of bills of exchange and are not specifically mentioned in the act. The principal of transference by endorsement is a key concept enshrined in the Act as is the unconditionality of the instrument. Section 16 of the Act establishes the legal right to sell a bill without recourse, by endorsement to third parties.

Geneva Convention

The Geneva Convention on Conflicts of Laws articles 2, 3 and 4 differs in one crucial aspect on the subject of without recourse indorsement. It permits endorsers to have no liability in the event of future default but maintains an exporter's liability even if he or she has sold the bill by endorsement to a third party.

It is questionable whether a forfaiter as holder of a dishonoured bill would seek redress from an exporter, as in purchasing it the exporter's without recourse endorsement will have been accepted along with those of previous holders. However, it causes enough concern to some exporters to insist that bills should be supported by a *waiver letter* which is passed on with the instrument itself each time it changes hands. This specifically insists that all subsequent holders of the bill will waive their right of recourse to the exporter.

Variations of Notes and Bills

The examples of a bill and note given above are the instruments in their simplest form. There can, however, be variations on the theme which are commonly seen and freely traded.

Interest terms

These can include provisions such as: 'This [note or bill] shall bear interest at the rate of . . . x . . . per cent per annum payable . . . x-monthly in arrears.' The rate of interest may be *fixed* or *floating* but the vast majority bear interest at a fixed rate.

Interest may also be payable under a separate set of parallel instruments which have maturities matching those of the principal ones. Interest can alternatively be wrapped up in what appears to be the principal sum. This may be used to avoid any *withholding tax* on interest payable by a party to the bill or where there is a wish to disguise the fact that interest is being charged to the buyer under the deferred payment arrangement.

Multiple payment notes or bills are common. In this form a single, perhaps one-page instrument will document a series of maturities. For a five-year transaction, ten repayments of principal and/or interest will be shown on the note, payable at fixed dates or with reference to a date in the past – so many days or months after shipment, for example. Similarly interest may or may not attach.

SUPPORTING DOCUMENTATION

Shipping Documents

The purpose of shipping documents in the context of a primary or secondary forfaiting transaction is to connect the payment instruments to their underlying trade transaction. This lends transparency to the transaction as a trade financing operation and enables the face values of the bills or notes to be related to the value of the cargo.

Copy documents are usually sufficient provided they conform with the originals. The originals themselves may have been used for a presentation under a documentary credit or passed to the buyer of the goods by some other means. Typical supporting copy documents would be: bills of lading or other transport documents; commercial invoices; or packing lists.

It should be possible to match the descriptions, weights and packing configuration of the cargo shown on the bills of lading with those shown on the packing list and/or the invoice. The invoice will show the value of the cargo and from this the value of the bills should be able to be deduced. For example, a forfaiting transaction may finance 85 per cent of the value of a cargo. This proportion of the invoice value becomes the principal value of the notes or bills with interest calculated at the interest term specified. Thus the instruments can be linked with the trade in goods.

In addition to documents relating to goods, other important documentation may support the transaction, for example:

- any separate bank or other guarantee attaching to the instruments;
- verification of the signatures of the importer and/or exporter where they appear on the instruments;
- verification of the signatures on behalf of the avalisor or guarantor;
- verification of the signatures of any previous endorser of the paper.

Separate guarantees have been dealt with above in the section on trade-related standby L/Cs and so will not be repeated here. Suffice to say that the guarantee should clearly relate to the forfaiting transaction in hand and the signatories should be valid.

The verification of all signatories to the notes, bills, avals and guarantees is of crucial importance in establishing the background to a transaction. A transaction which has passed through the hands of several previous endorsers will be supported by a series of signatory verifications rather as an old master painting carries a recorded history of previous owners to confirm its provenance.

The exporter's bankers may confirm the signatures of the exporter and perhaps also those of the guarantor/avalisor. The signatures of the exporter's bankers may be confirmed by the primary exporter who may hold a signature book and signing protocol for that bank. The signatories of the primary forfaiter will be checked and confirmed by the next holder of the paper and so on. Most forfaiters and banks engaging in forfaiting maintain a library of bank signatories and their signing authorities. This enables them to verify any previous bank or forfaiter's signatories to their own satisfaction. The importance of careful verification cannot be over-emphasised. Again, like a painting, the more complete the history the stronger price it can command and in forfaiting terms the more liquid the paper is likely to be, assuming all risk considerations have been dealt with.

Each forfaiting transaction is different and may for one reason or another require a certain variation in documentation. This lack of standardisation on the one hand inhibits large-scale trading as for some other capital market instruments such as bonds or commercial paper. However, it allows the requirements of the trade transaction to determine the formal documentation rather than forcing it into an inappropriate form.

Forfaiting structures are relatively flexible and use simple, less rigorous documentation as compared with letters of credit and state-supported export credits in particular. This may account for the steady spread in the use of forfaiting as a technique for financing international trade.

6: Buyer's Credits, Lines of Credit and Supplier's Credits

DEFINITION

These structures have evolved to provide credit terms to buyers to support their purchase of bigger ticket imports. They are often, though not necessarily, guaranteed by a state Export Credit Agency (ECA) from the exporter's country. ECA support will be dealt with later but will be mentioned where it is relevant to the structures described in this section.

Typically, larger amounts of funding are made available by these means. Given the legal and executive time costs involved in drafting and negotiating loan agreements it would normally be uneconomic to use such structures for transactions of less than about US$3 million. In practice smaller value agreements are used and the costs are saved by using standard form documents which require little drafting and input from lawyers. Most funding of this sort is made available by banks, or by a club or syndicate of banks therefore it has been assumed in dealing with the subject that lenders are banks rather than other types of export finance houses or institutions.

BUYER'S CREDIT

A buyer's credit might best be described as a rather specialised form of eurocurrency loan, where the borrower is the buyer of goods. Indeed where there is no ECA involved many of the conditions may be the same as a commercial loan but for those referring to the specific trade transaction being financed.

The Borrower

The buyer may be a company, ministry, government or other entity and will usually be defined as the borrower in the loan agreement. The borrower enters into the agreement for the specific purpose of obtaining funding for the

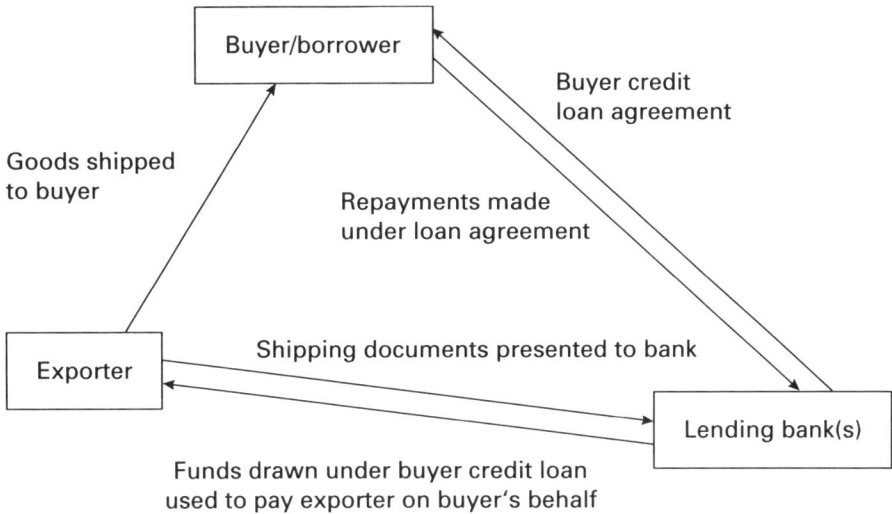

Figure 6.1: Buyer's credit structure

purchase of goods, equipment or services which is conventionally set out in the preamble to the agreement. Although loans for a period as short as 18 months are not unknown longer terms are often provided for, extending to 15 or 20 years. Five years would be a common term for a buyer credit loan.

The Guarantor

The buyer's credit borrower may benefit from a guarantee from a stronger entity such as a parent company or sovereign government. In the case of loans, where the support of an ECA is sought the guarantor needs to be acceptable to the ECA and this often means that it needs to be a government guarantor in its own name, a ministry or state-owned or other first-class bank.

Disbursement

Unlike a conventional domestic loan which you or I might borrow from our banks, the funds are not normally disbursed directly to the borrower under an export-related buyer's credit. Instead, drawings are disbursed to the exporter, as payment on behalf of the borrower for goods shipped. Such payments are accounted for in a bank's books as loans to the borrower.

In order to ensure that funds are correctly disbursed the loan agreement will normally set out a drawings procedure. This may involve completion of a drawings form or payment request by the exporter to be presented with supporting shipping documents, such as original bills of lading, insurance certificates, invoices and packing lists rather like a letter of credit. Other drawings protocols may involve the disbursing bank receiving written permission from the borrower/buyer before disbursement of funds.

Repayment

Repayment will tend to be by equal semi-annual instalments of principal with the commencement date being defined in the repayments paragraphs of the loan agreement. Monthly, quarterly, annual or bullet repayments are possible and may either date from specifically defined dates or be determinable by reference to trigger points in the underlying supply contract, for example: 'Repayment will be by ten equal consecutive semi-annual instalments of principal commencing on 2 January 1996.' Or: 'Repayment will be by ten equal consecutive semi-annual instalments of principal, the first to take place six months from date of signature of the loan agreement.' Other trigger points could be 'date of effectiveness of the loan agreement', 'date of shipment', 'date of provisional acceptance of the equipment' and so forth. It is quite common to see a 'grace period' of months, or in some cases years, before the first repayment is due.

Provision may also be made for repayments to be calculated as a proportion of the outstanding balance of the loan. In this case such a balance will usually be divided by the number of remaining repayments to produce equal principal repayments. This will be the case where shipments and drawings continue after the buyer has already begun to repay the loan.

Agent and Syndication

The laboursome process of setting up the buyer's credit means that it will normally be carried out by one bank, 'the agent bank', which will also administrate the loan throughout its life, handling all disbursements and repayments and receiving an agency fee for doing so.

In a substantial loan the agent may make the loan on behalf of a group, club or syndicate of lenders dealing with the borrower and the guarantor. When a disbursement is to be made the agent will advise the syndicate members of their participation amounts. They will pay their proportion to the agent which lumps them all together for disbursement in a single tranche, to the exporter.

Interest

Interest is usually payable at the same regular intervals as the repayments of principal. Where there is no repayment of principal, perhaps because there is a grace period and repayments have not yet begun, interest is normally paid six monthly or at another frequency.

Interest can be paid at a floating rate, usually priced at a margin over the lender's cost of borrowing or over a market funding rate such as London Interbank Offered Rate (LIBOR). As London is a major financial centre for eurocurrency loan funding this would be a common funding term. Alternatively if the loan is being funded in another market one would expect cost of funds in that market to be the basis for fixing the price.

ECA Subsidised Rates

Under ECA-covered loans a floating rate can still apply but it is likely that the ECA will pay a subsidy to the bank in order to manufacture a low, fixed rate which will be applied to the loan. In such circumstances the interest subsidy or 'interest make up' paid by the ECA concerned will be the difference between the fixed rate applying to the loan and the real cost of funds to the bank plus the bank's margin, for example:

Fixed rate on loan   = 5% per annum
Cost of bank funds plus margin = 10%
Subsidy payable by ECA   = 5%

Alternatively, under an ECA-supported export credit a so-called 'CIRR' rate can apply. This Commercial Interest Reference Rate applying at the time of contract signature as agreed with the supporting bank can sometimes be lower and therefore more attractive to the borrower than the ECA subsidised fixed rate. ECA subsidised fixed or 'consensus rates' are agreed every six months by the ECAs which are members of the consensus (see later section on export credit agencies).

Covenants and Warranties

As a buyer credit loan agreement may run to anything from 20 to over 40 pages of legalese, covenants and warranties cannot be dealt with in depth here. There are, however, one or two features which crop up in most agreements, whether they are bespoke tailored export credit loans or derive from eurocurrency loan documentation.

Conditions precedent

The signing of such loans does not usually open the way for drawings to be made. Certain other documents referred to as conditions precedent usually need to be collected before the loan can be declared effective by the agent to the borrower and all other parties to the loan.

Some examples of CPs (though not an exhaustive list) are as follows:

- board resolutions of the borrower and the guarantor that they have agreed to enter into the agreement;
- powers of attorney empowering the persons signing the agreement to do so on behalf of the borrower and the guarantor;
- ECA credit guarantee documents which support the loan;
- documents relating to interest subsidies payable by an ECA in support of the loan;
- agreements relating to fees payable to the lenders and/or the agent;
- agency agreement empowering the agent to act as such on behalf of the lending banks;
- payment of all fees due and expenses incurred which may be required before the banks will be prepared to make the loan effective.

Interest rate determination

Where the loan bears interest at a floating rate (see above) interest rates are normally established as if the loan were structured as a series of consecutive, automatically renewable loans of six months each – assuming that the interest is payable six monthly. Two days before renewal (or 'rollover') of the loan the agent bank obtains two or sometimes three 'reference rates' which the loan agreement will define as the rates at which significant participants in the eurocurrency deposit market will offer deposits in the currency for the period required under the loan agreement. The agent will calculate the average of these rates to determine the 'LIBOR' or other funding rate as defined in the agreement.

Market collapse

Often lengthy and convoluted, this part of the loan agreement boils down to what to do if it becomes necessary to establish some other way of funding the loan. It describes how to fix interest rates if the interest rate determination as discussed above cannot be carried out due to exceptional circumstances, such as collapse of the eurocurrency market.

Negative pledge

A clause for which World Bank loans are famous, the negative pledge is a warranty by the borrower that the assets defined in the agreement will not be pledged as security for other borrowings. Loans made by the World Bank have traditionally included a negative pledge as they are usually made to risky sovereign borrowers over whose national natural resources the Bank retains a lien.

Acceleration
Should the borrower and guarantor fail to make a payment of principal or interest when it falls due, then the entire loan plus accrued interest will fall due and payable within a defined, short period after the present failure to pay.

Cross default
Normally loathed by borrowers, this can take various forms. The most severe provides that if the borrower or the guarantor should default under this or *any other loan agreement* the present loan will immediately fall due and payable in its entirety.

Application of recoveries
In the event that amounts are recovered, following default for example, this clause will define how they are to be credited against the loan outstandings. Typically, they will be applied firstly against outstandings including interest on outstandings, then against interest on the loan and finally against any due and unpaid principal.

Governing law
Will normally refer to the jurisdiction where all parties would feel most comfortable for legal action to be taken if the worst came to the worst. The three most popular are 'the Law of England', New York law and law applying in a particular financial or legal centre in Switzerland.

There are numerous other provisions of buyer's credit loan agreements. Many are quite standard elements which mirror or overlap those of standard eurocurrency loans which are purely for funding purposes and are not linked to either the supply of goods and equipment or to ECA guarantees.

Further documentation
One of the key differences between buyer's credit loans and 'plain vanilla' eurocurrency loans is that being export-related, administration, including drawing procedures, cause buyer's credits to be more cumbersome. They also tend to be drawn in odd amounts to match the value of shipments rather than in round amounts of funds which can be the case with eurocurrency loans.

Where buyer's credits benefit from an ECA guarantee a further level of documentation and bureaucratic delay is added. Because, in effect, two buyer's credits are unlikely to be the same there is not the same ease of bench-marking against similar instruments for the same borrower in the marketplace. For these reasons it is fair to say that export-related buyer's credits are complicated and belong among the export financier's specialist techniques rather than capital market funding instruments such as eurobonds.

Applying Swap Techniques

Because a buyer's credit loan agreement, once it is drawn, represents a series of future cashflows there may be scope for using it to match interest rate or currency swap opportunities. There must of course be no doubt that the funds will be received on the due date. It has to be admitted that highly-rated borrowers who could assure such cashflows are relatively unlikely to be borrowers under buyer's credits because they are likely to have access to cheaper funding by other means via the capital markets. Government borrowers and guarantors might have the credit standing however and the need, in the context of large purchase contracts for capital goods, for attractively-priced buyer's credits.

There have been occasions where a buyer's credit loan structure has evolved to make use of interest rate and currency swap opportunities in order to cheapen the cost of the export finance. Where an ECA is providing a predictable subsidy flow at good rates and the structuring bank has the expertise in both export credits and swaps, a definite cost advantage can be delivered to the borrower and/or the exporting client at a profit to the bank.

Pricing Buyer's Credits

There are a number of ways in which banks profit from buyer's credits. Here are the most common ones:

Interest margin
Whether or not an ECA subsidy is involved, a spread over costs of funds is conventional and is priced in relation to the credit risk and the duration of the loan.

Commitment commission
Where a bank has committed itself to making funds available under a buyer's credit a commitment fee would be chargeable to the borrower. This would carry on being paid, usually quarterly or half-yearly in arrears, until either the committed funds had been fully drawn or the drawdown period had expired, whichever was the sooner.

It would be charged at a percentage per annum which may vary between as little as 0.25 per cent to perhaps as much as 0.75 per cent depending on what can be negotiated. If there are several banks or a lending syndicate involved each will be paid in direct proportion to its commitment to the transaction.

Management commission

If the loan structure has had to be developed with the client and subsequently managed through to effectiveness, a management commission can be collected. This is usually payable as a fixed percentage of the loan value.

If there are several banks or a lending syndicate involved it is conventional for those with the largest participations to receive a higher proportion of the management commission. To give an indicative idea, in a transaction of US$100 million a lender of US$20 million might receive 0.75 per cent flat on the value of the participation whereas the bank lending US$5 million might receive only 0.5 per cent flat.

In a further twist to the management fee distribution, the agent bank, whose job it will be to place participations with banks and agree the fee split among them, may well take a further proportion often referred to as a 'praecipium' in addition to that proportion of management fee relating to his or her participation on the lending. Management fees are often called 'front end fees' because they are usually payable on the effectiveness of the loan.

Agency fee

The agent may charge an annual fee of a fixed amount to cover the ongoing management and agency function which he or she performs throughout the life of the loan. Looking at the fees listed and at the amount of control and reward the agent bank has in the arrangement and administration of buyer's credits it is not surprising that agency roles in arranging buyer's credits, especially substantial-sized ones, are hotly fought over. Traditionally buyer credit loans have been led by merchant banks, investment banks and larger international banks with specialist skills in loan arrangement and syndication as well as export financing.

LINES OF CREDIT

Description

Buyer's credits as described above tend to relate to one piece of equipment or one set of goods, even if there are multiple shipments and drawings under the facility. They usually involve one supplier or one main contractor who co-ordinates the supply arrangements agreed in the supply contract and the loan drawings. Lines of credit ('LOC' or 'line') are, however, more wide-ranging.

A buyer may wish to establish a LOC to cover a range of purchases. It signs supply contracts with several individual suppliers, the payment terms of which will be upon presentation of shipping documents under the line. The buyer directs the supplier to the agent bank for the line and, rather like making a drawing under a documentary credit, the supplier will present documents to the agent bank and be paid, typically at sight, if the documents conform to its terms.

Buyers will typically be large corporations, governments or their ministries with substantial purchasing needs. Goods covered under the line may range from items costing several millions of dollars each down to spares costing a few thousand.

There is no reason why more than one buyer should not be covered under the line provided the ultimate credit risk is a single buyer or guarantor. Thus, for example, a government may set up a line of credit to cover purchases of vehicles by several of its ministries. The government may be responsible for the overall payment or be the guarantor standing behind the ministries. A corporation might adopt a similar plan to finance purchases by several of its subsidiaries or branches.

Disbursement and Repayment

Just as for the buyer's credit, disbursements to suppliers will be debited to the buyer/borrower's loan account in the bank's books. The buyer/borrower agrees to repay the loan according to the loan agreement in the same way as a buyer's credit.

Goods Covered

The LOC is then a kind shopping facility which can cover a variety of goods sold by a number of suppliers to one or more buyers. How it is configured will obviously depend on the particular circumstances of the transaction.

Where the definition of the goods is deliberately left vague in order to cover as wide a range of goods as possible the financing arranged may be termed a *general purpose line of credit*. If the purpose of the facility is to pay for goods, plant, equipment and/or services for a particular project it may be called a *project line of credit*. Some lines are established in respect of a buyer's particular sectoral requirements, for example to pay for medical goods, in which case the line may be called a *medical line of credit* and so forth.

ECA Cover

Many lines of credit are supported by ECAs. They may be viewed as tools of government aid policy – as can any form of export credit assistance – making available finance tied to exports from that country. Like buyer's credits they can benefit from guarantees which cover the risk of non-payment of the loans' principal and interest. They can also be supported by interest rate subsidies payable to the financing bank in order to make available fixed and/or preferential interest rate finance to the borrower.

Arrangement and Management

A bank arranging and managing an LOC may also syndicate the lending among a group or syndicate of banks. Each bank will pay its participation proportion to the agent bank in respect of each drawing and will, over the life of the loan, receive its proportion of interest and repayment as well as its fees as for a conventional buyer's credit.

The agent is likely to be involved in a substantial amount of administration if there are many disbursements to suppliers. It may be necessary to define a minimum drawing limit for the line, for example. If a line of US$100 million allows for minimum drawings of as large an amount as US$1 million there is still the possibility of 100 drawings being made. This means that 100 sets of shipping documents will require inspection and account being kept of what are, effectively, 100 separate loans.

It would be normal to aggregate the loans once all the drawings have been made. The loan would then repay by equal instalments of the aggregate value of the drawings. Thus if a five year US$100 million line was full drawn, it would then be treated as one loan repayable by ten equal semi-annual instalments of US$10 million over the five-year period.

SUPPLIER'S CREDITS

Description

As we have seen, both buyer's credits and lines of credit are loans to the buyers of goods, equipment and services. A supplier may also provide a customer with credit arrangements allowing the customer to pay for purchases over several months or years. Forfaiting, as we saw in Chapter 5, is a form of supplier's credit finance where the seller receives promissory notes or bills of exchange as evidence of the future obligations of the buyer to pay for the goods over time. In such cases the supplier discounts the paper

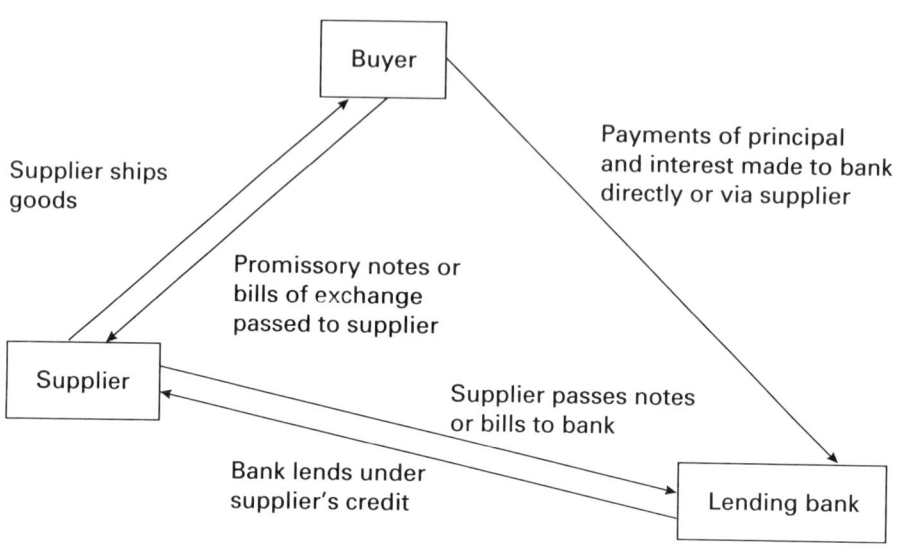

Figure 6.2: Supplier's credit structure

in order to refinance himself or herself. A supplier's credit loan (SCL) similarly refinances the supplier but in this case for the full amount under a loan agreement.

Effectively an SCL is a back-to-back funding operation whereby the supplier passes through, or assigns, to the lending bank(s) the credit risk and the funding requirements of the transaction. Bills of exchange or promissory notes will still be employed as evidence of the buyer's payment obligation. The payments made by the buyer under the notes will be assigned to the bank and will probably be paid directly to the bank under a standing arrangement, although they may reach the bank via the supplier. The supplier will assign the rights to such payment although it may be obliged to pursue payment on the bank's behalf in the event of default.

Disbursement

Practically speaking the mechanics of drawing will be placed in the hands of the lending bank as follows:

- A loan agreement is signed between the lender and the supplier of the goods in respect of the supply contract which exists between the supplier and buyer.

- As a condition precedent to effectiveness of the loan, pre-signed notes or bills in blank will be deposited in trust by the buyer of the goods, either with the same bank or with another bank.
- Upon shipment(s) of goods the note(s) or bill(s) will be completed by the trustee bank under agreement with the buyer to reflect the value payable for the shipment. The notes will also reflect interest payable for the credit period allowed for under those instruments.
- The notes or bills will be released to the seller against presentation of documents defined in the supply contract which will be likely to include evidence of shipment, invoices, packing lists and so on.
- The seller will then be in a position to make a drawing under the loan agreement by passing the bills or notes to the lending bank. It may endorse the notes to the bank or, if this cannot be done for some reason, will have entered into a separate agreement with the bank, agreeing to assign the proceeds of payments made against the instruments to the bank.

The effect of this supplier's credit structure is that credit is made available to the buyer by the supplier but the supplier has been able to avoid becoming the buyer's banker for what may be several years after the supply of the goods and consequent delay in cashflow. The supplier receives payment as soon as he or she presents shipping documents.

Guarantees

Where other collateral guarantees are received by the exporter, these are also either signed over to the bank (if they are transferable by endorsement) or the future benefit payable to the exporter (in the event of a claim), assigned to the bank. Such guarantees might take the form of standby letters of credit (see letters of credit above) or bank guarantees issued in favour of the exporter on behalf of the buyer. An ECA guarantee may also be available to the supplier.

ECA Guarantees

In the case of ECA guarantees several issues arise. Firstly, an export credit guarantee policy must be issued in the exporter's favour. This could either be a general policy covering export turnover as a whole, under which the transaction in question can be placed, or a transaction-specific policy relating directly to this one-off deal.

In the event of a claim, the supplier makes the claim and processes the paperwork in the normal way. The bank which has advanced funds under

77

the SCL will receive the proceeds of the claim either indirectly via the supplier or directly from the ECA as loss payee. The exact system will vary from one ECA to another but the structure will remain pretty much the same.

There may also be an interest make-up or subsidy available to the supplier enabling the interest rate payable by the buyer to be fixed at consensus rate. In this case arrangements are made for such subsidy to be paid on again to the SCL lending bank, either by the supplier or directly by the ECA, depending on the system of the ECA which is supporting the transaction.

Confirming House Supplier Credits

A further structure which can be used is that the bank effectively inserts itself or an associated company between the buyer and seller for the purpose of gaining ECA cover. The bank's company, which we will call 'Bank Export Services' (BES), is often termed a 'confirming house'. BES will buy the goods from the supplier and sell them to the overseas buyer in a back-to-back transaction. Effectively replacement invoices will be used to document the transaction. The exporter's invoices will be replaced by those of BES which will accompany the shipping documents to the hands of the buyer.

BES will have its own ECA policy or will be the exporter for the purposes of a deal-specific one issued by the ECA. BES will also receive the interest subsidy. To complete the structure the bank will lend to BES, which will appear as the borrower under the SCL agreement. For practical purposes both the loan and the functions of the BES company will be performed and administrated by the bank which will have the whole transaction fully under its control. The exporter will enter into a separate agreement with BES and will receive payment against shipping documents which will be simultaneously presented to the bank under the SCL.

7: State-supported Export Credits

INTRODUCTION

State support for the finance of a country's exports is the subject of a great deal of literature and comment. A common form of such support is via the individual Export Credit Agencies (ECA) of each state which, together with tied aid funding and other forms of support, are aimed at promoting donor countries' commercial interests with the target market. This section will deal with the basics of who the ECAs are, what they do, how they are governed and structured and how they work.

Details of specific markets covered, premium rates or particulars of the operations of the separate agencies have been omitted, firstly because the subject would require a separate volume to list them all and secondly because the ECA sector is in a state of flux. Some ECAs are slated for privatisation. In the UK this has partially happened already with the sale of ECGD's short-term operations to Dutch insurer NCM. Cost controls and the need for a profit imperative have seeped into a number of ECAs as mounting losses, funded by tax payers, have been recognised as unsustainable. With a Europe-wide export credit bank under discussion and other new trading blocks being formed the ECA game is one where the rules are likely to change quite quickly and radically over the next few years.

THE BERNE UNION AND THE CONSENSUS

The Berne Union, The International Union of Credit and Investment Insurers as it is properly called, was founded in 1934 and boasts 40 members worldwide. It is a forum where state organisations and private political risk insurers meet to discuss the rules governing the insurance of world trade. Specifically it fosters 'sound principles of export credit insurance', maintains 'discipline in the terms for international trade credit', encourages co-operation to enhance a favourable international investment climate and promotes 'sound principles of foreign investment insurance'. Export finance banks and officials of national export credit agencies will often refer to the Berne Union, particularly when asked to support out-of-the-ordinary transactions which they are prevented from helping with.

The Organisation for Economic Co-operation and Development (OECD) also plays a central disciplinary role in agreeing the Guidelines for Officially Supported Export Credits – commonly referred to as the 'Consensus'. This particularly concerns levels of interest rate subsidy which governments may make available in support of export sales and the length of credit periods which governments may guarantee. The term 'Consensus' is frequently used in discussions about officially supported export credits and its guidelines on terms and conditions for export credit cover should be adhered to by the individual agencies.

EXPORT CREDIT GUARANTEES AND COUNTRY CATEGORIES

ECAs, principally from the industrialised world, are prepared to issue guarantees in favour of exporters or their bankers that payments due to them in respect of exports will be made. The guarantees are usually issued in respect of overseas governments' obligations or those of their agencies or their banks which are acceptable to the ECA involved.

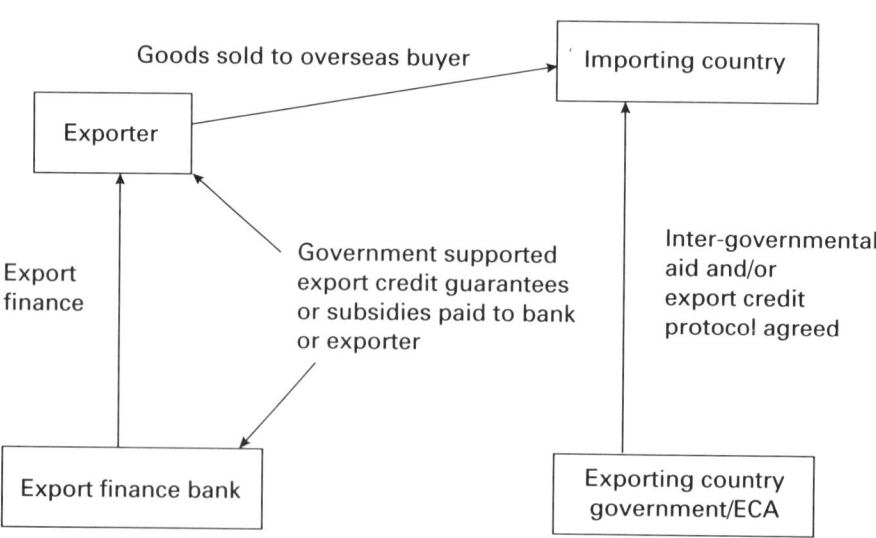

Figure 7.1: Export credit structure

ECAs monitor the track records for overseas debtors of this sort. An exporter or export financier contemplating applying for export credit cover is well advised to check with the ECA concerned at an early stage as to what it can cover before entering into discussions about the availability of finance or the pricing of an underlying contract of sale. The following factors may all be subject to alteration: risks covered, premium levels, duration of credit covered and the amount and rate of interest subsidy available.

Typically ECAs will cover:

- political factors affecting risk of non-payment due to a government's actions, such as government restrictions on foreign exchange availability;
- principal and interest due from debtors and/or guarantors and sometimes delay interest payable in respect of non-paid principal and interest.

The terms of cover differ from one ECA to another. Some coverage is more comprehensive than others, some waiting periods following claims are longer than others, some ECAs will cover markets which others will not. All of them are committed to providing no more than 85 per cent cover in respect of export contract values. Some in fact will only insure up to 90 per cent or 95 per cent of 85 per cent of contract values.

The 15 per cent not covered by export credit guarantees is usually paid as a downpayment, either as a direct payment on account, or under a letter of credit. Indeed it is often a term of the effectiveness of ECA cover that such downpayment has been received by the exporter or the exporter's bank.

These broad definitions leave ample scope for differences between one ECA insurance coverage and another. It can therefore be advantageous for an exporter with manufacturing, assembly or sub-contracting operations in several different countries to check the availability and scope of cover from the ECAs of each source market.

In this regard and bearing in mind that ECAs are tools of governments' trade policies, it is often easy to identify the ECA government's political interest or commitment in whether it is prepared to cover certain market risks. An outstanding example in recent years has been Italian government support for massive natural gas pipeline operations in Algeria and in the former Soviet Union.

Italy supported its exporters in bidding for the construction of the necessary infrastructure with large export credit limits. Italy, of course, has a shortage of energy fuels on the one hand which it can go some of the way to resolving by negotiating long-term supply contracts with such producer countries as part of the 'export credit package'. Secondly, it has a strong interest in seeing stable political and economic conditions in neighbouring Mediterranean states and in central and eastern Europe. It also has an oil and gas related construction industry which is currently largely controlled

81

by the state hydrocarbons agency, ENI, which is able to marshal strong Italian government support for its export sales operations.

In the same way the scope of coverage available to German exporters for sales to countries in eastern and central Europe is far more substantial than for others because of Germany's political interests in those regions. US Eximbank's support for its neighbour and NAFTA partner Mexico is similarly more substantial than that which any other ECA provides to its exporters.

In order to further regulate the degree of guarantee cover they can make available, ECAs categorise overseas territories in three groups:

- Group 1 countries are the wealthier markets which qualify for support;
- Group 2 are the less wealthy or medium emerging countries; and
- Group 3 are the poorest countries which are in need of the highest level of support.

Countries may be re-categorised from time to time in recognition of their economic re-emergence and improved credit status or their deterioration.

INTEREST RATE SUBSIDIES

ECAs or their associate government-backed institutions will often enable the exporter or his or her banker to offer fixed rate finance to the overseas buyer. These fixed rates, which are governed by the consensus and published periodically, are called *consensus rates*. In addition there are CIRR rates – Commercial Interest Reference Rates – which are also supported by ECAs.

When choosing the rate to offer a client along with the credit terms conceded under a credit sale, an exporter has the option of offering the consensus rate or the CIRR rate whichever is the lower. ECA support for interest rates is achieved by paying a subsidy to the exporter or the exporter's banker to make up the difference between the interest rate offered and the matching market rate plus the banker's margin.

Thus a bank may make a loan to an overseas buyer to enable it to pay for an exporter's goods over several years (a buyer's credit, see Chapter 6). The loan may carry interest at 5 per cent per annum payable every six months. If the six month interbank rate for that currency is 7 per cent per annum and the banker's margin is 1 per cent per annum the bank may receive a subsidy of 3 per cent per annum, the difference between the fixed rate of 5 per cent per annum and the interbank rate plus the margin totalling 8 per cent per annum.

The manner and organisation of the payment of such subsidy differs between ECAs. Thus the UK's ECGD both grants guarantees and pays the subsidy. Other agencies, such as those of Italy and Spain, separate the guaranteeing and subsidy functions into different entities. Moreover ECAs may or may not make the two types of support available in tandem. ECGD allows the interest subsidy to be paid only when linked to its guarantee, whereas Italy and Spain allow exporters to make use of either or both to match the transaction involved.

The clear message from all this is that exporters and their bankers should check the terms and conditions of whichever ECAs they or their subsidiaries or sub-contractors have access to, in order to see which one provides the most suitable arrangements.

PREMIUMS

Yes, you've guessed it. Not only do premium rates differ from one agency to another but so do the methods by which they are calculated. There are considerable differences in overall cost to exporters obtaining ECA guarantee cover from respective country ECAs. This is another reason why a contractor or firm with several different supply locations will shop around to see if sourcing products from different markets can be of advantage.

To illustrate the point, when Mexico was still in early-emergence phase and most ECAs were operating with restricted cover, a protocol was signed between Mexico and Spain which gave birth to the so-called 'King's Line' to cover exports of Spanish origin to Mexico. The result was that a number of substantial international companies with Spanish operations switched their sourcing to Spain in order to take advantage of the available cover.

There is no reason, of course, why a firm needs to produce goods *itself* in the market of the export cover. It may source them there and then invoice them to its overseas customer. Provided that the goods can be defined as having the origin of the country concerned the firm should be able to gain the support needed if acceptable to the ECA.

CREDIT TERMS

ECAs may cover short-, medium- and long-term credit in support of capital goods. In fact most agencies handle much more short term business than the headline-grabbing major power, bridge or road projects which can be financed over terms in excess of a decade. With shorter-term business the ECA is at risk for a shorter period of time and has the option of revolving its limits for succeeding contracts and charging premium each time.

These days commercial thinking has become a necessity among ECAs (see above). However, while the UK's ECGD was sold to NCM the UK government agreed to extend a reinsurance treaty to NCM for a limited time. It therefore remained, at least during the handover phase, the risk-taker of last resort. As other countries attempt to balance their budgets and reduce central government control of such functions, they may well follow suit and put out export credit operations to private management and control. Their intention will be to back away from risk taking on delinquent overseas debtors.

Privatising of the medium- and long-term ECA guaranteeing entities does not look as hopeful. Attracting investment to loss-making public sector entities is unlikely to be blessed with success unless the pill is sweetened in some way, which might prove costly and defeat the object of the exercise. This is especially so if one considers that unless the risk of an underlying commercial operation was not fairly high ECA cover would not have been sought in the first place. In any case most exporters would prefer to avoid having to negotiate export credit cover from their governments and deal with the bureaucracy involved if the commercial realities of their overseas sales allowed.

TERMS FOR GOODS

ECA cover is typically for exports of capital goods. Again however, agencies may back facilities of other types where special protocols have been agreed. General purpose lines of credit (see Chapter 6) are used to fund the procurement of a range of goods. Lines of credit have been used in respect of pharmaceutical equipment and for the purchase of foodstuffs as well as for engineered products such as small-scale machinery and spare parts. Exporters and export financiers should contact their national ECAs to ascertain whether lines of credit are available for particular types of goods exported to particular territories.

GRANTS, AID AND MIXED CREDITS

Government support for exports can also take the form of long-term, low interest rate loans which fall more within the definition of 'aid' than under the terms of the consensus. These are called *soft loans*. Where there is no obligation to repay the funding the term is *grant aid*. An export support package which includes elements of export credit, soft loans and grant aid is called a *mixed credit*.

Most exporters are unlikely to use mixed credits as they are generally arranged in support of large infrastructural projects. Mixed credits, aid packages and so forth are politically motivated. This can be to the exporter's advantage and to that of their bankers if an atmosphere has been created where their government wishes to be seen to provide needed help. If, however, it is another country's government which acts as 'donor', this can have the reverse effect.

Another side effect is that where one country has provided soft terms in support of previous contracts a buyer may expect similar terms for new business from a new exporter. This distorts the credit negotiation considerably. It is worth noting, however, that in general the modern tendency among donor governments, aid agencies and ECAs is to offer more commercially-priced export credits and decrease their aid budget.

PROJECT FINANCING AND COUNTERTRADE

Separate sections of this book are devoted to these techniques: however, export credits in support of revenue-driven projects are becoming more common. Where a project can be proved to be self-financing, ECAs may cover the risks of the project itself rather than take only the political risk of the sovereign government in whose territory the project is being carried out.

This has been partly the result of the 1980s debt crisis when the notion that 'governments don't go bust' was disproved. It is also partly the result of more prudent housekeeping at ECAs. Project financings, 'build, own, operate and transfer' and other variations are currently the fashion, especially in Group 2 (medium risk) countries where the political risks may not be as high. In fact, the amount of project work carried out in Group 3 (poorer) countries has diminished considerably over recent years.

Countertrade risks are also of a different order than those of straightforward sales contracts. There may be a political risk involved in delivery of goods from developing countries which are being exchanged for imports. ECAs are in principle able to cover these risks, especially if they are short-term and the political will is present. For most exporters and trade financiers, however, countertrade plays a small or non-existent part in the facilities they need to draw on.

8: Countertrade: Forms and Structures

INTRODUCTION

Traditionally countertrade has been used to facilitate trade where conventional exchange of cash or credit for goods has proved difficult. It is in that sense the market of last resort. But as we shall see below that isn't quite the whole story. Forms of countertrade and barter are now becoming common in wealthy western markets such as the United States and Europe.

Traditional countertrade structures make use of available commodities, materials, manufactured or semi-manufactured goods in place of currency as the means of purchase. It is something of a specialist art form where the use of experienced help can be advantageous in achieving the best result.

It has been estimated that 10–15% of the world's trade is transacted by means of countertrade. However, there is no way of accurately verifying this estimate as countertrade could be said to encompass a range of commerce from the exchange of vegetables by neighbouring gardeners to billions of dollars worth of arms traded for oil exports. However, about 100 countries have established rules and regulations to govern the use of countertrade, indicating that its use is quite widespread.

Countertrade was much favoured in the former eastern bloc, aligned countries and other markets with centralised economies. Forms of it are still used in those countries and in other emerging markets around the world. Its principal attractions are:

- to stimulate demand for the products of centrally controlled industries;
- to create a market for surplus production or for low quality products;
- to balance trade where there was an imbalance in favour of suppliers from western, developed market economies;
- to overcome a dearth of commercial credit.

Countertrade is certainly not an 'off the shelf' solution for financing overseas trade. Every deal is different, and there are many pitfalls. There are some conventions and very few rules. However, it does facilitate trade where otherwise it might not have been possible and can be rewarding for trading counterparties, banks and intermediaries who can successfully structure deals. Some of the common structures and examples of their use are given in the following sections.

STRUCTURES

Barter

Index of value

The pure exchange of goods for goods between two parties is called barter. Having said that, there remains the question of what each party's goods are worth and the evaluation method to be used. How, for example, could the value of a cargo of oil be reckoned against a consignment of rice?

This can be resolved where the goods concerned are traded on a recognised exchange. Where oil is exchanged for imported goods the value of the oil can be linked to the quoted price for that specification of oil say, in London or Rotterdam, as published at an agreed time and place; likewise if the goods are metals, minerals, tea, coffee, soya beans and so on. If the goods are not traded on an exchange or there is not an accepted world reference price mechanism then it becomes a matter of haggling to reach a mutually acceptable pricing. The establishment of an *index of value* is a pivotal issue of any countertrade operation.

The index of value will almost inevitably be the price of the goods to be exchanged, denominated in US Dollars or other hard currency. Often the

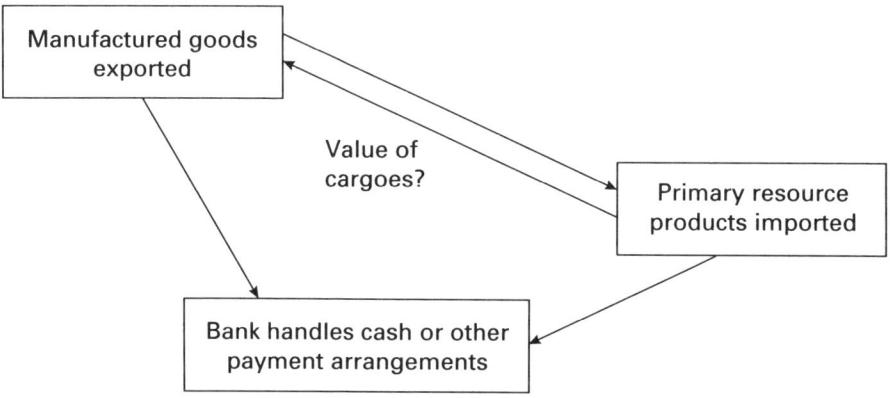

Figure 8.1: Structure of a simple barter

goods from one side of the transaction are difficult to price. There were numerous examples when trading with the former eastern bloc, where the manufactured goods were of low quality compared with similar articles for sale in the west. The party line from the eastern European sellers was that the goods were worth far more than they could have fetched in the west, even if it had been possible to find a buyer. The process of establishing a hard currency value therefore became a bone of contention.

Delivery risk

Having established the price then *delivery* becomes a prime concern. How can the buyer and the seller be sure that the goods will arrive where and when agreed?

Delivery risk can be insured against in the commercial insurance market. This is fine provided an underwriter is prepared to take such a risk, perhaps on the basis of prior experience. Where an underwriter has no prior experience and the seller has a poor or non-existent track record insurance will not be an option.

Perhaps a guarantee from a third party could be arranged. For example where the exported goods are the property of a government, ministry or state organisation a government guarantee from the exporting country might be arranged. More often than not no guarantee is available, in which case timing becomes crucial.

Timing

Timing is a key factor in delivery and therefore in the security of the transaction. If one of the parties is in greater need of the goods than the other – as will often be the case with priority imports such as oil, food and arms – then he or she may be prepared to be the first one to export goods in order to generate funds to get the transaction started.

Alternatively if the party delivering a cargo of goods has sufficient trust in the buyer to export his or her goods before recieving the buyer's goods then the delivery risk can be covered. In either of these cases one party will have to take a risk on the other. This is not ideal and would be unlikely in a first transaction between counterparties without the use of an intermediary trusted by both parties. Such an intermediary would effectively act as trustee for the goods of the counterparties who might in any case arrange for payment to be made at shipment by their respective letters of credit opened in each other's favour.

Quality and quantity risks

These can be dealt with by using an inspection agency which can send an expert assessor to test and/or measure the goods before dispatch and issue a certificate of inspection or 'clean report of findings' to the effect that the cargo is correct. Three of the best known international inspection agencies are Cotecna Inspection SA, SGS – Société Generale de Surveillance SA and Bureau Veritas. The contact details of these firms are given in the names and addresses section.

Trading companies
The chances that parties in a barter transaction are in complementary businesses is remote. The seller of rice, for example, probably will not have a great deal of use for a consignment of plastic buckets offered in the countertrade. Off-loading the unwanted goods can be time-consuming and it may be difficult to find a buyer who is prepared to pay a decent price for amounts of unwanted goods. One of the advantages in dealing with centralised economies is that, in principal at least, the government is the buyer of the imported goods and the seller of the export side of the deal. In practice it can be difficult to co-ordinate unless all foreign trading relations are in the hands of one centralised foreign trading entity. Even then getting unrelated departments within the same bureaucracy to speak to each other may not be easy.

To overcome this sort of problem *trading companies* or merchants are often counterparties in barter transactions. A trading company experienced in countertrading can perform the function of evaluating the goods being taken in the exchange and disposing of them on behalf of a principal.

If for example our seller of rice is offered that consignment of buckets, the trading house will locate a buyer for the buckets, negotiate a price for them and arrange delivery and payment with the end buyer of the buckets. The seller of the rice does not then need to become involved in the pricing and sale of the buckets at which, most likely, he or she has less skill than the trading company which carries out such operations regularly and knows a great many counterparties. In large corporations a trading subsidiary may perform this function, especially if the corporation is actively trading its goods into territories where countertrade is often requested as a solution to paying for imports.

Use of escrow accounts
Barter in its purest form is bound to be rare because of the unlikelihood of matching transactions being able to be structured. It is easier to use exports from the weaker country to produce funds which are subsequently used to fund the purchase of imports. In other words the export revenues are already gathered in before the import side of the countertrade takes place.

In such cases the funds arising from the exported goods are held in an *escrow account*, a specifically designated account opened with an international bank for the specific purpose of buying imports. The funds can only be disbursed from the escrow account once the seller of the imported goods has met certain pre-agreed conditions. The following is an example to illustrate how such a structure might work:

Freedonia is an African country whose finance ministry wishes to have its banknotes printed in Switzerland. Swissprint, the supplier, is not sure that it will receive payment as Freedonia has considerable outstanding foreign debts. However, Swissprint tries harder; it looks at a countertrade solution.

Freedonia happens to have large deposits of copper which it usually exports, selling through its normal agent in London. Swissprint suggests to the Freedonian government that it can pay the proceeds from the sale of copper into an escrow account with a Swiss bank which will hold the funds to the Freedonians' instruction.

These funds are then used to provide confirmation for a particular contract which the Freedonians agree with Swissprint. The bank holding the funds will either pay cash or issue a confirmed, irrevocable, cash-collateralised letter of credit in favour of Swissprint to cover payment for the Freedonian order.

Upon shipment, Swissprint claims its money from the bank and is paid. Swissprint will only print Freedonian notes if the trustee bank confirms that it holds sufficient funds to cover the order.

This crude example covers both parties' needs. It is noteworthy that Swissprint has not become involved in deciding on an index of value. Nor has it had to haggle with the Freedonians about the copper's actual market price. The advance payment of the cash revenue from the copper sale into the escrow account has been key to the whole transaction.

Also significant is that the two apparently irreconcilable elements of copper and printed banknotes have turned out to be complementary. It is often the lateral thinkers who succeed in trading into difficult markets by pulling disparate factors into a deal. The late Armand Hammer's early forays in Russia trading American grain for the starving populace against Russian furs, already hold a secure place in the annals of countertrade.

Counterpurchase
Counterpurchase is a technique which has been widely used in some countries and is relatively flexible but again may involve disparate elements. A buyer, in all probability a government or state-controlled entity in a developing country may wish to buy capital goods of some description. It agrees to do so on the basis that some of its exports are taken in lieu of all or part of the payment. The sales contract for the capital goods and purchase contract for the counter-purchased goods are separate but linked. They may be drawn up in the context of a framework agreement covering the two

contracts. The following imaginary example can serve to illustrate how the counterpurchase would work.

A government in a developing country wishes to purchase trucks for its ministry of transport. It approaches a European truck manufacturer with whom it agrees that it will pay for the trucks 50 per cent by confirmed irrevocable letter of credit and 50 per cent from the proceeds of sales of its banana crop. The advantage for the government here is that it can pay a local producer of the bananas in its own local currency. The banana grower may or may not be a state-owned plantation.

The bananas will not be bought by the truck manufacturer, however, as it has no use for them. Instead they will be bought under a separate contract with a fruit merchant with two provisos: that the proceeds from the sale of the bananas will be placed into an escrow account and used to pay the truck supplier and that the two contracts, for the purchase of the trucks and the sale of the bananas, will be linked under a framework agreement which defines the structure and operation of the counterpurchase.

There is one further complication and that is that the bananas may in fact be overpriced in the context of the market in which the fruit wholesaler has to resell them. In this case the seller of the trucks raises the price of the vehicles to allow for a

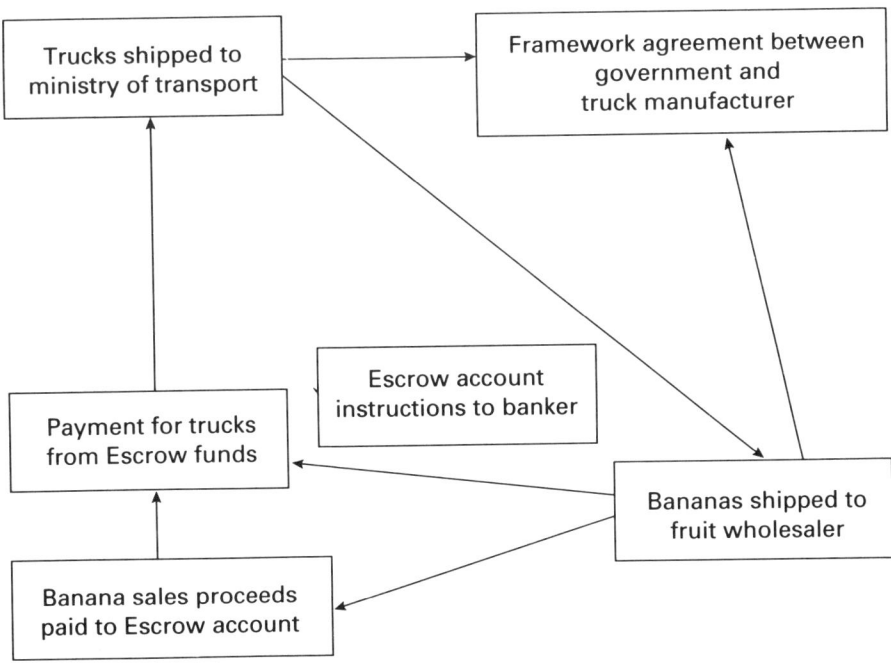

Figure 8.2: Counterpurchase of trucks for bananas

disaggio or subsidy to be paid to the banana wholesaler to level up the price. Without the disaggio the banana side of the counterpurchase would not work because the price of the bananas would be too high.

This example illustrates several key features of counterpurchase:

- The sale of the trucks can go ahead but flexibility is required on the part of the truck manufacturer to make it work.
- The trade of trucks for bananas looks, on the face of it, to be outlandish and unhopeful. In fact, with two linked contracts the very different elements in the counterpurchase can be reconciled.
- The disaggio is a key element to a realistic deal being struck. It is a way of solving the index of value/value for goods puzzle.

Buy-back and off-take arrangements
Also sometimes referred to as compensation, this technique can be used to pay for imports of capital plant and equipment. The goods produced by the capital plant are taken in part payment. It would be unlikely that 100 per cent of the plant would be paid for in off-take products.

Here is an example of how such a structure might work:

Papcom is a bankrupted Russian paper company which owns a dilapidated paper mill near the Baltic Sea. The mill is badly in need of refurbishment. Finmills is a Finnish company with the required technology in paper milling equipment. It can see an opportunity to gain a foothold in Russia, taking advantage of cheap timber and labour there. It has the opportunity of acquiring a controlling stake in the mill and of upgrading the mill to produce paper of internationally saleable quality.

Knowing that Papcom has no money, Finmills invests in a controlling stake in the mill and supplies the machinery on condition that it will be paid back in paper produced by the mill. It will have exclusive rights to the paper produced.

As Finmills has other divisions which are major paper suppliers internationally with a thorough knowledge of the world paper markets it is confident that it will be able to generate the revenue from selling the paper and that the whole scheme can be made to work.

This example would entail resolution of issues such as political risk and foreign ownership which we will side-step for the sake of this example. The key word in this buy-back is *control*. Finmills will control the production, probably supervising every stage in order to ensure the quantity and quality of the output. It may also own the proprietary process which will be used in making paper at the mill. By taking delivery of the paper produced at the plant, perhaps at a suitably low price negotiated as a key element in the initial arrangement of the transaction, Finmills will get its money back plus a profit. Finmills' ability to control every aspect of the operation by virtue of its own competencies in paper production and sales enables it to complete this transaction successfully.

Bilateral clearing accounts and switch trading

Much talked about and rarely achieved, these techniques involve counter-trading on the macro scale. It works as follows.

Two countries agree to trade together, importing from and exporting to each other. In order to keep track of the flow of goods and payment, bilateral clearing accounts are set up and maintained with their respective central banks. Each time goods are shipped in either direction an account of their value is logged, usually denominated in US Dollars, Deutschmarks or other convertible currency. These bilateral arrangements will include a periodic balancing of the books. If there is a surplus in one direction or the other then a payment of the surplus value will be made to zero the account.

Clearly a high degree of centralisation in each country is required or alternatively they agree to trade only with the products of state industries where their respective governments have control of production, shipment and payment. An imbalance may occur which for some reason cannot be rectified and a credit remains in the central bank which is not utilised. In this case, assuming the funds are actually available, they may be able to be accessed by other exporters wishing to sell to that country. This is called *switch trading*. A simple case study best illustrates the structure:

An eastern European country enters a bilateral arrangement with a Latin American state. It is a general agreement but has been principally set up to facilitate the exchange of Latin American minerals for vehicles and other engineered products from eastern Europe.

When the arrangement comes to an end there is a balance in the Latin American country's central bank showing that it has exported US$20 million more goods than it has imported.

Having become aware of this imbalance and negotiated access to it, a German company agrees that it will export goods to the Latin American country and receive payment from the eastern European country's central bank.

The money and goods come full circle. The German company sells US$20 million worth of the goods and the payment it receives from the eastern Europeans has the effect of zeroing the bilateral accounts between the two countries. Balances held in such accounts can be substantial, and if they can be accessed, trade can be financed where perhaps funds would not be available otherwise.

Modern or US-style barter

The use of countertrading techniques was widespread in eastern and central Europe before the disintegration of the centralised economies. Their use continues now in some of those territories, not because of state control and policy, but rather as a result of the lack of creditworthiness. The use of the proceeds of mineral export sales to fund imports into various parts of the former Soviet Union is believed to be quite widespread.

Countertrade structures based on the use of exports from emerging markets in Africa, Asia and Latin America are being applied to overcome similar credit considerations. It is generally true to say, however, that the spread of emerging markets investment and the associated more open mindset in relation to developing countries has made conventional trade finance more easily accessible. Exporters and export financiers who are able to think in terms of using goods as payment will always be better equipped to solve the more intractable trade finance problems.

The most exciting recent developments in countertrade have, however, been in highly developed countries. In the United States barter of goods and services is now reckoned to account for US$7 billion worth of trade annually. The key lies in marginal production cost. Here is an example of how a barter deal might work:

Hotels Inc. is a chain of hotels across the United States. Planes Inc. is an airline with a network of country-wide scheduled passenger services. The executives and staff of the Hotels Inc. have to travel widely on business, which they do by air. The staff of Planes Inc. have to use hotels regularly in the course of their work. It makes sense for both firms to enter into a reciprocal trading arrangement so that instead of paying cash between themselves they trade their services.

The appeal for each is that they can exchange marginal capacity. It is likely that Hotels Inc. will always have spare rooms in its hotel which would otherwise remain vacant and produce no income at all. Likewise Planes Inc. will have spare seats on its flights which would otherwise be unoccupied. Thus Hotels Inc. gains travel value for its unoccupied hotel beds while Planes Inc. gains accommodation value for its unbooked aeroplane seats.

The outstanding issues are to decide the value of the rooms and the seats. This will be a matter for agreement but considering that both companies would have gained nothing from their spare capacity otherwise they can afford to be quite flexible. Any value is better than none assuming additional related costs are covered, such as cleaning the rooms, changing bed linen, in-flight service and so on.

The second issue is the amount of usage. The barter needs to be balanced and again this will depend on what each party's needs and usage are likely to be over the term of the deal. As this prototype transaction is being carried out in the domestic market where US Dollars are the currency there is no index of value issue to discuss.

The future

The potential for this 'modern barter' type of countertrade is immense. Bilateral deals like our example are only the tip of the iceberg. There can be a chain of counterparties each providing goods or services which would eventually come full circle. Alternatively brokers can act as pools of exchange capacity, matching various counterparties with the goods and services they need to acquire and which they have to contribute. The greatest potential for barter and countertrading worldwide may lie in such exchanges of value in the developed world although, ironically, countertrade is usually associated with lack of creditworthiness.

9: Multilateral Aid Agencies

INTRODUCTION

It would be incorrect to describe multilateral aid agencies and the funding they provide for development projects as 'export financing techniques'. However, with the total funds made available by these institutions for the purchase of goods and services being in the region of US$30 billion per annum its contribution to funding world trade cannot be ignored.

This section introduces the largest multilateral institutions including the World Bank and its affiliates, European Bank for Reconstruction and Development, European Investment Bank, Asian Development Bank, African Development Bank, Inter-American Investment Bank and OPEC Aid Institutions. We will look at who the aid agencies are, how they work and how they select projects for funding.

Membership of the multilaterals is made up of 'shareholder' countries which are either net donors or net borrowers of funds. Apart from capital supplied by members, funding for on-lending to projects is raised through the international capital markets. They can achieve fine borrowing rates because their supra-national status and their strong credit ratings give them investor appeal. Their credit standing stems from their policies of predominantly sovereign lending, to government borrowers who are their members. They are also highly sophisticated in using financial swapping and hedging techniques which enable them to further lower their costs of funds.

THE WORLD BANK

The World Bank is the largest and most prestigious multilateral development institution and is a model for most of the regional development banks. Its procurement and approval procedures, for example, have often been copied and adapted to the needs of particular regional institutions. Therefore a study of the World Bank's methods is worthwhile both in its own right and for the purposes of extrapolation.

96

Table 9.1: World Bank – essential figures June 1994 (US$)

Total capital resources	Funds outstanding in the capital markets	Total funds currently disbursed or committed	Number of projects and investments currently being funded	Number of member countries
170bn	101bn	164bn	982	156

The World Bank Group

The World Bank Group is made up of four institutions.

- The International Bank for Reconstruction and Development (IBRD) – often referred to simply as the World Bank – the main funding agency.
- The International Development Agency (IDA). Its borrowers are the poorest countries which do not qualify for World Bank support. It lends over long terms which may extend to 30 or 40 years.
- The International Finance Corporation (IFC) – the Bank's profit-making commercial lending and equity investment arm.
- The Multilateral Investment Guarantee Agency (MIGA) which provides guarantees to support foreign investment in developing countries.

World Bank lending
The Bank lends to government borrowers or to agencies of governments which can obtain an acceptable sovereign guarantee. They can include any of its 156 member countries which have an annual per capita income below the borrowing threshold limit which, as at March 1995, was US$4,866.

Fund raising
The World Bank itself raises funds by issuing AAA-rated bonds and on-lending the proceeds at half a percentage point above its average cost of funds. The Bank implements roughly 2,000 financed projects at any one time and approves approximately 200 new loans annually.

It finances only the foreign exchange costs of projects usually to the extent of 30–40 per cent of project costs. This adds up to about US$15 billion per annum in World Bank lending and a further US$5 billion in IDA credits. Loans are usually structured over 12 to 15 years and include a grace period of three to five years.

Procurement and project funding

By understanding project procurement needs, suppliers can identify business opportunities to provide goods, equipment, services and consultancy.

Proposals to the World Bank for new projects need to come from the sovereign borrowers themselves. Companies cannot simply request Bank funding for projects. However, in practice the initiative may begin with proposals, suggestions or approaches being made to potential borrowers by third parties who have an interest in the success of a particular venture. These can be consultants, construction firms, other commercial companies and banks. Borrowers then bring projects to the Bank for their consideration.

In many cases the potential availability of loans, cash, aid funding, export credits or a workable financial structure is the driving force behind a project. Projects co-funded through bilateral intergovernmental aid of one sort or another are common. It has been argued that this produces 'white elephant' developments which are inappropriate either in their size or technology to the context of their construction. The developing world is littered with useless hardware and machinery in various stages of decay or dismantling. This is certainly a hotly debated issue. As far as getting projects agreed and funded someone has to take the initiative, arranging the initial trade and with the experience and abilities to access funding. People promote projects ultimately rather than amorphous governments and multilateral bodies.

Information

There are many types of project funded by the World Bank across sectors as varied as agriculture, education, the environment, health, population, power, telecommunications, transport and urban development. Projects must be technically and financially sound. Impractical ones will be screened out at an early stage. The Bank's selection procedures are necessarily tough and long-winded and there is no shortage of proposals put up for consideration. To find out about projects there are two useful sources:

- International Business Opportunities Service (IBOS) – a subscription service offered by the Bank which provides frequent news, updates and information on procurement, bidding, project development and financing.
- Development Business – a bi-weekly publication of the United Nations Department for Economics and Social Information (see below) which covers both World Bank and other regional development agencies.

Apart from information available from these sources it is important to make contact with the Bank itself in order to fully understand the available opportunities. It may be worth visiting regional and sectoral officers in Washington and keeping in touch with them regularly. In that way it is possible to monitor the state of play of transactions and to get to know the World Bank system. It is worth noting that a considerable number of people make the pilgrimage to Washington and World Bankers are busy people. A general presentation from yet another firm of consultants may be felt to be an unreasonable use for their time unless it can be short, focused and clearly sets out the unique abilities and benefits of the firm to the Bank, its clients or in the contexts of particular projects.

Tracking World Bank Projects*

Once development of a project has started it is important to track it through its evolution within the Bank. A six-phase cycle is followed and this can be monitored from identification through to disbursement of funds and completion:

1 Identification: recognising high-priority projects suitable for Bank support.
2 Project preparation: the borrower prepares an initial proposal. Consultants may be hired at this stage to prepare feasibility studies.
3 Project appraisal: required goods and services are identified as the Bank appraises the project.
4 Negotiation and approval: the terms of the Bank's support are agreed with the borrower and approved by the Bank's Executive Directors. Loan agreements are signed.
5 Implementation/supervision: goods and services are procured, funds are disbursed.
6 Completion/evaluation of project.

The total cycle can take several years to complete depending on the project.

Bidding Procedures

As far as individual sourcing arrangements for plant and equipment are concerned International Competitive Bidding (ICB) is the method usually used in procurement tenders.

The borrower is responsible for procurement under Bank-financed projects. This applies where procurement is 'of a size and nature that would interest eligible bidders outside the borrower's country'. Borrowers

---

* For greater detail see World Bank booklet *The Project Cycle* by Warren C. Baum.

are required to advertise their requirements internationally and to specify their needs in bidding documents. Contracts are let to the lowest bidder subject to its ability to perform its obligations and having met the terms of the bidding documents. Bids are opened at a public meeting where bidders are allowed to be present. Bids are read out and recorded and cannot be altered after they have been opened.

There are two other methods of bidding: Limited International Bidding (LIB) and Local Competitive Bidding (LCB). LIB is used if there are very few manufacturers known to be able to meet the specifications of a procurement contract. In this case they are approached directly by the borrower or the borrower's agents and there is no need for the bid to be advertised.

Under LCB, the opportunity to bid is publicised locally only where the operation is small in value or thought not to be of interest to international bidders. Local language and currency may be used by the borrower. Foreign bidders may also bid for LCB governed business.

Who may bid for World Bank funded business
Companies of all sizes can bid for Bank-funded business. There is no registration system for manufacturers, suppliers of goods and contractors although pre-qualification is often required for particular civil works contracts. The Bank does keep a computerised record of consultants called Data on Consulting Firms (DACON).

In all cases the borrower is responsible for preparing the bidding documents which suppliers and contractors need to request from the borrower or the purchaser under the project once they become aware of procurement taking place. The onus is on the supplier/contractor to follow projects through their project cycle.

IDA

Borrowers under World Bank facilities are necessarily developing ones but need to have achieved a certain level of creditworthiness. The poorest countries which are not sufficiently creditworthy may benefit from IDA funding. Once again IDA credits are made available only to sovereign borrowers. The terms of any loans are very much softer. Credit periods are likely to be in the range of 35 to 40 years with ten years' grace. No interest is charged although there is an annual service charge of 0.75 per cent. The project cycle and bidding for procurement under IDA-supported projects are the same as those for World Bank-supported loans.

IFC

The International Finance Corporation describes itself in its 1994 annual report as 'the largest multilateral source of loan and equity financing for projects in the developing world'. IFC's capital is in excess of US$2.2 billion and it has total assets of US$10.3 billion. It is to all intents and purposes a commercial bank but with a difference.

Lending and commercial bank syndication
Although it functions as a profit-making lender it benefits from its status as a division of the World Bank Group, as do the projects in which it becomes involved. This means that it often provides funding for infrastructure and private sector projects at terms which are more adventurous than those offered by most commercial banks. However, were a borrower to default on a facility extended by IFC it could damage its standing with the World Bank, seriously impairing its ability to gain the Bank's support in the future. Therefore IFC's participation in a project is often viewed by commercial banks as a risk enhancement and this often encourages them to provide funding by joining lending syndicates led by IFC.

Under its loan participation arrangement IFC signs a loan document with a borrower which makes funding available in two tranches. Under one it provides its own funding at long terms or with longer grace periods than other banks involved in funding a project. Under the second it makes funding available at commercial bank terms which encourages banks to join a club loan or syndication, the terms of which are closer to those in the eurocurrency loans market for comparable risks. Banks may complain at the fine pricing which reflects the additional credit strength of IFC's involvement. Participating banks sign a participation with IFC by means of which they share the commercial risks of the transaction. If, however, the borrow defaults it does so towards IFC itself. It is noteworthy that IFC loans and participations have never been rescheduled under any country debt restructuring.

IFC as equity provider
IFC may provide equity which commercial banks may not be prepared to do. This can, for example, be in the context of revenue-driven projects such as build, own, operate and transfer (BOOT) structures for developments such as power generation and water treatment operations. IFC may also operate as sole underwriter for corporate securities.

Applying for IFC funding
Unlike the World Bank, companies and entrepreneurs may apply directly to IFC for funding. IFC will appraise the proposal on its merits, requesting a business plan, feasibility study, history of a company or project and details of the promoters' competence in the business proposed.

IFC takes a highly detailed, analytical view of proposals put to it and has the abilities to act as corporate financier, venture capitalist, long-term lender and project funder. At the present time it is particularly keen to support revenue-driven privatised infrastructural developments. This sits well with its articles of agreement which describe its purpose as 'to further economic development by encouraging the growth of private enterprise in member countries'.

EUROPEAN BANK FOR RECONSTRUCTION AND DEVELOPMENT

Established in 1991, the mission of the London-based EBRD is to 'foster the transition toward democracy and open market-orientated economies in central and eastern Europe'. EBRD describes its role as:

- lending and investing in the countries of central and eastern Europe;
- having particular concern for the promotion or democratic institutions and human rights in those countries;
- offering a combination of merchant banking and development banking;
- being committed to promoting environmentally sound and sustainable development;
- providing funds within commercial decision-making time frames, according to sound banking and commercial principles.

EBRD Funding

EBRD may provide either debt or equity and sometimes both. It can provide guarantees, underwriting and technical co-operation. Projects co-financed with other organisations, such as export credit agencies, governments, commercial banks are common.

Table 9.2: European Bank for Reconstruction and Development (EBRD) – essential figures as at 31 December 1994

Total subscribed capital resources	Funds outstanding in the capital markets	Total funds approved, committed or disbursed	Total number projects and investments approved and currently being funded	Number of member countries and organisations
ECU 10 bn	ECU 3.6 bn	ECU 17.4 bn	251	57

Specific public sector projects need to be sponsored by member governments or public authorities where they are in the state sector. Requests for support need to be made by the public sector sponsor. Private sector projects can be submitted directly to EBRD by commercial organisations from any part of the world. Although no two projects are alike EBRD employs a standard 'operation cycle' for all proposals. It is similar to the World Bank's project cycle.

EBRD's Operation Cycle

* Identification and preparation: a proposal is viewed in the light of EBRD's country and sector strategies. It encompasses analyses of credit, equity and economics. It leads to a formal appraisal.
* Appraisal: to satisfy EBRD's policy criteria and the risk and rewards a project presents to it. This will include a detailed procurement plan presented by the clients/borrower/project sponsor.
* Approval: the operation is approved by EBRD's board. Legal aspects are completed. Funds are made available.
* Implementation: This is the responsibility of the borrower. EBRD monitors procurement although it is not a party to any procurement contract.

Timetable
In terms of the timetable of this operation cycle EBRD says it normally processes proposals within two months of its receipt of full project information. Public sector transactions may take longer but the majority are processed during a period of between four months and one year.

Competitive bidding
Competitive bidding procedures normally apply to all contracts of ECU 200,000 or more in respect of goods and services and ECU5 million for works. Public tendering criteria are similar to those for the World Bank. Procurement notices must be advertised publicly in newspapers with wide circulations and in official gazettes and trade publications. EBRD itself arranges for procurement notices to appear in: *Procurement Opportunities*, its own newsletter; *Development Business*, published by the United Nations; the Supplement of the *Official Journal of the European Communities*.

Contracts are awarded to the lowest bidder subject to the terms of the tender. Procurement for public sector operations usually follows a six-part procedure:

1　notification of a tender;
2　pre-qualification;
3　invitation to tender;

4   receive and evaluate tenders;
5   award of contract;
6   administration of contract.

There are some other procurement methods which do not follow international competitive bidding procedures. These are:

- selective tendering open only to pre-selected suppliers or contractors in particular specialised fields;
- single tendering or direct purchase when proprietary equipment is only available from one supplier;
- international and local shopping for off-the-shelf, low-value items where three quotations are normally required;
- local competitive tendering where the work or supply is unlikely to appeal to international bidders. Foreign firms may participate.

Becoming involved in procurement and financing operations requires getting to know of the opportunities or proposing projects for EBRD's support. Like other development banks, EBRD is a large bureaucracy whose board represents many different interests. It is important to get to know the country and sector officers and to learn how best to table proposals for their support and to gain their help in getting through the systems and procedures. It is generally true of the EBRD, as for the other multilaterals, that everything takes a long time to be applied for, approved and funding made available. Don't expect results overnight.

EUROPEAN INVESTMENT BANK

As the European Union's development funding institution, the European Investment Bank holds the purse-strings for major projects throughout Europe and also throughout the rest of the world. This represents a massive potential source of export finance funding.

During 1993 loans from the Brussels-based EIB towards capital investment within the member States was ECU50 billion (US$63.37 billion), 5 per cent of the total spent. Of EIB financing totalling ECU19.6 billion (US$24.83 billion) made available in 1993, ECU17.7 (US$22.43 Billion) was spent in member States.

Infrastructure Investment

Established in 1958, EIB's prime purpose is to provide long-term finance for large projects which match with the Community's development objectives.

One of its main priorities has been to concentrate resources on the development of efficient communications which facilitate free movement of persons, goods and information. Railway infrastructure is, for example, at the top of its shopping list. EIB has contributed towards the European high-speed rail network, particularly in Spain, Belgium and France and towards the Channel Tunnel.

EIB's role in supporting developments of this sort is important because it represents EU commitment to the Euro-infrastructure. No one country has the European overview to co-ordinate pan-European projects of this magnitude nor the funds to carry them through. Exporters who make it their business to align their thinking with EIB's activities and track its projects and initiatives can gain valuable marketing data.

Apart from railways EIB is promoting trunk road and motorway building projects among which the Great Belt fixed link project is one of the most noteworthy. European air traffic control systems and urban transit projects are also beneficiaries of the Bank's support as are telecommunications links. EIB's sponsorship of Inmarsat and Eutelsat are examples of satellite communications investments and it has also contributed funding to cabled telephone links to North America, the Middle East and Africa.

Environment

Water management schemes are the main focus for EIB's environmental investments in Member States. In the period 1989 to 1993 EIB invested ECU15 billion in the environmental sector as a whole and this is steadily accelerating year by year.

EC Directives on water quality in rivers and around European coasts has prompted increased investment as has public pressure on all environmental matters. Atmospheric pollution, industrial site clean-ups, effluent control and treatment and solid waste disposal are areas where EIB expects to invest further in the coming years.

EIB's environmental approach also extends to those areas which fringe the EU, particularly in the Mediterranean Sea. Its Mediterranean Environmental Technical Assistance Programme has funded studies which have led to projects, often in co-operation with other multilateral agencies in countries such as Egypt.

Energy

In the quest for reliable, economic and non-polluting energy for Europe, EIB has committed ECU415 million (US$526 million) to the Maghreb-Europe

Gasline connecting Morocco to Spain and the Snam-Transmediterraneo pipeline from Tunisia to Messina in southern Italy. British subcontractors, particularly with North Sea experience, have been able to bid for and win business in these two projects. Pipeline projects bringing gas to Europe from Siberia and the North Sea have also received EIB funding.

SMEs

In order to stimulate employment throughout the community EIB has pledged ECU1 billion (US$1.267 billion) towards subsidised loans to small and medium-sized enterprises for capital investment. Beneficiary companies must be located in Member States, be active in industrial, agro-industrial, tourism and service sectors and have less than 500 employees.

Central and Eastern Europe

Since 1990 EIB has made loans of more than ECU1.7 billion (US$2.15 billion) to the ten CEE countries and Albania. The focus for the Bank's investments in this area is similar to that for projects within the EU. Favoured sectors include infrastructure, communications, water supply, wastewater treatment and operations with an environmental focus. Like the European Bank for Reconstruction and Development, EIB is assisting CEE countries to adjust to market economic conditions by promoting economically viable projects.

European Development Fund

EDF is the EU's most important pool of European aid funding available to support projects in African, Caribbean and Pacific (ACP) countries. EDF is established periodically by a financial protocol forming part of the Lomé Convention agreed between ACP countries and EU Member States. The current pool, known as 'EDF VII', was agreed under so-called 'Lomé IV'.

In the period 1991 to 1995 EDF VII provided a total of ECU12 billion (US$15.20 billion) to ACP countries. EIB manages ECU2.30 billion (US$2.9 billion) of this in the form of loans, risk capital resources and interest subsidies. The rest is managed by the Commission of the European Communities and covers grants for national and regional programmes, structural adjustments, emergency aid, and other economic aid.

Initiatives and applications for project funding arise from the ACP state itself. It is therefore important to gather information locally in the country concerned. Once projects have been identified direct contact with EIB is recommended.

ASIAN DEVELOPMENT BANK (ADB)

Table 9.3: Asian Development Bank – essential figures December 1994 (US$)

Total capital resources	Funds outstanding in the capital markets	Total funds currently disbursed or committed	Number of projects and investments currently being funded	Number of member countries
50.8bn	17.4bn	51.5bn	1,239	55

Manila-based ADB covers the region which has the world's fastest-growing economies but also the greatest concentration of the world's poor. It makes loans and equity investments to promote the social and economic advancement of its member countries. Infrastructure projects, agriculture, education and health are the main sectors in which ADB invests. It makes loans to both public and private sectors.

Lending

ADB makes two types of loan; Ordinary Capital Resource (OCR) loans and Asian Development Fund (ADF) loans. OCR funding accounts for the majority of funding operations. Borrowers are generally more highly developed countries and the loans are at a floating rate based upon ADB's cost of funds in the capital markets. ADF loans are made to less developed member countries. They are interest free, often extend over 35 to 40 years and carry an annual service fee of 1 per cent per annum.

Both types of loan are designed to have what ADB describes as a 'catalytic effect'. ADB's involvement often causes other national or multilateral institutions to become involved in funding projects. For every dollar it lends US$1.50 is provided in the form of co-financing from local governments, other aid agencies and export credit authorities.

Procurement

ADB's charter requires that procurement shall be from member countries unless a specific dispensation is made. Procurement follows a project cycle similar to that followed by the World Bank (see above) and projects need to be tracked in a similar way. International competitive bidding is used for

107

contracts for goods and related services valued above US$500,000 and for civil works valued above US$1,000,000.

Other forms of bidding include:

- international shopping for low-value, off-the-shelf items;
- local competitive bidding for procurement which is thought unlikely to interest international bidders;
- direct purchase in respect of proprietary equipment or technology.

Information about ADB funded projects and procurement can be obtained from the following sources:

- *ADB Business Opportunities* lists various projects under consideration by ADB (see contacts section);
- *Development Business* produced by the United Nations (see contacts section);
- General procurement notices and news releases put out regularly by ADB.

AFRICAN DEVELOPMENT BANK (AFDB)

AFDB contributes to projects which are sound and which clearly benefit its Member States, many of which are among the poorest on the planet. In many cases projects such as road building, water supply, bridge building, hospital and housing developments might not be carried out at all were it not for AFDB's support. It particularly favours operations which operate to the benefit of the poorest of its 50 African country members and which may benefit two or more countries. This is to foster inter-African co-operation.

Table 9.4: African Development Bank – essential figures as at 31 December 1993 (US$)

Total capital resources	Funds outstanding in the capital markets	Total funds currently disbursed or committed	Number of projects and investments currently being funded	Number of member countries
22.3 bn	8.1 bn	17.3 bn	1,894	75

Funding

Funding for projects must be applied for by the borrower directly to AFDB. As with other development banks its funding criteria usually require that the borrower country contributes at least 50 per cent of the project value from it own resources. Thus tracking of projects by potential suppliers requires research through the AFDB but also direct liaison with the borrower. There is no substitute for thorough and regular research of all available information in order to spot funded business opportunities.

At time of writing AFDB is going through a particularly difficult period. The proportion of its non-performing loan portfolio has grown to a level which is causing its shareholders to question its management. In this climate it is doubtful that the institution will be able to function efficiently as a development funding institution until these issues have been ironed out.

INTER-AMERICAN DEVELOPMENT BANK (IADB)

Closely modelled on the World Bank, IABD is also based in Washington and it covers the Americas and the Caribbean.

It has a similar raison d'être to the other regional development banks. In 1993 its loans supported procurement under more than 2,000 contracts and it disbursed US$3.3 billion. It is therefore well worth examining the projects which it supports with a view to identifying suitable supply opportunities. Its use of international competitive bidding is based on that of the World Bank.

Table 9.5: The Inter-American Development Bank – essential figures as at 1994 (US$)

Total capital resources	Funds outstanding in the capital markets	Total funds currently disbursed or committed	Number of projects and investments currently being funded	Number of member countries
61 bn	25.2 bn	27.53 bn	358	46

OPEC AID INSTITUTIONS

Lower oil prices have restricted the scale of funding made available by the several aid agencies associated with the Organisation of Petroleum Exporting Countries (OPEC). Nevertheless they represent a potential, indirect source of funding for suppliers of goods and services.

Table 9.6: OPEC aid institutions – essential figures as at December 1993 (US$)

Total authorised capital endowment of OPEC institutions	Total funds currently disbursed or committed	Number of projects and investments currently being funded	Number of OPEC member countries
46.332 bn	53.604 bn	n/a	12

OPEC Fund

The OPEC Fund for International Development (OPEC Fund) has concentrated its loans, investments and grants in support of 96 of the world's poorest countries in Africa, Asia, Latin America, the Caribbean and southern Europe. It funds local projects and promotes co-operation between member states.

Islamic Development Bank (IsDB)

Islamic Development Bank (IsDB) operates according to Islamic Shariah principles which eschew the payment of interest. So funding operations often take the form of interest free loans, equity participation, leasing, technical assistance and finance for trade in commodities. The objective of the IsDB is to foster development and social progress in 45 member countries which are also members of the Organisation of the Islamic Conference.

   In total there are 14 funds which fall under the umbrella of OPEC Aid Institutions. They have been constituted for a variety of reasons which are not necessarily trade-related. It is therefore advisable to approach the OPEC Fund for International Development in Vienna, Austria for information about their aims and objectives and the means by which to access funding.

10: Project and Infrastructure Financing

DEFINITION

All and any of the export financing techniques dealt with so far could form a part of the financial package assembled to fund a project. Project financing involves structuring the financial aspects of an entire construction project, such as, for example, building and operating a toll bridge. Procurement of raw materials, plant and equipment which might involve importing them from elsewhere contributes only a limited part of the overall financing package. Other examples of projects might be the revamping and running of the water supply and waste treatment for a small town or a large city. Perhaps the project is to provide and run a public transport or telephone system for an entire country. The project may continue to operate over a number of years and even decades. The essence of the financing structure, however, is that the cash-flow derived by the project pays for its construction and operation. In other words it is *revenue driven*.

Projects based upon the cash they generate are not a new idea. In a sense the construction of a factory or other business establishment anywhere in the world would be financed on the basis of the cash it could generate to a greater of lesser degree. We will, however, concentrate on the essential characteristics of financing major infrastructure operations. These are not only very much in fashion in the mid-1990s but represent a huge international spend on hardware and services. This is especially the case in developing countries. In early 1994 market opinion among project financiers estimated that US$100 billion worth of projects stood a good chance of being structured in the foreseeable future. This figure excluded the 'possibles', the projects which were still on the drawing board but could eventually see the light of day.

Typically, the financing for large infrastructure projects takes a great deal of time to develop from conception to realisation. It is concerned with the entire sweep of project planning, development, procurement, construction, maintenance and management. The main players involved are often governments, regional or local authorities, project financing banks, multilateral aid agencies, development banks, major contracting firms and teams of lawyers. It is a highly specialised field requiring skills in cash flow projection, computer modelling, corporate finance, using local and international capital markets and the law of several jurisdictions.

Finally, a note on terminology. Newly constructed infrastructure projects involve building, ownership and operation throughout their life and eventual transfer back to a public authority or the sponsoring government. Depending on its particular structure a project may be termed;

- BOT – Build, Own and Transfer,
- BOO – Build, Own and Operate or
- BOOT – Build, Own, Operate and Transfer.

PROJECT DRIVERS

Privatisation

Setting up and running infrastructure has usually, in the past, been the concern of the public sector. This is understandable because of the importance of infrastructure – such as the provision of water, electricity, gas, telecommunications, ports, airports and transport systems – to a country's economy as a whole. Moreover, only governments, national, regional or local could afford the sums of money involved in infrastructure construction, maintenance and operation and only they could take long-term views of policy based upon national interest. However, the mood has changed.

Indebted national governments found the financial burden a severe drain on their national resources. Having to raise taxes for funding was always an unpalatable, if necessary, option. There were accusations of inefficiency and even corruption which placed political leaders and bureaucrats in the firing line (sometimes literally). And then along came the idea of introducing private funding and management which at one stroke, if handled correctly, could address the political and fiscal issues and maybe do a more efficient job. The introduction of private capital and professional management have been the most important spurs to the development of revenue-driven infrastructure projects in recent times.

Efficiency, Regulation and Tariffs

The drive for greater efficiency has also been a prime mover in introducing private management and funding for infrastructure. Private management has been able to attack problems such as leakages in water and sewerage systems and private individuals tapping into power and telephone wiring. In addition private firms with international expertise have been able to transfer their experience gained in other markets to good advantage. The French and British water companies have been particularly successful in doing this.

Proper regulation of private projects to ensure quantity and quality delivery standards for public services has been important in tempering the risks of involving firms whose prime concern is profit and making an adequate return on shareholders' funds. In many countries a regulatory structure has had to be built from scratch and regulating agencies established. One function of proper regulation has been the pricing of services which has been a highly sensitive political issue and a key factor in project feasibility.

Tariff structures in a revenue-driven project are, after all, a main determinant of financial viability. There has to be sufficient income to cover existing service delivery, capital investment and all other project costs including service for debt providers and profit for investors and lenders. At the same time tariffs have to be set at levels which are reasonable for the customer to bear. The development of a tariff determination formula and the fixing of the tariff itself are both issues which demand detailed examination and careful structuring both from political and financial perspectives.

FINANCING

Funding

Recourse and non-recourse
In many projects the sponsoring government or other entity provides a measure of support. This is termed 'recourse' or 'limited recourse'. In fact most infrastructure projects are limited recourse to a greater or lesser degree. This may take the form of payment guarantees for example, where the sponsoring government remains the ultimate risk for lenders and agrees to underwrite regular payment for debt service. A government may also provide a guarantee to purchase a fixed amount of the product from the project for its own or its citizens' use, effectively guaranteeing income to the project. This might take the form of a 'take or pay agreement'. The nature and extent of the recourse will depend on the particulars of the project.

Where there is no such guarantee in place and the financing stands entirely on it own as far as cash flow and performance risks are concerned this would be referred to as 'non-recourse'. Purely non-recourse operations would be relatively rare because of the political, regulatory and other localised risks which can be involved in infrastructure projects. It would, for example, be difficult to attract investors and lenders to projects in developing countries which retained such long-term risks as expropriation of assets, future nationalisation and foreign exchange restriction. Comfort would therefore be sought from the government concerned which effectively represents a form of government guarantee or underwriting.

Equity
In project scenarios involving privatisation and the establishment of a project specific limited company, shareholders are often sought from among domestic and foreign investors. On many occasions equity providers are also actively involved in the operation of the underlying project. A gas or electricity provider in one country might become a shareholder of a similar privatised utility in another. In this way it would enjoy a measure of control over the performance of the project from which it would expect to draw dividends.

The ratio of equity to borrowings is often an important measure in assessing a project. There is no hard and fast rule about what the proportions of each source of project funding should be although research by IFC in 1994 calculated that the average across 70 projects in which it was involved

% of total project cost

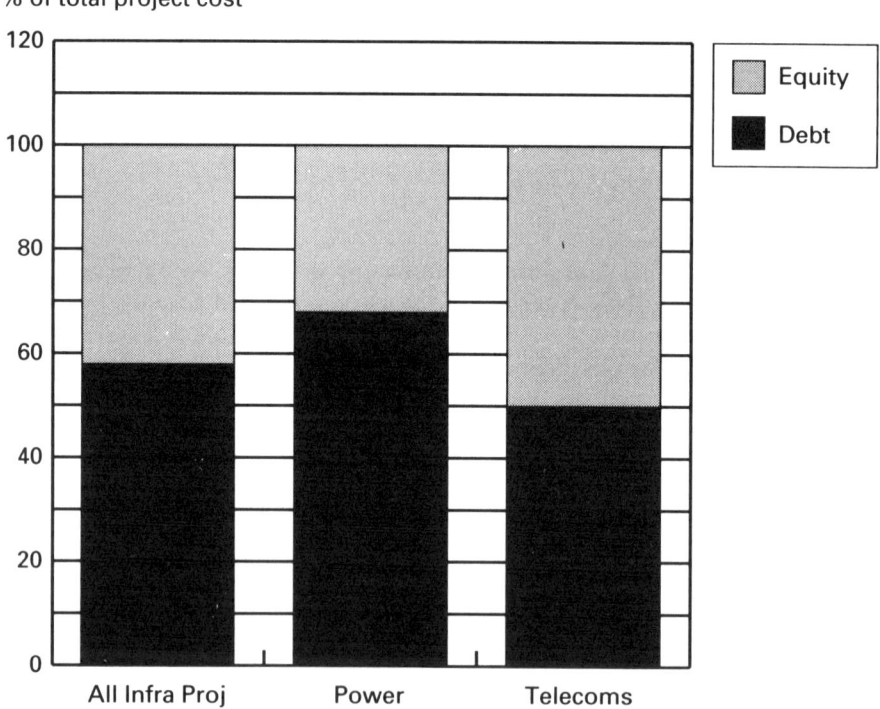

Figure 10.1: Debt: equity ratios in infrastructure projects
Courtesy of International Finance Corporation

was 59 per cent debt to 41 per cent equity. Rehabilitation of a railway project required a debt to equity ratio of 41:59 while for a pipeline project in Zimbabwe the ratio was 50:50.

Equity investors stand to gain from success achieved by the project, but need to temper the scale of their investment by obtaining funding from banks and other lenders. Equity investors will have direct risks on the project, the country of the project and the currency of that country. How equity is raised will depend again on the project concerned. Some will be placed with private or corporate investors, others with institutions such as insurance companies or investment funds: IFC itself has often been an equity provider and share issues on local and international stock markets are other sources.

Debt

Most conventional export financing would fall under this category. Long-term commercial lending would be relatively rare unless the risk was particularly strong or was linked to an export credit operation. Parallel financings led by the IFC may involve commercial lending but are perceived by lenders as risk-enhanced because of IFC's World Bank affiliation.

Buyer's credits, lines of credit, soft loan support and mixed credits may all form part of the debt structure where government-to-government trade or aid protocols may exist. These would allow for a long-term debt profile, perhaps extending 10, 15 or even 20 year credit at lenient fixed rates. Such terms of credit would be likely to match long-term operating concessions granted to the project company.

Funding by means of letters of credit or forfaiting could also be incidental to the supply of plant or equipment for a project. Generally, however, this would relate to specific supplies made by sub-contractors to whom payment could not be made by any other larger and probably more cost-efficient debt financing, such as export credits (see above). It is likely that bids invited from sub-contractors or suppliers would require a financing proposal to be attached to them in order that the project could take advantage of any attractive credit terms which were offered.

It must again be stressed that international procurement financing will only form a part of a project's costs. The operation of, say, a 30-year water and waste treatment project concession would involve a great many other local costs such as employees' salaries and wages, payments to local contractors, billing and cash collection systems and so forth. The operators of such projects are likely to be most concerned with the management and operation of projects on the ground.

Domestic capital markets: Equity and bonds

The development of domestic capital markets throughout the world has directly paralleled privatisation initiatives and new project financing opportunities. Indeed in some capitalist markets utility stocks resulting from privatisations represent a large proportion of stock market capitalisation.

Whether a stock market existed originally or not, once established it provides a platform for raising equity for infrastructure project equity funding. Project specific companies can be listed and, especially where they effectively provide monopoly services, are regarded as safer stocks than those of industrial companies although upside potential may be restricted.

Local currency denominated bonds can be attractive to investors especially if they are rated by an international rating agency. For the issuer they typically have the advantage of bearing interest at fixed rates with known maturity dates allowing funding requirements to be determined well in advance. Such instruments may be issued in the form of public sector instruments if the government stands behind the transaction or as corporate bonds or project bonds. An example of locally issued project-related bonds was Mexico's toll road construction funding in the early 1990s which raised US$14 billion to fund the building of 6,000 km of highways.

International capital markets: Equity and bonds

Raising funding in the international capital markets has the advantage of reaching a much broader spread of investor. The disadvantages are that offshore investors are likely to be much more sensitive to political and foreign exchange risks. Many institutions, for example, choose only to invest in 'investment grade' bonds.

On the other hand emerging markets investment now has a significant place in investors' thinking. In the relentless search for higher yields, private individuals, institutions and investment funds have embraced emerging markets' equity and debt instruments. While these may form only a limited proportion of funds under management they can provide a higher yield element to help increase the overall portfolio return where funds have otherwise been invested in cash, government stock or other 'safe' but relatively uninspiring instruments.

While not strictly project-related the London listings of Ghana's Ashanti Goldfields and the Kazakhstan gold mining venture, Bakyrchik Gold PLC, were successful in raising funds for their respective ventures. Latin American new issue bonds have also been taken up in large amounts. These demonstrate that the international capital markets are open to emerging markets' issues in a way which, in the debt crisis years of the eighties, was unimaginable.

Structures

Overall financing structures will vary with each project. Figure 10.2 sets out a typical ground plan which will be useful to examine in detail.

Equity sponsors will not only contribute capital but will be the principal force behind the project. They may have conceived the project perhaps. They carry out independent cost reviews, study similar projects, research the market for the products of the project and co-ordinate the project, especially at its outset. Their undertaking to complete the project is a vital link in the structure of the deal.

The equity sponsors along with their investment banks, securities firms or investment advisors may also bring in other equity investors and together will provide capital to the *project company*. There may be other shareholders such as the national government itself. The project company becomes the focus of the operation both in the set-up phase and throughout its operational life. *Contractors* may provide a variety of services to the project company both in construction and on-going services such as metering, billing

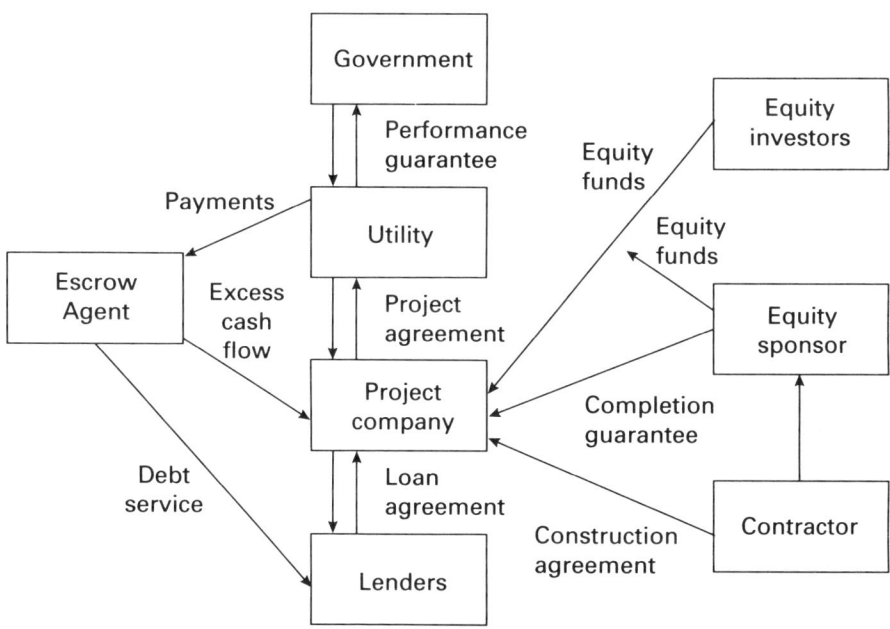

Figure 10.2: Structure of a BOT project
Courtesy of the International Finance Corporation

117

and other practical services (if the project company does not incorporate these in house).

The project company is also the borrower for the funding banks whether for commercial loans, export credits or other forms of borrowings. In the example structure we are using the project company has a project agreement with the *utility* to carry out certain functions such as the delivery of the service, water or electricity or the operation and management functions of the utility itself. For its part the utility provides an undertaking that it will buy services or supply from the project company, so assuring its cash flow.

The manner in which the payments are made is important. In our example they are paid to an *escrow account* held with the *escrow agent*. This means that any funds to be paid by the utility will be held in trust by a nominated bank and will be earmarked for the specific purpose of paying interest and principal to the lenders. The lenders will take security over these funds up to the sums they require.

It may be, for example, that after a *grace period* during which funds are drawn down from the loan agreements, the escrow agent builds up sufficient funds to secure a certain number of payments to the lenders. A year's cash cover might be envisaged in an agreement which will establish and define the role of the escrow agent. Over and above the cover required, excess funds may be paid back to the project company. Such excess funds would represent profit to the project company. It might repay any debt which it had raised to finance itself and will pay dividends to the equity providers.

The role of the government in our structure will depend on the extent of its involvement/recourse in the project. As a minimum it would expect to receive a guarantee of service provision from the utility in exchange for support for the project. This support could take the form of various guarantees or undertakings which would form the bedrock of the project underpinning the cash flows themselves. Guarantees against political risks mentioned above under 'recourse' would be likely to be established.

Overall the project centres upon the provision of a vital, infrastructural service for which a regular, reliable cash tariff is paid by customers. That the services provided are essential to the customers' everyday lives is the practical reality on which the project succeeds or fails.

Part II
Analysing and Assessing
Credit Risk

11: Introduction

This part deals with the risks to take into account when appraising export financing operation. These risks have been separated out for the purpose of explanation and ways of countering and controlling them have been suggested. However, in practice most transactions are made up of elements of several different overlapping and intersecting risks. Transactions may often require balancing several of these risks against the reward for the export financier who shoulders them to a greater or lesser degree. No transaction is totally secure. If it was it wouldn't be worth carrying out, as export financing is usually structured to grant credit or to minimise a client's risk.

12: Commercial Risk, Corporate Risk and Credit Insurance

This is the risk that the buyer of goods may not pay for them or repay any financing made available when it falls due. Such default results from the state of the buyer's own business and character. There are several methods which can be used to examine the customer to assess the state of health of the business.

BANKER'S REFERENCES

Formal bankers' references are usually suggested in credit assessment manuals but are on the whole rather vague. A request for a state of health report made to a customer's bank may produce one of the following typical responses:

> In reply to your enquiry, the information herein is given in strict confidence, for your private use only, without any guarantee or responsibility on the part of the Bank or its officials and, where the information has been obtained from another bank, or informant, without responsibility on the part of themselves or of their officials . . .

> xyz is a respectably constituted private limited company which has an account with us and its directors are considered respectable and trustworthy. We consider that the Company is good for the purpose of your enquiry, i.e. $....... credit.

> The Bank is not a credit reference agency within the terms of Section 145(8) of the Consumer Credit Act, 1974. Disclosure of the content and source of this opinion is not required by that Act . . .

> Subject is considered respectable and good for its normal business engagements, although the amount of your enquiry is thought to be excessive . . .

In practice a bank's duty of discretion to its client often prevents a full and frank written response. Furthermore a customer's express permission may be required by a bank before they can answer a status enquiry. All in all banker's references may be an element in a firm's credit procedure but contribute little to the accurate assessment of commercial risk.

However, a little more light can be shed on the credit risk if an informal inquiry is made. The banking network is in fact rife with rumour. Who better to ask about a risky customer than the banker who is facing a bad debt? A word of caution however. Very often bankers are themselves kept in the dark, especially if they don't visit their customers very often or rely on out-of-date figures. If they hold the customer's current account and can track cash moving through it then that is a very useful tool, but it is unlikely that a sophisticated customer will hold only one account or puts all the business's eggs in one financial basket. Indeed this may demonstrate an over-reliance on one institution which, as we shall see in the section on bank risk below, may expose the business to new risks if the bank changes direction or withdraws its support.

To summarise, it is of some value to include bankers' references as part of a policy on risk assessment but only to a limited extent.

CREDIT AGENCIES

If a customer has a formal credit rating from one or more of the major credit rating agencies such as Moodys, Standard & Poors or Duff & Phelps then the business is likely to be reasonably substantial in size. Neither the rating nor the size of the firm should be relied upon, however, as a guarantee of creditworthiness. Large companies can run into problems and credit agencies merely provide an opinion based upon their own research.

However, the view of a credit rating agency does contribute to the overall creditworthiness picture built up by the various means set out in this chapter. The information they make available is likely to be detailed and they have well-developed systems and well-trained analysts on their staff. They are able to place a business in the context of its sector, its country and the economic macros which affect its business. If a rating agency has been commissioned by the firm in question to give it a credit rating, to enable it to access funding at finer rates for example, then it is likely that information will have been provided to the agency to enable it to do its job thoroughly and to issue as accurate a rating as possible without risking its own credibility. This additional background is indirectly of benefit in assessing a firm's commercial standing.

Dunn & Bradstreet is another credit agency which can provide a full credit report to subscribers, including details such as recorded defaults under bills of exchange and latest available financials. The weakness of a D&B report is that it is standardised and therefore there may not be a box on their form for the question you would have asked.

FINANCIALS

Financials are important . . . as far as they go. A balance sheet, profit and loss account and sources and applications of funds statement are only snapshots in time. The balance sheet summarises the assets and liabilities of a firm at the end of the firm's accounting period. Profit and loss accounts, otherwise known as income statements or operating statements, show totals for the broad categories of income and outgoings in the business during the year to the reporting date. These include 'total sales' or 'turnover', the various costs to the business during the year and the 'bottom line', net or after tax profit. Sources and applications of funds statements show what the cash in the business was used for during the year and where it came from. It may also be called the sources and uses of funds statement.

The basics of how these statements are put together are easy to grasp: it is how they are used, manipulated and sometimes abused which make them of limited value in assessing risk. Creative accounting is widely used whether it is called that or not. A study of one or two books on how accounts are manipulated, stuffed, restated, juggled or otherwise crafted is a fascinating insight into deception which will convince you that financial statements are of very limited value indeed when it comes to understanding how a company works and how healthy it is. *Creative Accounting* by Ian Griffiths and *Accounting for Growth* by Terry Smith are recommended reading on this subject.

Trends and cycles in a company's activities emerge from comparing several years' accounts. A view over at least three years is recommended. A simple spreadsheet can be assembled to match one year's numbers against another and there are many credit analysis software packages into which the reported figures can be keyed and which go further in producing ratios to help formulate the comparison year-on-year. As tomes have been written on financial analysis and ratios it is sufficient here to recommend a basic grasp of them as tools for our purpose in analysing risk.

The greatest weakness in using financials is that they will be out of date by the time they are made public. For example, if it is now late February and your customer's year end is 31 December the latest audited annual report is likely to relate to the year ending December 31 the year before last because last year's have not yet been released. When last year's are ready they will, of course, be out of date.

Larger, public companies will produce interim figures at six monthly or quarterly intervals. These will be useful, although they will again be historical and a brief résumé to be superseded by the full year's accounts. Bankers should be able to gain access to more recent management accounts. Bearing in mind that they won't be audited, at least they should be more up to date. As the name implies, they are merely a guide to management.

If the customer is a limited company then the chances are that there are statutory regulations in his or her country requiring that accounts be filed within a defined period after the end of the company's financial year and in an approved format. However, many countries do not require formal auditing. Even if they do then the audit may merely declare that the manner of the accounting has been correct. What if there is skulduggery, offshore accounts, two or more sets of books hiding a crucial weakness in the company? You never know until it's too late and legion are the cases of banks who have advanced funds to companies and then learned very shortly afterwards of the arrival of the receivers.

BROKER'S REPORTS

If the company is listed on a well-regulated stock exchange there may be other reporting requirements laid down as a condition of its stock being traded, but then again stocks have been known to be suspended. Brokers' reports may also be available which will analyse facts and figures at their disposal. Beware again. Remember those brokers' lunches hosted by the chairman who exudes bonhomie in order to prompt a buy recommendation?

While maintaining a healthy scepticism about the broker's arguments which are propounded in order to encourage trading a company's shares nevertheless brokers' analysts spend their entire lives putting companies under the microscope, dissecting accounts, discussing the sectoral trends and applying measures of different sorts to companies. They are experts and we can make good use of their expertise.

INDUSTRY GRAPEVINE

The industry grapevine can be most instructive. Who has supplied your customer lately and what was their experience? Have they been paid on time? What will they say privately that can't be said or written elsewhere?

PRESS CUTTING SERVICES

Press coverage is well worth looking at. It may be sensational, it might conceivably be untrue, but it provides another aspect on a company. A terse statement released by the company such as 'Alexander Bloggs, Chairman and Chief Executive of XYZ importers is stepping down after 30 years' loyal service to the company. We thank him for his leadership over the years' is not terribly informative. A press report headlined 'Bloggs ousted in board room coup' and a discussion of the succession crisis at the debt-strapped company adds something to our collage of company analysis.

Press-cutting services, especially on-line ones such as Reuters Textline, Lotus One Source, and the *Financial Times* can rapidly bring you up to date with information reported in a wide range of publications. It is usually possible to search references to the company over a period of time going back months or even years.

VISIT THE CUSTOMER

There is no substitute for visiting the risk. A company visit can reveal a variety of new factors. Look around the plant, meet several members of the workforce – at all levels and in as many functions of the business as possible. Look for tell-tale signs of neglect, overspending, overstocking, recent rationalisation, pickets and union banners at the gate, gauge staff morale and so on.

A visit may be difficult if the risk is located in another territory, but as a general rule if you can't get a decent handle on the risks proposed, don't do the deal. Banks have a history of being seduced by overseas risks usually to their detriment. Short cuts to lending decisions based on such woolly ideas as 'we have spare country limit', 'it is a state owned company' or 'we want to establish a presence in the market' really do not wash. They are about as valid as the notion that 'countries don't go bust' which contributed to the aggregation of Latin American lending and which culminated in the debt crisis following Mexico's default in 1982. There are no short cuts to a sound credit judgement.

By the time the company's commercial/corporate risk has been analysed from all these angles the chances are that a pretty clear picture of its state of health will have emerged. The exercise is one of risk minimisation to a point where the likelihood of non-payment is strongly improbable.

CREDIT INSURANCE

If export finance is being made available to a company either in terms of offering credit to it, or to its customer, credit insurance can provide a further risk enhancement. A customer's credit insurance policy will cover the possibility of it not receiving payment due to becoming insolvent or being in 'protracted default'. Cover is given up to an agreed indemnity level and over agreed credit terms. This could mean anywhere between 75 and 95 per cent of the invoice value and up to 360 days of credit. The benefit of the credit insurance can be assigned to the bank formally or a bank can merely take it into account when gauging the risks of non-payment.

As distinct from state-supported insurance schemes and political risk insurance which tend to cover individual, one-off deals, and which are dealt with elsewhere in this book, commercial credit insurance takes on the risk of a trading company's entire portfolio of receivables for an annual premium. The terms of cover are set once a year in negotiation with the insurer, including how large a 'first loss' the customer shoulders when a claim is paid; rather like an excess on a domestic insurance policy. The higher the first loss the lower the premium.

Before a policy may be taken out the customer has to demonstrate to the insurers that it has a competent credit control and debt collection set-up within the company and is capable of running its business so as to minimise the risks of non-payment. This has obvious risk-enhancing benefits for its bankers.

A hidden advantage lies in the fact that credit insurers keep information on a very wide range of companies, both from formal and informal sources and from their own experience. A known bad risk will not be covered under the policy. This can be useful to the customer in deciding who to do business with and again has a collateral spin-off for the financing bank in terms of minimising the likelihood of default.

In underpinning a credit judgement with a customer's commercial credit insurance policy a bank needs to be confident that its customer will run the policy properly and not imperil the cover through any breach of the policy's terms. It needs also to look through the customer and the policy to the insurer's risk. It must feel comfortable that if a claim were to be made under the policy the insurer would be likely to pay.

Increasingly credit insurance policies are becoming international. If a proportion of a customer's turnover is, for example, in another European or North American territory this could easily be covered from a political risk perspective. The terms of the policy must be studied carefully to be sure of the extent of the cover provided. For many international trade financing operations, especially those involving large sums of money, longer credit terms, large or unique cargoes or buyers located in distant or emerging markets it will be necessary for the seller to take out political risk insurance.

13 Political Risk and Emerging Markets

DEFINITION

For the export financier the question of political risk is that of asking whether the country or region in which a buyer is situated poses risks of non-payment under a financing arrangement. The following examples illustrate political risks of different sorts:

- In 1982 the Mexican government withheld payment on its debt to foreign commercial banks, precipitating a debt crisis which swept through Latin America and reverberated around the world's financial markets.
- Prior to perestroika and the eventual collapse of the USSR, the Soviet Union's credit was one of the best in the world. The end of the centralised system and the resulting political and economic transition has resulted in a weakening of the credit standing of many countries in central and eastern Europe.
- Civil war in Mozambique affected the ability of Tanzania, Zambia and Zimbabwe to export and import through the Indian Ocean port of Beira.

There are numerous other examples of political risks which we could consider and the issue does not only arise with emerging markets. Changes of political regime, government legislation or monetary policy can quickly alter the viability of an export deal altering the risks facing a financier supporting the deal.

RESEARCH

It is important to keep up-to-date with local events in the markets where risks may be taken and in neighbouring territories or those which may have knock-on effect for the market under consideration. For example, financial difficulties faced by the Mexican government in late 1994 led to shocks being felt elsewhere in Latin America, as overseas investors lost confidence in those markets too. This in turn affected emerging markets on other continents where it was felt that similar risks existed and investors got cold feet. There are so many factors which can affect political risk that it is difficult to know where the next shot is coming from. There can be no substitute for visiting a territory. Better, on-the-ground representation can mean quick reporting of significant developments for the better or for the worse.

Political events will affect the exporter's ability to obtain insurance cover, a banker's willingness to lend or a government aid or export finance package being available. Exporters can make it a policy of the company for those involved in the export decision-making process to keep some handle on the markets to which the company exports, then there will be less likelihood of being caught out.

POLITICAL RISK INSURANCE

The commercial insurance market can cover political risks although it is often considered to be 'the market of last resort' among other risk coverage options such as bank risk-taking, state-supported export credits and the forfaiting market. Some risks, however, can be more easily covered in the commercial political risk market than otherwise.

No centralised statistics are available to define the scope of the political risk market so it is not possible to offer a view as to the overall volume of business transacted annually. When considering the size of the market it is usual to refer to the coverage capacity for a single transaction, which today would be about US$15 million. If the risk is a strong one, the term short and the insured (an exporter) has a track-record of successful dealing in the market it may be possible to access cover of a larger scale. Likewise if an exporter intends to cover a basket of different transactions and risks under a single umbrella policy the available 'global limit' to underwrite the entire package may extend to much greater figures.

The main political risk insurance markets are, respectively by size, in the UK, USA, France, Germany and Singapore. Lloyds of London has the largest share of world political risk business estimated by market practitioners to be around 35 per cent. The system operates through a network of brokers who work with exporters and present transactions to underwriters. The underwriters assess the risks and then spread them among a syndicate of insurers who in turn reinsure themselves with reinsurance companies.

Types of Cover

Several types of risk are typically coverable in the political risk market:

- *Public buyer default* covers the failure or refusal of a public sector buyer to honour any of its contractual obligations.
- *Public bank default* covers the failure or refusal by a government bank to honour its guarantee, draft or letter of credit.
- *Public supplier default* indemnifies an insured against losses incurred due to non-delivery of goods to be supplied by government suppliers. This typically concerns supply of minerals and other commodities where mines or production facilities are government-owned.
- *Unfair calling of bonds* covers the contingent liability of an exporter's on-demand bond being called unfairly by a government. Alternatively unfair calling may stem from a government intervention or change in legislation.
- *Exchange transfer embargoes* covers situations where a government controls and withdraws foreign currency funds allocation, preventing importers from meeting their obligations.
- *Import/export restrictions* where government restrictions result in withdrawal of import or export licenses.
- *War* covers contract frustration or termination due to outbreak of war, civil war, insurrection, rebellion and/or revolution which directly prevents performance under a contract.
- *Arbitration default* insures against an arbitration award being made but not honoured.
- *Confiscation/expropriation/nationalisation/deprivation* applies where an overseas investment is affected by government intervention such as nationalisation of natural resources.

In practice insurance of political risks is quite flexible and a policy can be structured to match perils not listed here. Alternatively coverage can be tailored to meet particular contractual circumstances which might involve one or more of the above risks.

One advantage which the commercial market has over state-supported schemes is that cover is not restricted to capital goods. Goods of any nature can be covered including perishables, other commodities and used plant and equipment. Where commodity cargoes such as minerals, oil and grains are involved, an underwriter may be able to justify coverage based upon a good track record in a territory which might otherwise seem risky. This stems from the fact that non-payment for oil and food cargoes is relatively rare in otherwise highly risky territories because were it to occur other suppliers might refuse to deal with the buyer in future. This would be politically risky for the government concerned.

Typical policy terms

Policy conventions are relatively standard across the market, with variations:

- 90 or 95 per cent of contract value may be insured but not 100 per cent. This is because of the 'insured's loss' principle. That the insured should retain a share of the risk for his or her own account.
- Waiting periods between claim and indemnity pay-out are normal for political risk policies.
- The more exotic the risk, the longer the waiting period. This can extend to 540 days after the date when claim is made.
- Delay interest is not normally paid during waiting periods as it may be under certain state-supported schemes, and therefore needs to be allowed for in costing a transaction, as does a contingency for 'insured's loss'.
- The credit period covered will extend to three years maximum, although it may be possible to roll forward the cover annually, subject to the under-writer's discretion.
- For pre-credit risks contract frustration cover can be given for risks which are present prior to shipment. For example where there is a long manu-facturing cycle for a specific piece of machinery.
- It is noteworthy that many banks will not accept pre-shipment contract cancellation risks which the commercial market can.

Premium costs vary as do all the other terms of the policy depending on the nature of the cover given. Indications for political risk coverage can be obtained from brokers such as Colburn, French & Kneen and Sedgewicks. Brokers and sub-agents are present all over the world.

Emerging Markets

The risks posed by transactions involving payment receipts from emerging markets are a compound of both commercial and political risk with an emphasis on the latter. The growth, for example, of the forfaiting market into a broader range of country risks has involved becoming increasingly familiar with the political risks posed by changes in the economics and politics of emergent economies. Of course credit risks on a range of guarantor banks have had to be measured and monitored.

Part of the difficulty of dealing with trade-related emerging market trans-action risks, apart from that of getting good information quickly, has been 'liquidity'. Where risk is taken for any period beyond a few weeks or months holders of debt have to face being stuck with potentially bad debts on their books if the market for paper dries up. Turkey, Iran, Mexico and Venezuela are all examples of markets which have recently, within quite a short space of time, effectively gone off-limits as far as placing risk is concerned.

Because trade receivables are not as easily bought and sold, due to the nature of their market, as rescheduled debt, Brady bonds, CDs and equities, financing emerging market trade is still fraught with perils. Political risk insurance may be a solution, with exporters as insureds assigning claim proceeds to financing banks as loss payees. But banks tend to prefer to make their own judgements accepting as inevitable, 'accidents' which occur from time to time.

Banks may prefer to trade out impaired debt at a discount if necessary rather than pay premiums, suffer a waiting period and receive only partial recovery under an insurance arrangement. Currently, passed due trade-related receivables in the form of letters of credit, forfaited paper and loan obligations are traded for a number of market risks. Some specialist firms indeed make a market in just such instruments recovering overdues on a 'best efforts' basis in return for a hefty fee. The consequence for the loss-taking bank is often merely a profits-deductable trading loss which can help to minimise the corporate tax bill. In addition to the benefit of at least being able to claw something back for the defaulted receivable, this way out of defaulted debt helps to increase the scope for financing new markets.

The petrified loan portfolios of the decade following the 1982 debt crisis were eventually dissolved by banks taking losses, forgiving a proportion of the debt and trading away their impaired debts. Liquidity was the key to the growth of emerging markets investment in the 1980s and early 1990s. It could be the way forward for trade debt into the 21st century, so bringing into play many more emerging markets. As the World Trade Organisation promotes freer trade on an immense scale across the globe, new players will require finance to get on their feet. Some will stumble and require a helping hand.

14: Performance Risk

On the basis that it takes two to tango both sides of the international sales contract will face a performance risk on the other party. A financing bank may, unless it structures its financing carefully, find itself paying for the failure of one or other party to perform.

Excluding the failures of counterparty banks which will be dealt with in a later section, it is important to remember that banks are not usually parties to the commercial contract. Indeed why should they be? They provide funds, credit and the mechanism of payment but neither goods nor the payment itself.

A bank would wish to be insulated from the failures of either party to perform. Under letters of credit, as we saw earlier in this book, banks are involved with documents and not goods and documentary credits are entirely separate operations from the sales contracts in the context of which they facilitate payment. Likewise in forfaiting transactions, discount will only take place following shipment. Guarantee of payment against avalised bills or notes is unconditional and irrevocable. In a buyer's credit transaction again a guarantee or state-supported export credit arrangement should be separate from obligations under the financed supply contract.

If, however, the financing is secured by products or pre-export financing is made in advance of manufacture, harvest or processing then it is important that a financing bank focuses very clearly on where its risks lie and what its recourse is in the event of non-performance. Enforcing legal actions in overseas territories for non-performance is often time-consuming and expensive. If the sums involved are small, the costs of recovery by legal action may be uneconomic.

In public and other large contracts, performance security such as bonds will often be called for as part of the tendering process. No performance bond – no deal. Typically these will involve a first-class bank issuing the bond on behalf of a contractor in favour of an overseas buyer. If the exporter fails to deliver the goods or services in keeping with the contract then the bond can be called by the buyer. A bank issuing the bond is bound to pay and should take recourse to the exporter. This recourse faces the financing

133

bank with commercial/corporate credit risk considerations which have been discussed above. Alternatively if security is taken over property, plant or equipment then an accurate appraisal of the worth of that security needs to be made.

Another common feature to protect the buyer is the use of payment retentions. The buyer withholds a certain proportion of the contract price until pre-agreed steps have been taken, such as full operation of all plant and equipment, testing or formal acceptance by the customer after a lapse of time.

The risk of non-payment is, of course, a risk of non-performance by the buyer, which can be dealt with in various ways. As a general rule a bank has very little influence on questions of performance under sales contracts. For this reason banks should avoid taking performance risk altogether. Client relationships may on occasion oblige an export financing bank to shoulder a performance risk and in that case the track record of performance by the client must be impeccable.

15: Shipment Risk

There are many risks which arise during the shipment/delivery process. Whenever a cargo is stored or in transit by road, rail, air or sea it could be damaged, lost or stolen. The loss of goods or equipment is likely to be costly for their owner and the cause of dispute between the buyer and seller. It is important that goods are fully insured at all stages of production, transit, delivery and post-delivery storage. Indeed it is a term of many supply contracts that goods will be insured by one or other party. Failure to do so is an actionable breach of contract.

Who owns goods before, during and after delivery, is responsible for insuring them and paying for the costs of delivery is defined by the terms of shipment. Specialist works on shipping practices and maritime law should be referred to for detailed commentary on this complex subject. Essential reading, however, is *Incoterms* published by the International Chamber of Commerce where shipping terms are explained and to which many shipping terms actually refer in their definition, for example 'c.i.f. (Incoterms)'.

Shipping costs can substantially affect the cost of exported goods. In a secured transaction an export financier should be fully aware of the make up of the cost of the cargo as it will affect the forced resale value of this security.

For example, if a lien is taken over a cargo to secure an advance and it becomes necessary to foreclose on that cargo its price at auction *in situ* is likely to be substantially less than the cost to the buyer under the sales contract where delivery and insurance to a distant destination were costed in.

Insurance and freight are also negotiating pieces in an export sale. They can be haggled over to arrive at the eventual terms of business. Thus 'I can deliver it to your premises in Backwoods, Michigan for $5,000 but if you arrange for it be collected from our warehouse near London's Heathrow airport it's yours for $3,999.'

Bearing all this in mind here are the basic shipping terms outlined and graded from the easiest, nearest-to-home with the minimum of responsibilities for the exporter to the most onerous and costly.

Ex Works, Ex Warehouse or Ex Store
Under these terms the buyer agrees to collect the goods from the works, warehouse or store where the goods are manufactured or kept. The supplier must pack and supply the goods in keeping with the supply contract and make the goods available at the time and place agreed. The supplier must give reasonable notice to the buyer of the goods' readiness for collection.

The buyer agrees by such terms to collect the goods and accepts all charges for doing so including customs import duties, taxes, transportation costs, insurance and the costs of obtaining documents.

In essence the supplier has a pretty easy time of it. In negotiations concerning delivery an exporter would prefer to agree such terms.

FOR or FOT (named point of departure)
Free On Rail and Free On Truck mean that the supplier delivers the goods to the railway authority at a named place. There is a slight difference between the two terms which we need not explore here. The supplier still has no responsibility for actually exporting the goods as such although he or she bears all the costs and risks as far as FOR or FOT requires.

Delivered at Container Collection Depot (named place of depot)
The supplier is responsible for all charges and risks prior to acceptance by a combined transport operator at the container port named.

FAS (named vessel in the port of shipment)
Free Alongside Ship. The supplier transports the goods to the side of the named vessel at the named port of shipment. The actual loading of the goods across the ship's rail is at the risk and expense of the buyer.

An important point to note here is that where in any of the terms mentioned a named place of delivery is to be given both buyer and seller should be clear as to what the term encompasses. Ports differ one from another in size, depth of draught, loading facilities and so on.

FOB (named port of shipment)
Free on Board is one stage further than FAS. This time the supplier is responsible for all risks and associated costs of delivering goods 'over the ship's rail'.

There is a considerable literature on FOB arising from local customs and peculiarities. In addition, although the exporter has, strictly speaking, no responsibility for insurance and freight beyond the ship's rail it may be inconvenient for the buyer to arrange them. Therefore an FOB clause can involve 'additional services' language which reflects agreement between the parties that the seller will act as the buyer's agent in obtaining insurance and freight.

FOB is often used as a pricing term between buyer and seller, especially at the initial stages of discussion. However, before final agreement is reached both parties should make sure they understand precisely what their responsibilities are and the costs involved.

FOB airport

This is similar to FOB but concerns delivery by air. In this case the 'handover' normally takes place, not at an 'aeroplane's rail' but at the air carrier's transit facilities.

Note: Under this clause, were the goods to be damaged after delivery to the airport of departure, say on the tarmac of the runway, the buyer would bear the risk which should therefore be insured against.

CIF (named port of destination)

Along with FOB, Cost, Insurance and Freight is a commonly used term. It means that the exporter is responsible for the cost of the goods, insurance and freight to the agreed point of delivery. It should be borne in mind that the supplier is obliged to ensure safe shipment – not safe arrival – although marine risks should be insured against.

Once the goods have been shipped and the bill of lading has been made available to the exporter he or she will usually be in a position to present documents under a documentary credit and so receive payment, if payment terms were at sight. The importer will normally require an original bill of lading to obtain title for the goods upon delivery. This will typically be routed through the banking system unless other arrangements have been made.

Insurance and freight aspects of the CIF contract are complex areas in themselves and the reader is recommended to consult specialist material on these subjects.

C&F (named port of destination)

This is similar to CIF except that the buyer agrees to insure the goods.

If the buyer is a state organisation where the state concerned insures its own cargoes such terms would be common. Alternatively where a buyer felt that it could insure the goods more cheaply or appropriately than the seller it might prefer to take out its own insurance cover.

Beyond C&F there is a series of delivery terms which are more advantageous to the buyer than the seller, almost a mirror image of the terms ex-works, FOT and so on, explained above.

Arrival, or Ex Ship (named ship and named point of arrival)
Differing from CIF the goods are 'caused to be delivered' to the buyer rather than subject to any documentary provisions. The terms therefore imply a greater degree of trust on the part of the seller that the payment will be secure.

Ex Quay (named port of delivery)
As for 'arrival' except that the seller also accepts responsibility for import duties and unloading costs at the named port of arrival.

Delivered at Frontier (named place of delivery at frontier)
This clause is self explanatory. It is commonly used in continental Europe.

Delivered or Franco Domicile or Free Delivery (named place of destination in the country of importation)
The mirror image of 'Ex works' above. The seller delivers the goods to the buyer at the agreed place.

The importance of Incoterms and a clear understanding of the shipment responsibilities cannot be over-emphasised. Especially where remote, inland or island destinations are concerned the delivery can be costly and difficult to arrange. Failure to properly insure up to the responsibilities of the shipment terms is a costly oversight best avoided.

Cargo Insurance

The full details of the risks covered are shown on the insurance policy relating to the cover taken out. The list normally includes 'perils of the sea' such as accidental loss or damage caused by sea water, storms, stranding, collisions, fire related risks, jettison in times of emergency and 'assailing thieves'. There are numerous other risks which can be insured against which are specifically mentioned and additional premium is payable to cover them.

16: Currency Risk and Hedging Techniques

Definition

A currency risk is present wherever a revenue is to be received by a party in a currency other than that in which the party normally accounts. You cannot for example know how much an incoming fee received in US Dollars is worth until selling it for your own accounting currency, say Deutschmarks, Sterling, or Hong Kong Dollars. As you do not know what it is worth to the profit and loss account it could turn out to be less than that budgeted for.

For banks and export financing houses currency poses a double risk. The first is not knowing what their own revenue will be. Secondly and more importantly they are faced with an additional aspect of customer/borrower credit risk. A shift in exchange rates can mean that a customer or borrower may be faced with higher obligations to the financier than was allowed for. This can affect all types of customer from the smallest trader to the largest sovereign borrower in the world. There are two golden rules:

- Never take on open exposures to currency risk unless you are absolutely certain that it will turn out in your favour – and short of using a crystal ball you can never be sure.
- Always make sure that those to whom you are exposed understand currency risk and how to avoid it. This means, for a banker or financier, giving sound advice and perhaps selling a client a currency hedge alongside export finance.

Because sales of goods and services from one country to another almost always involve some currency risk, choosing the currency in which to invoice is often a matter discussed in relation to the commercial contract. Those negotiating it may be quite happy to concede the buyer's own currency if it will add strength to the sales proposal. Alternatively they may have no choice. But the currency risk implications of offering medium or long payment terms can be that a profitable contract can turn into a loss if the seller's currency appreciates.

Likewise if a buyer, particularly in a territory with a weak local currency, takes on foreign currency obligations, his or her ability to service the debt may be impaired if his or her own currency loses value.

Natural Hedge

If a firm receives foreign currency but also has outgoings in the same currency there is a natural hedge. This is true for importers, exporters and finance providers alike. Thus if an emerging market oil producer buys-in capital equipment in US Dollars but also receives revenue for its oil exports in dollars there is a degree of protection from currency risk. How much will clearly depend on the actual amounts of dollars coming in and going out, whether they match wholly or partially and other budgetary considerations within the firm, for example, the market price of oil.

Forward Cover

Where there is a predictable, short-term currency flow the forward foreign exchange market can be used. The currency to be received can be pre-sold to a bank at an agreed exchange rate such that the seller of currency, probably the exporter, can be sure of the revenue that will be received in his or her own currency.

The reverse is also true. If an importer needs to make payment in currency at a predictable future time, foreign currency can be bought or fixed forward safe in the knowledge that the price in the importer's base currency will not change.

Where the term of payment is relatively short and in a major financing currency for which a forward market exists this will be a sufficient currency hedge. But it may be difficult, even impossible to use forward contracts if a forward market does not exist for the currencies concerned or if it does not extend far enough into the future. In this regard the less-developed countries with weak or soft currencies are disadvantaged.

Currency Swaps

Where stage payment flows of foreign currencies can be predicted it may be possible to sell these to banks in the currency swaps market. Practically banks will be unlikely to enter into swaps agreements with counterparties who's credit rating is not acceptable, which excludes a large number of exporters. For banks or export finance houses with good credit ratings this is a hedging option.

Match Funding and Book Funding

Banks or export financiers such as forfaiters which have a constant flow of currencies may chose one of two strategies to hedge their exposure. They will tend to have natural hedges, as described above, in any case but for large transactions they may be able to 'match fund' the cash flows. This means that they borrow in the interbank market to fund the purchase of the foreign exchange-denominated asset, repayment for which exactly matches the inflow of funds from the asset. The asset might, for example, be a forfaiting transaction or loan with six monthly repayment terms.

This works well for transactions of a reasonable size where it is possible to find an interbank market counterparty to provide the funding. A transaction of US$5 million repayable in ten equal semi-annual instalments of US$500,000 should be simple to match fund. Bank's deposit dealers have a tendency, however, to argue that where cash flows are small or in unequal amounts they will have difficulty in matching them. In this case banks themselves and forfaiting companies tend to 'fund their book'. This means aggregating sets of cash flows falling due at more or less the same times so that they can similarly be funded and hedged against currency fluctuation. These techniques are also used to cover interest rate risks, which will be dealt with in Chapter 17.

Bank Fees and Commissions

Lastly, many banks and finance houses receive their fees and commissions in currencies other than that in which they account. Because the pricing and profitability of transactions are often calculated well in advance of receipt it may be as well to consider how to deal with the currency risk to such receipts. Many companies take a 'swings and roundabouts' point of view, selling currency income spot (immediately) for their own currency as soon as it is received. If the exchange rate has gone up or down since the fee was charged then they net the benefits with any loss sustained. It can be worth considering selling substantial fees forward or retaining them in currency once they are received if the rates are moving in the right direction. This obviously presents risks but as the market in the major currencies is highly liquid the fee can be sold off quickly if the rates take a turn for the worse.

It is quite easy if you work for a large bank with its own currency dealing operations to become blasé about foreign exchange risk. An export finance banker within a large British or American bank is accustomed to arranging transactions in foreign currency and passing the appropriate instruction to the dealing room which will automatically arrange cover. This can cause one to lose focus on how threatening currency risk can be

141

to the other parties in the transaction. The best practice, whether for a banker in a large institution or for the smallest importer or exporter, is to think carefully about the consequences of making or taking payment in foreign currency and to take the necessary measures to insulate the transaction from currency risk.

17: Interest Rate Risk

Definition

Where credit is made available in support of an export sale or contracting operation a double interest rate risk exists. On the one hand the financier faces a risk that interest receivable from a borrower or obligor may not cover his or her own funding costs. This would be a greater risk where the interest due was at fixed rate and the financier was funding his or her own lending with floating rate money. The second risk is that the borrower or obligor is faced with higher interest costs than those budgeted for and cannot afford to pay. This could occur where funding was made available at floating rates which have risen during the period of the credit arrangement.

With both risks the financier stands to lose and should therefore take steps to cover against them. As a general rule, as with currency risk, no risk should be taken at all unless the lender is quite sure of future rates (which is pretty much impossible unless the credit period is very short).

Fixed-Rate Funding

Therefore where fixed-rate funding is made available, such as in forfaiting transactions for example, a bank or export finance house can 'match fund' the transaction. Funds may be borrowed in the interbank market for the term of the deal and on-lent at a profit. The incoming interest cash flow will liquidate the interbank funding interest leaving the financier with a margin.

Alternatively a group of small transactions with similar maturities in the same currency may be funded as one 'critical mass' in the same way. The effect of such book funding is to neutralise the risk inherent in making credit available at fixed interest rates.

Floating-Rate Funding

Where floating-rate credit is provided, for example under a buyer credit or eurocurrency loan agreement, it would be conventional to define the interest rate as a margin over the cost of obtaining funds in a eurocurrency deposit market, London Interbank Offered Rate or LIBOR being the most common reference rate. The interest rate definition is usually linked to interest periods, typically one month, three months, or six months. The loan is 'fixed' or lent for the interest period, and then automatically renewed, or 'rolled over', for a further interest period. A rate of interest is fixed for the new interest period two days before it commences and the borrower is advised of the new rate at which the interest payable at the end of the interest period will be calculated. The interest rate is usually determined by calculating the average of three rates supplied by reference banks.

From the lending bank's point of view there is no interest rate risk involved in the funding operation as such funding is usually procured at the rate quoted. There can be a minor risk if the bank defines the interest rate as a margin over LIBOR but cannot itself in fact procure funds at LIBOR either due to market conditions or its own standing in the market. This risk can be eradicated by ensuring that the interest rate is defined in the loan agreement as based upon the bank's cost of obtaining funds in the interbank market rather than on LIBOR.

The risk with floating rate interest lies with the borrower. In the late 1970s, for example, US Dollar LIBOR rates were in the region of 20 per cent per annum; in the early 1990s they fell as low as 3.5 per cent. Borrowers therefore bear the brunt of interest rate rises and should be encouraged to hedge their exposure where possible. An interest rate swap might, for example, be put in place enabling a borrower to exchange its future floating-rate obligations for fixed-rate ones, so stabilising its outflow of funds over the term of the loan.

18: Secured Transactions

Many export financing structures can be collateralised using goods, equipment, vessels, commodities, the real property of either the exporter or the importer or indeed cash. Whatever the security for the transaction it should never be assumed that because the transaction is secured it is without risk.

The history of international banking, especially as it concerns property-related lending, is littered with impaired debt, distressed property and negative equity, especially since the property crises in London, Paris and Tokyo in the early 1990s. Security for loans turned out to be worth less than it was estimated to be when it was taken as security. The trouble is, of course, that the weakness of a secured structure may not be revealed until it is necessary to repossess and sell off the security, by which time it is too late to strengthen the risk. Nevertheless, some measures can be taken to protect the financier.

Check that the Security Exists

Crates filled with rocks, empty boxes, tanks of water which should have contained oil, buildings not yet built, machinery which is broken. There is no substitute for seeing and inspecting security to make sure it is what it has been pledged to be.

If it is held in another territory it can be inspected by an agent acting on a lender's behalf. Inspection agencies such as SGS (Société de Surveillance), Cotecna or Bureau Veritas are among the companies which offer such a service. They can inspect cargoes for quantity and quality and warrant that the goods have been seen and inspected by them. Property, likewise should be inspected and evaluated by market experts.

Valuing Security

Having determined that it exists, what is it actually worth? The benefit which security brings is that when and if it is sold it will produce sufficient cash to cover funds advanced. Therefore its value can only be determined by how much people would be likely to give for it in the current market and over the life of the credit which it secures. Those experienced in the market for such goods or property will be best placed to know what security will fetch and a banker should not assume that he or she knows the value of the bank's security without detailed reference to its market.

Furthermore, markets change. Security needs to be re-evaluated regularly. An outdated security valuation is an unseen risk the magnitude of which will not be understood until it is necessary to sell the security. By this time it may be too late to do anything about recovering further value from elsewhere, say if a company is in liquidation.

If, in the process of checking the value of security, it emerges that there is a shortfall of value versus funds advanced, taking further security or a repayment of the advance should be considered.

Loan to Value Ratio

In secured transactions it would be both unusual and dangerous to advance the full value of security. Although there are no hard and fast rules as to what proportion of value should be advanced it is worth looking at the market for the security again.

If the market for the goods, property or commodity has never been known to fall then it may be safe to assume that a larger proportion of funds can be advanced. Markets in which values fluctuate widely suggest a loan to value ratio should err on the side of caution. Of course looking backwards at market trends will always be like driving while looking in the rear-view mirror. As so many banks found when lending against property in centres such as London, New York and Tokyo even good old bricks and mortar should not be trusted, especially if no one seems keen to buy property any more.

Ownership

Once the existence and value of security have been successfully established and attested to in writing its ownership needs to be verified.

Proof of ownership should be proved to the financier before it is accepted as security. Ownership of property, for example, in countries with developed

146

land registries and legal documentation procedures, should be simple to establish. Where vehicles and other plant and equipment are concerned, again registration documents should be able to prove ownership. In respect of bulk commodity or mineral cargoes it will be important to establish ownership and to ensure that even if the ownership changes, perhaps as the cargo is traded while on the high seas, the financier retains a lien over it.

Where local or international documentation is put forward as proof of ownership it is important that this is based on good provenance. Local legal advice and opinion on documents of ownership and title are important and should be obtained from well-respected local law firms.

Ultimately, should it be necessary to prove or contest ownership a financier should have evidence that he or she took all necessary steps to establish ownership and obtained documents which were verified or appeared beyond all reasonable doubt to represent ownership by the person pledging the goods as security. While discussion of the law relating to ownership of property in various jurisdictions is beyond the scope of this book the important point is that every effort to ensure proof of ownership should be made prior to any advance being made against the security.

Already Pledged

Finally, having checked out all of the above, it is important to be certain that the security in question is not already being used as security for another financing arrangement. By use of negative pledge language in loan documentation or exchanges of letters relating to the security financiers in secured transactions should gain an undertaking preventing the same security being used as security for another loan or advance.

19: Documentation Risk

DOCUMENTATION – VITAL LIFELINE

Financing international trade is, at best, an arm's length business for most banks and financing institutions. The trade financier is likely to be thousands of miles away in one of the world's financial centres while the goods being financed are manufactured, moved about the globe, the vessels carrying them dock and embark, goods are transhipped and finally delivered to the seller. The trade financier may be involved in dozens of transactions at the same time and cannot supervise each one, minute-by-minute. He or she is linked to the transactions by a few all-important pieces of paper. If this documentation is faulty the entire structure may come unravelled and money may be lost – and perhaps the financier's job as well.

Documentation has firstly to be properly prepared. Letters of credit, bills of exchange, promissory notes and other standard instruments need to be correct in every detail. The documents themselves are discussed elsewhere in this book but if they are faulty, not properly checked or incomplete the documentation risk is very real.

Documentation Skills and Protections for Trade Financiers

It is reckoned that 60 per cent of documents presented to banks under letters of credit are faulty in some way. That is usually a risk to the exporter and perhaps the importer. However, paying out against such faulty documentation represents a risk to the bank or finance house. If it fails to correctly carry out its function in the documentation chain it can be held responsible for its failures. This points to several requirements:

- Documentation needs to be thoroughly and accurately prepared.
- Staff need to be adequately educated, trained and managed to handle the work.
- Operating and control systems need to be in position to double-check all work to see that nothing slips through the net.

148

When non-standard transactions are structured they often require detailed documentation to be drafted by legal advisors, either internal or external to the financing bank. It should obviously be legally correct and actionable if necessary and encapsulate the transaction, but it should also be practical. Ideally three parties should play a part in ensuring the documentation is correct from the lender's point of view:

- the trade finance officer negotiating the transaction on behalf of the financing institution;
- the lawyer instructed by the lender to document the deal; and
- a representative of the administrative department of the bank which will run the transaction throughout its life.

All three parties have a role to play and will have differing views of documentation. If the transaction provides medium- or long-term finance they should all aim to ensure that there will be no unforeseen difficulties, perhaps years after signature of a facility when it may be necessary take legal action. It is likely that none of these three parties nor the original representatives of a borrower, guarantor or other signatories will be around when, years hence, the documents come under scrutiny. Everything of significance in the life of the transaction should be logged in the form of file notes. This includes telephone conversations, written exchanges and communications, meetings and so forth.

Understanding Documentary Implications

It is also important that all parties to the financing understand the implications of a financing agreement's covenants. Guarantors, for example, may happily put their names to an agreement on behalf of a subsidiary assuming it to be merely a formal requirement of the bank. Records may not be kept properly by the parent company so that when the subsidiary does default much later the guarantors have a rude awakening when the guarantee is called. Having to remind a guarantor of its obligations can be unpleasant and certainly unwelcome but it can also be time-consuming and costly if it comes to litigation.

Safe-keeping

Another documentation risk arises from failures in safe keeping. If documents cannot be found when they are needed it is not only embarrassing but can prove difficult to substantiate a legal case. All original documentation should be kept in fire-proof storage in such a way that it can be quickly retrieved. This applies, incidentally, whether the document is an original bill of lading held overnight or a loan agreement held for decades.

If it is necessary to refer to documentation regularly then photocopies, microfiche or copies held on disk should be referred to. The risk of damage, loss or theft of originals, perhaps relating to financing of many millions of dollars must be protected at all costs and at all times.

Many transactions, particularly those which are complex or which have numerous parties to them, require sets of complementary documents to be drawn up. All of the documents in the set should be conserved safely – not just the original letter of credit, promissory note or main loan agreement. This includes side letters, subsidiary arrangements of different sorts and anything which in any way bears upon the transaction or facility.

Over the life of a transaction operational details may be all that it is necessary to refer to on a day-to-day basis. The more esoteric provisions hardly concern the facility administrator. But when it is necessary to set about litigation then it is absolutely crucial that every last scrap of paper is available, tightly drawn up and proves itself to be the airtight package which you always assumed it was. By then it is too late to redraft, renegotiate or unpick the arrangements.

20: Pricing Risk

The costs of financing international trade need to be adequately reflected in the pricing applied to transactions in the form of risk margins, discount rates, fees and commissions. There is a risk in not doing so.

The draw of higher margins, larger deals or the kudos of being an international trade financier can attract individuals and their firms to finance export transactions. It may also be that clients of a bank or a finance house request trade finance services which appear on the face of it simple enough to graft onto the corporate banking relationship. Practically speaking, however, it is a lot more expensive to engage in international transactions generally and trade transactions in particular than it would be to carry on domestic business.

Overheads

If business is to be done sensibly and safely it is necessary to expend considerable time, effort and consequently money on doing the job properly. Hiring expert staff with the right experience is a cost. So is training. There is a cost in research, analysis and monitoring of risks as well as in controlling aggregation of country and other risks described in this section of the book. The costs of travelling to markets in far-off places, accommodation and the enormous amount of dead time spent by executives waiting in airport lounges and outer offices all add up to costs to the business which need to be priced into transactions.

Competition and Volume

It is likely that a firm will underprice its export finance services, especially as competition for deals is so intense among banks, forfaiters and other export finance houses. Larger banks do have a distinct advantage in being able to set up systems within their banks to handle larger numbers of relatively low-risk transactions. The marginal cost of doing further transactions becomes minimal the more you do. At the other end of the scale a small project finance team in a bank may make very little money for months or even years while working on a substantial infrastructure project. Once, however, the transaction is finally closed and fees of several hundreds of thousands of dollars are paid then it all seems very worthwhile.

Pricing transactions can become quite a difficult matter despite cost/profit centre accounting and inter-departmental billing. Then there is 'the market rate'. With letter of credit confirmations or forfaiting well-known risks, for example, it is very difficult to charge more than the competition because business will simply transfer to the cheapest house.

Reflecting True Risk

Underpricing and overpricing
Where risk is being taken, how is it reflected in the margin or fee pricing? This is something of a mystery. Many banks charge extraordinarily low margins, tenths of 1 per cent for example, for advancing funds in loan transactions. No right-minded manufacturer would entertain that sort of return even if the volume of production was extremely high.

In pricing eurocurrency loans, export credits and transactions secured on property, for example, many banks will simply refer to similar transactions which other banks have carried out for analogous risks, increasing and decreasing the price to reflect changes in market conditions. A thoroughgoing empirical appraisal of market and price needs to be made. Banks may undercut each other to win market share and the perils of such an approach to pricing are realised only when the market as a whole becomes overheated. By then it is too late. Market collapse occurs and pricing is shown to have been inadequate; the last arrivals on the block with the lowest prices lose out most.

The effect of central bank rulings on risk asset weighting for determining the amount of capital banks should hold against their risk assets has had the result of focusing bankers' minds on the cost of capital and therefore the level of margins and total remuneration required to make a transaction worthwhile. From a pricing point of view this is to be welcomed.

Overpricing is also a risk. Bankers and financiers are immediately branded as usurers if they try to take too much reward from a transaction. Overpricing can affect credibility as an institution is labelled as charging too much for its labours. In the UK the question of how much merchant banks and brokers should charge for privatisation and new issue work has come in for public criticism, especially if the fees come out of the public purse in privatisation work, for example.

Reaching an adequate price for taking a risk over time, especially where it involves international risk factors and complex structuring, is not an easy task. In summary, trade transactions do carry a pricing risk. Attributing full costs to individual deals is tricky especially in a large organisation.

21: Transfer Risk

DEBT PIPELINES

The author was once involved in the task of reorganising the trade debt outstandings of an African country. In fact, considering the hundreds and hundreds of pieces of paper and the dust-covered, hand-written ledgers where the information was stored in bank branches throughout the country in question the basic arrangements were admirably well-organised. The 60,000 separate entries which were tapped into a new database represented amounts of money owed to foreign firms, banks and individuals, paid into banks by importers, some of them local affiliates of multinational companies but awaiting foreign currency allocation from the central bank.

Such a debt pipeline is common in countries where the economy is in a desperate state and there is a dearth of foreign exchange to pay for imports. The risk of not receiving payment until months or even years after it is due is a real one when financing trade to such countries. For the financier dependent on payment in hard currency this is a risk to be avoided.

When confirming letters of credit opened from markets which have debt pipelines, banks will insist on being cash-collateralised by the opening bank before adding their confirmation. Similarly before accepting local bank guarantees an international bank may wish to take a lien over any cash balances which are held with it over and above any banker's right of set-off. In some cases banks will call for security over a country's national foreign currency or gold reserves which they or a correspondent bank may hold before agreeing to finance the country's government purchases.

Such dissuasive measures are prudent in view of the risk that funds may be paid by a local payee and remain in limbo indefinitely.

Solutions

Debt for equity

If funds are blocked in this way there are one or two remedies which are available to banks and other parties to liquidate the situation. It may be possible to purchase local goods, services or investments with the local currency-denominated blocked funds. Where an investor wishes to develop a local operation it may liquidate its own blocked funds or purchase (usually at a discount to the face value) funds awaiting payment to another party.

Broadly termed a 'debt for equity swap' countries where it is possible to do this may have a formal scheme set up. Other informal arrangements are not uncommon. For an institution awaiting payment there are several advantages:

- at least partial payment is received where none looked likely for the foreseeable future;
- cancellation of a bad debt provision and final write-off of any loss;
- an end to the administrative nuisance of monitoring and chasing the debt;
- a more creative approach to dealing with blocked funds.

Trading impaired debt

The market in 'impaired debt' is global and enormous. Trading in rescheduled debt, Brady Bonds and a range of other commercial debt instruments has led to an opening up of trading of trade debt deriving from emerging markets. It may be possible to liquidate transfer pipeline trade debt in this way without becoming involved with local investment complications.

The downsides are that prices of purchasing trade debt of this sort are usually quoted as a percentage of the face value and these can sometimes be very low and can fluctuate widely and quickly. This is because the market is very often a thin one with relatively few counterparties available. It may also be the case that behind a purchasing bank or trader lurks the original debtor government, bank or importer owing the outstanding. The effect is that they buy back their own debt at the expense of a foreign creditor. The other side of the coin is that some payment in final settlement is better than none at all.

22: Bank Risk

DESCRIPTION

The risk we take on banks is not new but has forced itself onto our agenda over the last couple of years. This follows the collapse of BCCI, numerous savings and loans institutions in the USA, various Latin American banks and Barings, one of London's oldest and most blue-chip merchant banks. The manner in which banks have entered or withdrawn from certain types of banking business has also cast doubt on whether they will be around when we need them.

The considerations mentioned above in respect of credit risk apply to banks as to commercial companies. When accepting a letter of credit, or a bank-guaranteed bill of exchange or promissory note in expectation of future payment against it, then an independent credit assessment of the bank risk needs to be made.

INFORMATION

It is generally speaking easier to obtain information on banks' credit standing than on that of commercial companies. Many banks are rated by the international rating agencies. Many are obliged to produce quarterly financials which are reported in the financial press.

However, the average manufacturer/exporter is unlikely to transact with more than a handful of overseas banks. Meanwhile Italy alone has 1,000 banks, the USA 10,000 or so. Not all will be engaged in trade-related business but nevertheless when in doubt take measures such as obtaining counterguarantees from banks whom you have good reason to trust.

Bank-watching

Banks withdraw from business very rapidly. If you are relying on a bank for its support with a transaction which is taking some time to finalise, perhaps as a counterparty to buy a trade debt instrument such as forfaited paper, check regularly that the bank is still there with you. If a bank has not issued its formal, written commitment to carry out a certain piece of business do not assume that it is committed.

One should avoid the assumption that banks do not make mistakes. They can delay payments, mislay documents, transpose figures, misuse calculators and are peopled by folk with the same degree of human fallibility as you and I. Everything needs to be checked and delays in payment chased to ensure timely receipt.

Banks are keen to standardise procedures as much as possible. It is, however, a feature of export sales that business differs deal-to-deal. Therefore flexibility of the bank towards a transaction is important to you and to your counterparties whether you are trade financiers or exporters.

Work with More Than One Bank

Putting all of a company's banking business with one bank tends to make companies vulnerable, just as buying from one supplier or selling to only one customer does. Healthy competition for one's business leads to finer pricing for the exporter. It also encourages banks to generate new ideas in order to prove their worth. This can be very helpful for the banks themselves who will after all have a number of exporting clients and can apply the lessons learned from other peoples' transactions to yours.

From the export financier's point of view the market is becoming increasingly cut-throat. Transactions and relationships are hotly fought over and there are certainly no grounds for assuming that the deal is yours by right. The good news, however, is that more counterparties, such as emerging market banks, brokers and export finance specialists are playing a part in the trade finance market. Potentially if one counterparty can't do a deal then another will. This does of course mean that counterparties need to be checked and monitored carefully and regularly. The word 'bank' does not necessarily denote creditworthiness.

23: Summary of Risks

This Chapter has been intended to catalogue the risks. Risk assessment is a complicated business which is unfortunately often left to relatively junior staff to assess. This happens because it is time-consuming and sometimes considered menial. While it is excellent training for new staff, risk assessment is best done in teams, either formally or informally with senior and junior staff both involved.

The process of analysing risk can be so absorbing to those involved in it that it becomes an end in itself. There is little point in this unless the function of the organisation is the provision of risk analysis to clients. For export finance houses and banks the goal should be to fully understand the risks at stake with a view to doing safe business.

Many banks, however, see their role as finding reasons for not doing business. This, fortunately is becoming less prevalent as competition among banks and the pressure to reduce costs and up shareholder returns becomes more intense.

The goal then of risk analysis is to arrive at a position where the export financier can say:

- 'I have analysed this piece of business and understand all of the risks bearing upon it';
- 'I have structured the deal so as to minimise these risks'; or
- 'it is now sufficiently tightly arranged that we can carry it out profitably without undue risk to the firm'.

Part III
Documentation

24: General

In dealing with the structures and risks involved in financing international trade, we have referred to shipping and other complementary documents. This chapter describes and examines some of the most commonly used of those documents.

As far as letters of credit are concerned *Uniform Customs and Practice for Documentary Credits (UCP),* published by the International Chamber of Commerce (ICC Publication 500), effective from 1 January 1994, is the vital rulebook. Anyone who handles shipping and other documents involved in the financing of trade should be familiar with it. Although reference to UCP is not always made in the context of forfaiting, supplier's credits, buyer's credits and other financing structures, in the author's view it still provides the best yardstick and guide.

Documents can take a variety of different forms and there is not room here to deal with one example of each. Moreover, there are great many specialised documents which can be called for under letters of credit or in the context of particular financing arrangements. They may relate to specific types of goods and industries, for example, and we have insufficient space here to examine them in detail.

It is important to remember that the documents are prima facie evidence of a trade transaction which those involved in buying and selling goods and handling the payment mechanism use as proxy for the trade itself. It is all we have to go on much of the time, short of hauling down to the quayside or warehouse to inspect the goods themselves. For this reason documentation has to be complete, correct, must match and should not include extraneous material.

UCP Article 13a is clear and worth quoting in full:

> Banks must examine all documents stipulated in the Credit with reasonable care to ascertain whether or not they appear, on their face, to be in compliance with the terms and conditions of the Credit. Compliance of the stipulated documents on their face with the terms and conditions

of the Credit, shall be determined by international standard banking practice as reflected in these Articles. Documents which appear on their face to be inconsistent with one another will be considered as not appearing on their face to be in compliance with the terms and conditions of the Credit.

Documents not stipulated in the Credit will not be examined by banks. If they receive such documents, they shall return them to the presenter or pass them on without responsibility.

Article 13b goes on to allow seven banking days following date of receipt of documents in which to inspect them and to decide whether to take up or reject them.

Article 15 gives a comprehensive disclaimer of what banks are *not* responsible for:

Banks assume no liability or responsibility for the form, sufficiency, accuracy, genuineness, falsification or legal effect of any document(s), or for the general and/or particular conditions stipulated in the document(s) or superimposed thereon; nor do they assume any liability or responsibility for the description, quantity, weight, quality, condition, packing, delivery, value or existence of the goods represented by any document(s), or for the good faith or acts and/or omissions, solvency, performance or standing of the consignors, the carriers, the forwarders, the consignees or the insurers of the goods, or any other person whomsoever.

A triumph of exclusion and bankingese, this article puts the onus on all other parties to check and deliver appropriate documents which appear on their face to match the terms of the credit.

Finally, it is important that any parties involved with checking documents whatever their role in the process, inside or outside of banks, should make it a fundamental operational practice to double and even triple check documents. Obvious as this may sound, and however often this advice is repeated, more than 50 per cent of documents presented under letters of credit are still found to be discrepant in some respect. This produces delay and ultimately costs money, typically for exporters whose payment is delayed.

The documents reproduced here are courtesy of several parties to whom thanks are due for their permission to use them. SITPRO, the Simplified Trade Procedures Board, has been particularly helpful. SITPRO produces documents in aligned format so that the same template of transaction details can be applied to a range of documents. This is helpful in avoiding errors and enables documents presented to banks to appear in a familiar form which banks feel comfortable with. Thanks also to Barclays Bank PLC, Lloyds of London, the London Chamber of Commerce and Industry, NYK Line (Europe) Limited, Colburn French & Kneen and the Baltic and International Maritime Council.

25: Commercial Invoice

The commercial invoice is a basic piece of evidence for this trade transaction, whether it concerns sales of goods, equipment or services (see Figure 25.1).
   Commercial invoices are covered by Article 37 of UCP:

Unless otherwise stipulated in the Credit, commercial invoices:
• must appear on their face to be issued by the Beneficiary named in the credit (except as provided in Article 48)*;
• must be made out in the name of the Applicant (except as provided in sub-Article 49 (h));
• need not be signed.

Article 37b notes that unless otherwise stipulated banks can reject invoices with values in excess of the credit value. It is important to adhere precisely to the description of the invoice given on a letter of credit or which is set out in any form of payment request. Remember that a document is acceptable provided that it appears on its face to be what is required. Make sure that the invoice is in the right number of originals and copies and that any particular requirements with regard to signature, authentication and so on are adhered to.
   UCP Article 37c provides that:

The description of the goods in the commercial invoice must correspond with the description in the Credit. In all other documents, the goods may be described in general terms not inconsistent with the description of the goods in the Credit.

Where there are too many details to be included on the commercial invoice an invoice continuation sheet is used for as many pages as necessary. The top section of each page of the continuation sheet will contain the details of the seller, consignee, invoice reference, date, sheet number, buyer's reference and buyer in order to appear consistent with the main invoice.

---

* Article 48 concerns transferable credits. Please refer to Chapter 3 and to UCP.

INVOICE RECHNUNG FACTURE FACTURA فاتـــورة		

Seller (name, address, VAT reg no.)	Invoice number	
James and Smith Limited 256 Kenilworth Road East Wigan Lancashire BL7 9QR England	ABC-0011	
	Invoice date (tax point) 30.06.95	Seller's reference O/NO 2367/NY
	Buyer's reference P-657833	Other reference

(c) SITPRO 1992

Consignee VAT no.	Buyer (if not consignee) VAT no.
Kenworthy Industrial Products Inc. 1223 Wilson Boulevard Schenectady N.Y. 10823 United States of America	Kenworthy International Inc. Suite 1380 30 East Forty Third Street New York, NY 10017 United States of America

Country of origin of goods	Country of destination
U.K. (EEC)	U.S.A.

Terms of delivery and payment

DDP - Delivered Duty Paid
 (Schenectady)
Payment via: Bank of Foreign Trade
18-22 Valentine Place, London WC2

Vessel/flight no. and date Lucitania	Port/airport of loading Liverpool
Port/airport of discharge Boston	Place of delivery Schenectady

Shipping marks; container number	No. and kind of packages; description of goods	Commodity code	Total gross wt (Kg)	Total cube (m3)
KENWORTHY O/NO 4587 SCHENECTADY via BOSTON U.S.A.	1 x 20 ft.container Electrical apparatus		Kgs 217.00 Total net wt (Kg) 207.50	

Item/packages	Gross/net/cube	Description	Quantity	Unit price	Amount
1) Cases	2	Cat. E/1520. 13 amp 3 pin rubber plug (black) with 13 amp fuse	100	2.00 each	200.00
2) Boxes	8	Cat. E/1959W. 20 amp flush mounting switch (BS3676) - 1 gang, rocker dolly, with flex outlet	650	5.63 each	3659.50
3) cases	12	Cat. E/5588W. 13 amp trailing socket - 2 gang	250	2.08 each	520.00
TOTAL GROSS & NET WT & CUBE	-------- 217.00 207.50				--------- 4379.50
		Handling fees Documentation charge			200.00 125.00 --------- 325.00

	Invoice total	
It is hereby certified that this invoice shows the actual price of the goods described, that no other invoice has been or will be issued, and that all particulars are true and correct.	USD	4704.50
	Name of signatory AT Bell	
	Place and date of issue Wigan	30/06/95
It is hereby certified that this invoice shows the actual price of the goods described, that no other invoice has been or will be issued, and that all particulars are true and correct.	Signature	

SITPRO Licensee No. 000.   V6L

Figure 25.1: Copy of SITPRO invoice.

Courtesy of SITPRO © SITPRO 1987–1995

165

26: Packing List

As the name suggests, the packing list is an inventory of how the goods were packed when prepared for transportation whether by air, sea, road or rail. Packing lists are concerned with containers, crates, bundles, cases, packages and so on and will list them in detail including weights and measures. They do not show the value of goods.

To be able to match with the invoice both documents must contain details which are consistent even if the invoice will exclude full packing details and the packing list excludes value.

Packing lists often run to several pages, depending on the configuration of the goods and their containers. As required under a letter of credit, they will usually be defined in number and detail and whether they are to be originals or copies will be specified. An example is given in Figure 26.1.

PACKING LIST	LISTE DE COLISAGE VERSANDLISTE ESPECIFICACION DE EMBALAJE		
Seller (name, address)	**Invoice number**		
James and Smith Limited	ABC-0011		
256 Kenilworth Road East	**Invoice date (tax point)**	**Seller's reference**	
Wigan	30.06.95	O/NO 2367/NY	U
Lancashire BL7 9QR	**Buyer's reference**	**Other reference**	N
England	P-657833		I
Consignee	**Buyer (if not consignee)**		C
Kenworthy Industrial Products Inc.	Kenworthy International Inc.		
1223 Wilson Boulevard	Suite 1380		
Schenectady	30 East Forty Third Street		
N.Y. 10823	New York, NY 10017		
United States of America	United States of America		
	Country of origin of goods	**Country of destination**	
	U.K. (EEC)	U.S.A.	
	Terms of delivery and payment		
	DDP - Delivered Duty Paid		
	(Schenectady)		
	Payment via: Bank of Foreign Trade		
Vessel/flight no. and date	**Port/airport of loading**	18-22 Valentine Place, London WC2	
Lucitania	Liverpool		
Port/airport of discharge	**Place of delivery**		
Boston	Schenectady		

Shipping marks; container number	No. and kind of packages; description of goods	Commodity code	Total gross wt (Kg)	Total cube (m3)
KENWORTHY O/NO 4587 SCHENECTADY via BOSTON U.S.A.	1 x 20 ft.container Electrical apparatus		Kgs 217.00 Total net wt (Kg) 207.50	

Item/packages	Gross/net/cube	Description	Other details
ACLU3042873		1 X 20 FT. Container stc	
1 - 8	136.50 130.00 2.1500	8 Boxes 650 Cat. E/1959W. 20 amp flush mounting switch (BS3676) - 1 gang, rocker dolly, with flex outlet	85365000
9 - 10	15.50 15.00 4.4300	2 Cases 100 Cat. E/1520. 13 amp 3 pin rubber plug (black) with 13 amp fuse	85366900
11 - 22	65.00 62.50 7.6200	12 cases 250 Cat. E/5588W. 13 amp trailing socket - 2 gang	85366900
TOTAL GROSS & NET WT & CUBE	-------- 217.00 207.50 14.2000		

	Name of signatory
We warrant that the goods described above comply with regulation 4092 of 13 May 1994, and that packaging and labelling are to the specifications laid down in regulation 248 of 11 February 1990.	AT Bell
	Place and date of issue
	Wigan 30/06/95
	Signature

VSL

Figure 26.1: Copy of SITPRO packing list.

Courtesy of SITPRO © SITPRO 1987–1995

27: Export Cargo Shipping Instructions

These provide instructions about the shipment to the freight forwarder. They cover not only the cargo and the routing but also details of documentation, freight payment, stowage instructions and value of cargo and are helpful for completing customs formalities. Some forwarders have similar forms of their own although SITPRO forms are widely used (see Figure 27.1).

(c) SITPRO 1992

EXPORT CARGO SHIPPING INSTRUCTIONS

Approved by BIFA

A Exporter/shipper   VAT no.

James and Smith Limited
256 Kenilworth Road East
Wigan
Lancashire BL7 9QR
England

Customs reference/status

Pre-entry

Booking number | Exporter's reference

O/NO 2367/NY

Forwarder's reference

U N I C

B Consignee   VAT no.

Kenworthy Industrial Products Inc.
1223 Wilson Boulevard
Schenectady
N.Y. 10823
United States of America

D Other address   VAT no.

Kenworthy International Inc.
Suite 1380
30 East Forty Third Street
New York, NY 10017
United States of America

To ▶

C Freight forwarder   VAT no.

Livingstone Freight Limited
Lading House, 29 Evanston Road
Liverpool L8 0BQ

If required, this space may be used for other addresses, e.g. buyer, place of acceptance/ delivery, additional notify party.

Country of origin of goods

U.K. (EEC)

Country of final destination

U.S.A.

Other UK transport details

E If required this space may be used for extra addresses or other information

L. Dixon Spears Associates
1818 Brunswick Avenue
Elizabeth, New Jersey 17207

Vessel/flight no. and date   Port/airport of loading

Lucitania   Liverpool

Port/airport of discharge   Place of delivery

Boston   Schenectady

Please insure for

Unless otherwise instructed cover will be for ILU clauses "A" and will be charged to A

Shipping marks: container number	Number and kind of packages: description of goods *	Item No.	Commodity code			
			85366900	0		
KENWORTHY	**14 cases**		Quantity 2	Gross weight (Kg) 80.50	Cube (m3)	
O/NO 45654	Electrical apparatus		Procedure	Net weight (kg) 77.50	Value(£) 720	
SCHENECTADY	(plugs and sockets)		Summary declaration/previous document			
via BOSTON						
U.S.A.			Commodity code			
			85365000	9		
	8 Boxes		Quantity 2	Gross weight (Kg) 136.50	Cube (m3)	
KENWORTHY	Electrical apparatus		Procedure	Net weight (kg) 130.00	Value(£) 3660	
O/NO 45655	(switches)		Summary declaration/previous document			
SCHENECTADY						
via BOSTON			Commodity code			
U.S.A.						
			Quantity 2	Gross weight (Kg)	Cube (m3)	
			Procedure	Net weight (kg)	Value(£)	
			Summary declaration/previous document			

* DANGEROUS GOODS: Refer to IMDG, ADR, IATA, CIM and UK regulations as appropriate and specify: proper shipping name, hazard class, UN no; flashpoint deg C.

Identification of warehouse			Inland carriage to	Groupage depot/ICD	A	Trade Term	Invoice price	
	FREIGHT ▶			UK port/airport	A	DDP	USD	4704.50
Certificate of shipment	A	DOCUMENTATION ◀	Depot/ICD or port charges including unloading		A	Special Instructions	Total gross wt (kg) 217.00	Total Cube (m3)
Air, sea or other waybill	A							
Bill of lading	A	Indicate services required, and to whom charges should be debited, by entering	Freight to:			Stow away from excessive		
Consular formalities/certs. of origin			Pt.of dischge.		A	vibration.		
Other documentation charges						Transhipment prohibited.		
Customs formalities Export	A	A,B,C,D or E	Depot/ICD or port charges at destination		A	Part-shipment prohibited.		
Transit	A	in check box	Oncarriage at	Depot/ICD	B			
Import			destination to	Place of delivery	B			
STATUS Enter T1/T2/MIX or T2L (as applicable) ▶		Indicate who post enters if SCP ▶	Ocean Freight Payable at **Destination**			Name of contact and telephone number **James & Smith Ltd 0204 846**		
Make out documents as indicated and dispose of as follows:			No. of bills of lading required 3/3 Original 6 Copy			**AT Bell, Export Supervisor**		
All to A. Telephone A on departure of vessel.			I/we hereby declare that the above particulars are correct and agree to your published Regulations and Conditions, including those as to liability.			Date **Wigan 30/06/95** Signature		

SITPRO Licensee No. 000.

Figure 27.1: Copy of SITPRO export cargo shipping instructions.

Courtesy of SITPRO © SITPRO 1987–1995

169

28: Standard Shipping Note

This document travels with the cargo and is for use for non-hazardous goods. It supplies information to a shipper, carrier, forwarder and receiving authority about the shipment and can be used as a pre-shipment advice for customs authorities. The example shown in Figure 28.1 has been made out in standard form and therefore is consistent with the other documentation such as invoices and packing lists.

The standard shipping note is the precursor to the issuance of a transport document required under a letter of credit, such as a bill of lading or airway bill.

(c) SITPRO 1991   **STANDARD SHIPPING NOTE**   - FOR NON-DANGEROUS GOODS ONLY

IMPORTANT USE THE DANGEROUS GOODS NOTE IF THE GOODS ARE CLASSIFIED AS DANGEROUS ACCORDING TO APPLICABLE REGULATIONS SEE BOX 10A			

Exporter   [1]

James and Smith Limited
256 Kenilworth Road East
Wigan
Lancashire BL7 9QR
England

Customs reference/status   [2]

Pre-entry

Booking number   [3]

Exporter's reference   [4]

O/NO 2367/NY

Forwarder's reference   [5]

[6]
Kenworthy Industrial Products Inc.
1223 Wilson Boulevard
Schenectady
N.Y. 10823
United States of America

Freight forwarder   [7]

Livingstone Freight Limited
Lading House, 29 Evanston Road
Liverpool L8 0BQ

International carrier   [8]

For use of receiving authority only

Other UK transport details (eg. ICD, terminal, vehicle bkg. ref. receiving dates)   [9]

The Company preparing this note declares that, to the best of their belief, the goods [10A] have been accurately described, their quantities, weights and measurements are correct and at the time of despatch they were in good order and condition; that the goods are not classified as dangerous in any UK, IMO, ADR, RID, or IATA/ICAO regulation applicable to the intended modes of transport

Vessel/flight no. and date	Port/airport of loading [10]
Lucitania	Liverpool
Port/airport of discharge	Destination [11]
Boston	Schenectady

TO THE RECEIVING AUTHORITY - Please receive for shipment the goods described below subject to your published regulations and conditions (including those as to liability).

Shipping marks	Number and kind of packages; description of goods' non-hazardous special stowage requirements [12]	Gross wt (kg) of goods [13A]	Cube (m3) of goods [14]
KENWORTHY O/NO 45654 SCHENECTADY via BOSTON U.S.A.	14 cases Electrical apparatus (plugs and sockets)	Kgs 80.50	
KENWORTHY O/NO 45655 SCHENECTADY via BOSTON U.S.A.	8 Boxes Electrical apparatus (switches)	136.50	

For use of Shipping company only.

Total gross weight of goods	Total cube of goods
217.00	

PREFIX and container/trailer numbers [15]	Seal number(s) [16A]	Container/trailer size(s) and type(s)	Tare wt(kg) as marked on CSC plate [16B] [16C]	Total of boxes 13A and 16C [16D]
ACLU3042873	2313313	1 X 20 FT		

DOCK/TERMINAL RECEIPT Received the above number of packages/containers/trailers in good order and condition RECEIVING AUTHORITY REMARKS unless stated hereon.	Name of company preparing this note [17]
Haulier's name	James & Smith Ltd 0204 846 AT Bell, Export Supervisor
Vehicle reg. no.	Date
DRIVER'S SIGNATURE SIGNATURE AND DATE	Wigan 30/06/95 (Indicate name and telephone number of contact)

630 Non-completion of any boxes is a subject for resolution by the contracting parties.

SITPRO Licensee No. 000.

Figure 28.1: Copy of SITPRO standard shipping note.

Courtesy of SITPRO © SITPRO 1987–1995

29: CMR Note

CMR stands for *'Convention relative au contrat de transport international de Marchandise par Route'*. It is a transport document relating to shipment by road and is both a receipt of goods shipped and evidence of contract of carriage. However, it is not a document of title. Like the packing list it notes details of packing specifications and cargo weights, although it does not list values of goods carried. An example is given in Figure 29.1.

LETTRE DE VOITURE INTERNATIONALE **CMR** INTERNATIONAL CONSIGNMENT NOTE

(c) SITPRO, FTA, RHA 1992

Sender (name, address, country) Expediteur (nom, adresse, pays) **1**	Sender's/agent's reference Reference de l'expediteur/de l'agent **2/3**
James and Smith Limited 256 Kenilworth Road East Wigan Lancashire BL7 9QR England	Pre-entry O/NO 2367/NY
Consignee (name, address, country) Destinataire (nom, adresse, pays) **4**	Carrier (name, address, country) Transporteur (nom, adresse, pays) **5**
Kenworthy Industrial Products Inc. 1223 Wilson Boulevard Schenectady N.Y. 10823 United States of America	

COPY 1 SENDER
COPY 2 CONSIGNEE
COPY 3 CARRIER

Place & date of taking over the goods (place, country date) ILieu et date de la prise en charge des merchandises (lieu, pays, date) **6**	Successive carriers Transporteurs successifs **7**
Place designated for delivery of goods (place, country) Lieu prevu pour la livraison des merchandises (lieu, pays) **8** Schenectady U.S.A.	This carriage is subject, notwithstanding any clause to the contary, to the Convention on the Contract for the international Carriage of Goods by Road (CMR) Ce transport est soumis nonobstant toute clause contaire a la Convention Relative au Contrat de Transport International de Merchandises par Route (CMR)

NB FOR DANGEROUS GOODS SPECIFY

1. Substance identification number (if applicable)
2. Substance description,
3. Class,
4. Item number and letter (if any),
5. The initials 'ADR' or 'RID'
6. Other statement to be required by ADR or RID

Shipping marks; no & kind of packages; description of goods * Marques et nos; no et nature des colis; designation des merchandises* **9**	Gross weight (kg) **10** Poids brut (kg)	Volume (m3) **11** Cubage (m3)
KENWORTHY O/NO 45654 SCHENECTADY via BOSTON U.S.A. 14 cases Electrical apparatus (plugs and sockets)	Kgs 80.50	
KENWORTHY O/NO 45655 SCHENECTADY via BOSTON U.S.A. 8 Boxes Electrical apparatus (switches)	136.50	

Carriage charges Prix de transport **12**	Senders instruction for customs etc.. Instruction de l'expediteur (optional) **13** Stow away from excessive vibration. Transhipment prohibited.
Reservations Reserves **14**	Document attached Documents annexes (optional) **15**
	Special agreements Conventions particulieres (optional) **16**
Goods received Merchandises recues **17**	Signature of carrier Signature du transporteur **18**	Company completing this note Societe emettrice **19** James & Smith Ltd 0204 846
		Place and date; signature Lieu et date. signature **20** Wigan 30/06/95

SITPRO Licensee No. 000.

Figure 29.1: Copy of SITPRO CMR international consignment note.

Courtesy of SITPRO © SITPRO 1987–1995

173

30: Bill of Lading

Unlike other transport documents the marine or ocean bill of lading is a document of title. A holder of it is able to lay claim to goods. It is also a receipt for goods, evidence that the shipper received the goods for shipment and is signed by the ship's master, carrier or agent. It is also evidence of a contract of carriage.

Typically a 'shipped on board bill of lading' is called for. It can be matched with the commercial invoice and packing lists by comparing descriptions of the cargoes, packing specifications and weights. However, bills of lading do not list the value of the goods.

Bills of lading should not be claused unless specifically acceptable. A clausing suggests that the goods may be damaged, shipped on deck, have damaged packaging or some other shortcoming. When presented under letters of credit bills of lading are usually held to be 'stale' if presented longer than 21 days after shipment unless the credit stipulates to the contrary.

UCP Articles 23, 24 and 25 refer in detail to bills of lading. An example is given in Figure 30.1.

(Forwarding Agents)

Shipper	B L No.
SHIPPING & FORWARDING LTD ANCHOR COURT MILLHARBOUR LONDON E14	NYKS485000000

NYK *LINE*
NIPPON YUSEN KAISHA

Consignee

TO ORDER

BILL OF LADING

Shipped on board the Vessel, the Goods, or packages said to contain the cargo described below, in apparent good order and condition unless otherwise indicated herein, to be carried to the port of discharge or such port or place as selected by the Carrier under the terms and conditions of this Bill of Lading, with or without transhipment, as the Vessel and or other connecting conveyances may safely get, and to be delivered there in like order and condition unto order or assigns, subject to the terms, conditions and exceptions on the face and back hereof.

Notify Party

CHEMICAL PLANTS LTD
P.O. BOX 112
BLANTYRE, MALAWI

If required by the Carrier, this Bill of Lading duly endorsed must be surrendered in exchange for the Goods or delivery order.

In accepting this Bill of Lading, the Merchant agrees to be bound by all the stipulations, exceptions, terms and conditions on the face and back hereof, whether written, typed, stamped or printed, as fully as if signed by the Merchant, any local custom or privilege to the contrary notwithstanding and agrees that all agreements or freight engagements for and in connection with the carriage of the Goods are superseded by this Bill of Lading.

In witness whereof, the undersigned, on behalf of Nippon Yusen Kaisha, the Master and the owner of the Vessel, has signed the number of Bill(s) of Lading stated below, all of this tenor and date, one of which being accomplished, the others to stand void.

(Local Vessel)	(From) SINGAPORE CY	
Ocean Vessel: QUADRANT EXPRESS	Voy. No. 002	Port of Loading SINGAPORE

Port of Discharge DURBAN	*For Transhipment to (if on-carriage) BEIRA CY	*Final Destination (for the Merchant's reference only)

Marks & Numbers	No. of Pkgs or Units	Kind of Packages or Units; Description of Goods	Gross Weight	Measurement
			(KGS)	(M3)
CONTAINER NO. NYKU5558411 SEAL NO. 3333003 CHEMICAL PLANT BLANTYRE MALAWI	1	X20' FT CONTAINERS SAID TO CONTAIN 554 BAGS NON HAZ CHEMCIALS FREIGHT PREPAID SHIPPED ON BOARD	17,000.00	28.00
TOTAL NUMBER OF PACKAGES OR UNITS (IN WORDS)	ONE			

Particulars Furnished by the Merchant

FREIGHT & CHARGES	Revenue Tons	Rate	Per	Prepaid	Collect

ICS B/L	Ex. Rate	Prepaid at LONDON	Payable at	Place of B(s) L Issue LONDON	Dated 17.06.95
	@	Total Prepaid in Local Currency	Number of Original B(s). L 3 (THREE)	**NIPPON YUSEN** 𝒴	

(JSA STANDARD FORM B)

* See-Article 17
(TERMS OF BILL OF LADING CONTINUED ON BACK HEREOF)

B2NYO1S93

Figure 30.1: Copy of NYK Line bill of lading.

Courtesy of NYK Line

31: Letter of Credit

Figure 31.1 is an example of a letter of credit which has been prepared in line with the SITPRO documents in this part (though not with the Bill of Lading example shown in Figure 30.1).

It is clear to whom it is addressed, in respect of which credit, which documents are to be presented, how many and within what time frame. It also requires to be drawn on the confirming bank, Barclays Bank PLC. The credit also makes clear that it is drawn subject to UCP 500.

BARCLAYS BANK PLC
NORTHERN INTERNATIONAL BANKING CENTRE
PO BOX 84, 6TH FLOOR 4 EXCHANGE QUAY SALFORD M5 3PL UK
PHONE: 0161 911 6270 FX NO: 0161 911 6391
ANSWERBK: BARCGB G TELEX: 418139

BENEFICIARY:
JAMES AND SMITH LIMITED
256 KENILWORTH ROAD EAST
WIGAN
LANCASHIRE BL7 9QR

ADVICE OF
IRREVOCABLE DOCUMENTARY CREDIT
NUMBER: 105512/14
DATED: JULY 5, 1995

DATE OF EXPIRY: AUGUST 31, 1995
PLACE OF EXPIRY: UK
AMOUNT: UP TO USD 4,704.50
UP TO FOUR THOUSAND SEVEN HUNDRED
FOUR AND 50/100'S US DOLLARS

OUR ADVICE NUMBER: MRDC7002245

OPENING BANK:
BANK OF FOREIGN TRADE
18-22 VALENTINE PLACE
LONDON WC2

APPLICANT:
KENWORTHY INTERNATIONAL INC.
SUITE 1380
30 EAST FORTY THIRD STREET, NEW YORK, NY 10017

JULY 5, 1995

DEAR SIR(S)

THIS LETTER OF CREDIT IS AVAILABLE WITH BARCLAYS BANK BY PAYMENT AGAINST PRESENTATION OF THE DOCUMENTS
DETAILED HEREIN AND OF YOUR DRAFTS AT SIGHT DRAWN ON BARCLAYS BANK PLC, NORTHERN I.B.C. FOR 100 PERCENT OF
INVOICE VALUE.

DOCUMENTS REQUIRED:-

1.   COMMERCIAL INVOICE IN DUPLICATE.
2.   PACKING LIST.
3.   MARINE INSURANCE POLICY OR CERTIFICATE, BLANK ENDORSED
        COVERING 'ALL RISKS' PLUS 10 PER CENT.
4.   SEAWAYBILL COVERING A PORT TO PORT SHIPMENT BLANK ENDORSED
        MARKED 'FREIGHT PREPAID' AND NOTIFY KENWORTHY INDUSTRIAL PRODUCTS
        INC., 1223 WILSON BOULEVARD, SCHENECTADY, N.Y. 10823.

COVERING THE FOLLOWING GOODS:-

ELECTRICAL APPARATUS:-   DELIVER DUTY PAID US PORT

PARTIAL SHIPMENTS: ALLOWED   TRANSHIPMENTS: ALLOWED

SHIPMENT FROM: UK PORT NO LATER THAN: AUGUST 10,1995 FOR TRANSPORTATION TO: US PORT

DOCUMENTS MUST BE PRESENTED AT PLACE OF EXPIRATION WITHIN 21 DAYS OF ISSUE DATE OF TRANSPORT DOCUMENT
AND WITHIN THE L/C VALIDITY.

DOCUMENTS ARE TO BE ACCOMPANIED BY YOUR DRAFTS DRAWN ON BARCLAYS BANK PLC AT SIGHT MARKED 'DRAWN
UNDER IRREVOCABLE LETTER OF CREDIT NUMBER 105512/14 OF BANK OF FOREIGN TRADE AND QUOTING OUR REFERENCE
NUMBER MRDC7002245'.

IMPORTANT: PLEASE CAREFULLY CHECK THE DETAILS OF THIS CREDIT AS IT IS ESSENTIAL THAT DOCUMENTS TENDERED
CONFORM IN EVERY RESPECT WITH THE CREDIT TERMS. IF YOU ARE UNABLE TO COMPLY, PLEASE COMMUNICATE WITH
YOUR BUYERS PROMPTLY IN ORDER THAT THEY MAY ARRANGE A SUITABLE AMENDMENT WITHOUT DELAY. IF DOCUMENTS
ARE PRESENTED WHICH DIFFER FROM THE CREDIT TERMS WE RESERVE THE RIGHT TO MAKE AN ADDITIONAL CHARGE.

THIS CREDIT IS SUBJECT TO THE UNIFORM CUSTOMS AND PRACTICE FOR DOCUMENTARY CREDITS (1993 REVISION) ICC
PUBLICATION NO. 500.

YOURS FAITHFULLY

SPECIMEN   SPECIMEN

_____   _____
AUTHORISED SIGNATURE   AUTHORISED SIGNATURE

Figure 31.1: Copy of Barclays Bank letter of credit

Courtesy of Barclays Bank PLC

32: Letter of Credit Presentation Form

This is the form of a letter which could be used by the beneficiary when presenting documents to a bank under a letter of credit(L/C). In this case, unlike the credit shown in Figure 31.1, the documents are being presented to the Bank for Foreign Trade PLC. The letter makes clear which documents are being presented under which L/C and gives clear instructions as to where the proceeds of the successful presentation are to be paid. An example is given in Figure 32.1.

LETTER OF CREDIT PRESENTATION FORM

(c) BBA/SITPRO 1992

Drawer/exporter	Drawer's/exporter's reference(s)	
James and Smith Limited 256 Kenilworth Road East Wigan Lancashire BL7 9QR England	O/NO 2367/NY	ABC-0011
	Issuing bank L/C no.	Your reference no. FCA - 344543
	Issuing bank	

AUTHORISED BY THE BRITISH BANKERS' ASSOCIATION

To (bank)	Value of the drawing
Bank of Foreign Trade PLC Barton Chambers 18-22 Valentine Place London WC2E 3HP	USD 4704.50

DOCUMENTS ENCLOSED (state no. of copies)

Bill of exchange	Commercial invoice	Certified Consular Invoice	Certificate of origin	
	X		X	
Insurance policy/certificate	Transport documents	L/C for endorsement	OTHER DOCUMENTS	
			Document	Copies
X	2 + 3			

Dear Sirs,

We have much pleasure in enclosing the above documents related to the Letter of Credit referred to above.
We trust you will find the documents to be in order and look forward to receiving your settlement as shown below.
Should you discover any discrepancies please contact us as shown below BEFORE taking any action.

FOR TERM DRAFTS
We request you to *discount/negotiate (less interest)
Please *retain/return accepted draft(s) to us
*Delete as appropriate

PAYMENT INSTRUCTIONS

For GBP sterling items please remit proceeds to our account no. :
held with   :
                 :
                 :
Sort code no.   :

For GBP sterling items please remit proceeds to us by cheque

For currency items - (please specify)
:
:
:
Forward contact reference (if any)
:

OTHER - (please specify)
:
:
:

DISCREPANCIES/SPECIAL INSTRUCTIONS

Contact details (eg. fax. telex nos.)	Company/telephone no.
	James & Smith Ltd 0204 846
	Name of signatory AT Bell, Export Supervisor
	Place and date Wigan 30/06/95
	Signature

SITPRO Licensee No. 000.

Figure 32.1: Copy of SITPRO letter of credit presentation form.

Courtesy of SITPRO © SITPRO 1987–1995

33: Certificate of Insurance

The certificate shown in Figure 33.1 has been issued under a continuous insurance policy. It refers to the policy under which it has been issued and to the specific cargo which it covers.

Details of shipment, shipment date, insured value, marks and numbers are inserted in the sections provided. This also enables the insurance certificate to be matched with other documentation presented under a documentary credit.

Instructions are given on the reverse of the certificate.

ORIGINAL

LLOYD'S

CLAIMS SETTLEMENT INSTRUCTIONS

THIS CERTIFICATE
REQUIRES ENDORSEMENT IN
THE EVENT OF ASSIGNMENT

1. Lloyd's Agent at ....
is authorised to adjust and settle on behalf of the Underwriters, and to purchase on behalf of the Corporation of Lloyd's, in accordance with Lloyd's Standing Regulations for the Settlement of Claims Abroad, any claim which may arise on this Certificate.

2. In the event that Clause 1 is not completed claim papers should be sent to: J. O .B. Long & Co., Ltd., 999 Lloyd,s Street, Insurance Avenue, London ECO 0EC.

Certificate of Insurance No. C000/

This is to Certify that there has been deposited with the Council of Lloyd's a continuous Contract effected by *J. O .B. Long & Co., Ltd.,* of Lloyd's, acting on behalf of *The Short Supply Co.,* with Underwriters at Lloyd's, and that the said Underwriters have undertaken to issue to *J. O .B. Long & Co., Ltd.,* Policy/Policies of Insurance at Lloyd's to cover, up to *£100,000 (or equivalent in other currencies)* in all by any one *steamer and or sending by air and/or parcel post, Goods and/or Merchandise in connection with the Assured's business,* from any port or ports, place or places in *the United Kingdom,* to any port or ports, place or places in *the World,* and that *The Short Supply Co.,* are entitled to declare against the said Contract insurances attaching thereto on or after the *First* day of *January* 1987. This Certificate is not valid in respect of insurances attaching after the *Thirty-first* day of *December* 1989.

for the Council of Lloyd's.
Dated at Lloyd's, London, 31st February, 1987.

Conveyance	From	
Via/To	To	INSURED VALUE/Currency:
Marks and Numbers		Interest

SPECIMEN

We hereby declare for Insurance under the said Contract interest as specified above so valued subject to the special conditions stated below and on the back hereof.

Institute Cargo Clauses (A) or Institute Cargo Clauses (Air) (excluding sendings by Post) as applicable.
Institute War Clauses (Cargo) or Institute War Clauses (Air Cargo) (excluding sendings by Post) or Institute War Clauses (sendings by Post) as applicable.
Institute Strikes Clauses (Cargo) or Institute Strikes Clauses (Air Cargo) as applicable.
Institute Classification Clause.
Institute Replacement Clauses.
For the purpose of claims for general average contribution and salvage charges recoverable hereunder, the subject-matter insured shall be deemed to be insured for its full contributory value.

Underwriters agree losses, if any, shall be payable to the order of THE SHORT SUPPLY CO, on surrender of this Certificate.

In the event of loss or damage which may result in a claim under this Insurance, immediate notice should be given to the Lloyd's Agent at the port or place where the loss or damage is discovered in order that he may examine the goods and issue a survey report.

(Survey fee is customarily paid by claimant and included in valid claim against Underwriters.)

SEE IMPORTANT INSTRUCTIONS ON REVERSE

This Certificate not valid unless the Declaration be signed by
THE SHORT SUPPLY CO.

Dated

Signed

Brokers: J. O .B. Long & Co., Ltd.,
999 Lloyd,s Street, Insurance Avenue, London ECO 0EC.

Authorised Signatory
4742C

Figure 33.1: Copy of Lloyds certificate of insurance.

Courtesy of Lloyds of London Certificate Office

IMPORTANT INSTRUCTIONS IN EVENT OF CLAIM

DOCUMENTATION OF CLAIMS

To enable claims to be dealt with promptly, the Assured or their Agents are advised to submit all available supporting documents without delay, including when applicable:-

1. Original policy or certificate of insurance.

2. Original or copy shipping invoices, together with shipping specification and/or weight notes.

3. Original Bill of Lading and/or other contract of carriage.

4. Survey report or other documentary evidence to show the extent of the loss or damage.

5. Landing account and weight notes at final destination.

6. Correspondence exchanged with the Carriers and other parties regarding their liability for the loss or damage.

IMPORTANT
LIABILITY OF CARRIERS, BAILEES OR OTHER THIRD PARTIES

It is the duty of the Assured and their Agents, in all cases, to take such measures as may be reasonable for the purpose of averting or minimising a loss and to ensure that all rights against Carriers, Bailees or other third parties are properly preserved and exercised. In particular, the Assured or their Agents are required:-

1. To claim immediately on the Carriers, Port Authorities, or other Bailees for any missing packages.

2. In no circumstances, except under written protest, to give clean receipts where goods are in doubtful condition.

3. When delivery is made by Container, to ensure that the Container and its seals are examined immediately by their responsible official. If the Container is delivered damaged or with seals broken or missing or with seals other than as stated in the shipping documents, to clause the delivery receipt accordingly and retain all defective or irregular seals for subsequent identification.

4. To apply immediately for survey by Carriers' or other Bailees' Representatives if any loss or damage be apparent and claim on the Carriers or other Bailees for any actual loss or damage found at such survey.

5. To give notice in writing to the Carriers or other Bailees within 3 days of delivery if the loss or damage was not apparent at the time of taking delivery.

Note.- The Consignees or their Agents are recommended to make themselves familiar with the Regulations of the Port Authorities at the port of discharge.

NOTE.-The Institute Clauses incorporated herein are deemed to be those current at the time of commencement of the risk.

It is necessary for the Assured when they become aware of an event which is "held covered" under this Insurance to give prompt notice to Underwriters and the right to such cover is dependent upon compliance with this obligation.

Lloyd's Agents referred to herein are not insurers and are not liable for claims arising on this Certificate. The service of legal proceedings upon Lloyd's Agents is not effective service for the purpose of starting legal proceedings against Underwriters.

This Insurance is subject to English jurisdiction.

Figure 33.1 cont.: Reverse of certificate of insurance.

Courtesy of SITPRO © SITPRO 1987–1995

34: Certificate of Origin

The certificate shown in Figure 34.1 has been drawn in line with the invoice (Figure 25.1) and packing list (Figure 26.1) shown above. It is used to prove the origin of the goods. Certificates of origin are often required in order to conform to regulations in an importer's country and may also be needed in order to prove that goods can enjoy a lower import tariff rate where favoured nation treatment is applicable.

PLEASE READ THE RULES AND NOTES OVERLEAF BEFORE COMPLETING THIS FORM

1 Consignor (Name, or name of firm, and full address, as in the commercial register). JAMES & SMITH LIMITED 256 KENELWORTH ROAD EAST WIGAN LANCASHIRE BL7 9QR ENGLAND	**No. DA** 121873 **APPLICATION**
2 Consignee (Name, or name of firm and address if known or mention "to order"). KENWORTHY INDUSTRIAL PRODUCTS INC. 1223 WILSON BOULEVARD SCHENECTADY N.Y. 10823 UNITED STATES OF AMERICA	**EUROPEAN COMMUNITY** ——————— **CERTIFICATE OF ORIGIN**
	3 Country of Origin ("European Community" or country of origin concerned) EUROPEAN COMMUNITY UNITED KINGDOM
4 Transport details (Optional) SEA FREIGHT	4 Remarks

6 Item number, marks; numbers; number and kind of packages; description of goods (For goods not packed indicate number of "in bulk")	7 Quantity (expressed in gross or net weight or other units of measure
ELECTRICAL APPLIANCES	217 KGS WEIGHT 207.50 KGS NET WEIGHT

8 I, the undersigned,

9 Applicant (if not the consignor)

Place and date   Signature of the applicant
The signature of an agent must be followed by his name in block capitals

DTI/VJ5/5/1   LT PRINTING 051–647 8006

Figure 34.1: Copy of certificate of origin.

Courtesy of London Chamber of Commerce and Industry

Part IV
Case Studies in Structuring Finance for International Trade

35: Introduction to Case Studies

The foregoing chapters of this book have been concerned with the instruments used in financing international trade, assessment of the risks involved and the documentation used to evidence trade and gain payment. Part IV illustrates how financing techniques can be adapted and applied in the context of real deals.

All of the case studies in Part IV really happened. Duties of confidentiality and discretion owed to former employers, clients and colleagues require that the details of transactions and particularly the names of the counterparties be disguised. These case studies should adequately fulfill their purpose nevertheless.

36: Trading Scrap Metal – Using Letters of Credit

Schmidt, an experienced European trading company, had developed an ongoing business of purchasing large quantities of scrap metal from Braun Steel, a major steel producing firm.

Braun was pleased to get rid of its waste material. It loaded the cargo in 100 roughly equal consignments to be shipped by the same vessel. Schmidt, having bought an entire ship load of the scrap, would sell the individual lots to a wide variety of companies in several far eastern countries. Schmidt bought a cargo of scrap every four weeks.

TERMS OF THE TRADE

In this case the purchase price of a cargo was US$5 million CIF far eastern ports payable by Schmidt to Braun Steel 120 days after the date of the bill of lading under a usance letter of credit (L/C or Credit).

Schmidt sold the 100 lots at an average price of US$60,000 CIF far eastern port through its commission agent based in Asia who would earn 1 per cent on the selling price.

Schmidt paid no other charges on the transaction other than its corporate overheads which it accounted for separately. Therefore Schmidt's trading operation looked like this:

	US$
Sale price to 100 buyers @ an average price of US$60,000 per lot:	6,000,000
Less: purchase price payable to Braun Steel:	5,000,000
Less: payment to commission agent @ 1% on selling price:	60,000
Profit to Schmidt:	940,000

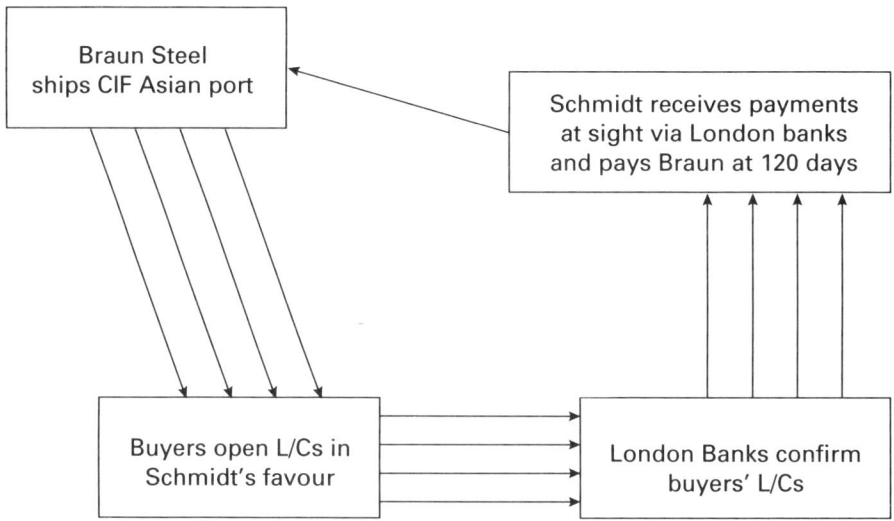

Figure 36.1: Trading and payment structure using L/Cs

TERMS OF PAYMENT

The purchase side of the trading operation was quite straightforward. Schmidt and Braun had been trading together for many years and had handled many transactions which usually went smoothly. Schmidt had always paid on due date under open account terms.

On the sale side of the transaction Schmidt received payment from its customers by means of confirmed irrevocable letters of credit payable at sight, drawn under Uniform Customs and Practice for Documentary Credits.

LETTERS OF CREDIT

Each customer opened its L/C at the time it placed its order. The L/Cs were opened through local banks in the buyers' countries and were advised and confirmed by either the branches of those banks based in London or other international banks in London. Schmidt would only accept confirmations from banks which were acceptable to it and on occasions it even sought to have its credits counter-confirmed by its own banks.

Each of the L/Cs required the documents listed below to be presented by Schmidt following shipment:

- commercial invoices in two originals and three copies;
- packing lists in two copies;
- full set of clean shipped on board bills of lading;
- certificate of origin issued by Braun's local Chamber of Commerce;
- weight certificate showing the weight of the consignment.

All charges relating to the credit and the payment were for the account of the openers of the credits, that is, the ultimate buyers.

DOCUMENTARY PRESENTATION AND CREDIT CONTROL

Schmidt usually presented documents within seven days of shipment, receiving payment within a further seven days. It was constantly pushing the shipping company and its own documentation staff to prepare documents for presentation faster and get them to the banks ever more quickly.

At the same time the company credit controller spent two or three hours each day pursuing the banks to make payment more quickly. Almost all payments were made electronically direct to Schmidt's bankers which saved time. Schmidt reckoned that at rates of 10 per cent per annum it stood to gain an interest advantage of roughly US$1,643 per day for each day that it could save in getting paid.

$$\text{US\$6,000,000 @ 10\% p.a.} = \text{US\$600,000 p.a.}$$
$$\text{US\$600,000/365 days} = \text{US\$1,643 per day}$$

Even though Schmidt was experienced with L/Cs it found that of the 100 documentary presentations it made each month ten of them were discrepant for one reason or another. These were the typical reasons given by the banks for not accepting the documents:

- name of buyer not as per L/C;
- address of buyer not as per L/C;
- value shown on invoice incorrect versus L/C;
- tonnage shown on packing list did not agree with tonnage shown on bill of lading.

These discrepancies usually resulted from clerical errors in Schmidt's shipping department in misspelling unfamiliar names and addresses and transposing letters or numbers. The pressure on staff to prepare and present 100 sets of documents as quickly as possible was the principal reason.

Where there were minor discrepancies of this sort the banks with which Schmidt dealt regularly usually paid against Schmidt's indemnity. Schmidt

Table 36.1: Risks and advantages to Schmidt

Risks to Schmidt	Advantages to Schmidt
If Braun does not ship according to agreement this presents Schmidt with a performance risk.	It profits from the difference between the buying and selling prices of the scrap.
It does not account in US$. This presents a foreign exchange risk to its profit although it receives and pays in dollars.	It gains liquidity by having the use of the incoming funds some weeks before it has to pay Braun.
If the banks handling the documents are inefficient or, at worst, go out of business, Schmidt is at risk.	It has a wide spread of customers who all pay by confirmed irrevocable letter of credit.
Documentation: Staff need to be expert in documentation.	
Schmidt is dependent on one source of supply for its scrap which is a threat to its ongoing business.	

would undertake to repay the funds if the buyer refused to take up the documents. Schmidt had never known of a case where the buyer did refuse. On rare occasions Schmidt had to request banks to send a telex tō the opening bank to obtain permission to pay against the discrepant documents. It was the commission agent's job to support Schmidt by arranging for the buyers to instruct their banks to pay and send a speedy reply to the telex request.

CONCLUSION

This is a classic trading company structure although it is not without risk. Practically speaking it worked extremely efficiently. The cash flow benefits to Schmidt were considerable and its high level of liquidity helped it to fund a number of other trading operations at the same time, where it was not able to negotiate such favourable payment terms from its suppliers. This also gave confidence to its bankers who were pleased to handle its outgoing and incoming L/Cs, its foreign exchange business and grant it substantial over-draft limits.

37: Pre-financing of Coffee Exports – Using Letters of Credit

Coffee prices were higher than normal due to frost and drought damage to crops in Latin America. An African coffee processor, Africof, wished to take advantage of this opportunity to get a good price on the international market. It did not have the working capital necessary to pay cash to the growers within a week of purchase and wait for payment under letter of credit to come through from the international buyers. A pre-financing facility needed to be arranged and in order to be able to cover a succession of shipments the facility had to be renewable after each drawing.

STRENGTHS AND WEAKNESSES

Africof was staffed by experienced coffee processors with excellent personal reputations in their country and among international coffee traders in London and New York. They had only just established the company itself however, and Africof was not a well-known name. It had leased a processing works which was in good working order and was known to be adequate to carry out the processing of the coffee.

International bankers were approached and were keen to finance coffee *per se* but were concerned about the ability of the new company to perform its processing task. They were worried about the security of the cargo while in processing and during transit. Lastly, bankers were unsure about the political stability of the exporting country. It had had always protected its coffee industry because it was a top priority foreign exchange earner but there had been political upheaval in recent times. The country did not have access to the international capital markets and was largely funded by multilateral lending and aid institutions.

Table 37.1: Strengths and weaknesses of the proposed transaction

Strengths	Weaknesses
Coffee: an internationally recognised commodity with ready market and recognised pricing formula.	Africof was a new company with no track record.
Africof was staffed by experienced people of good standing in the international market.	Africof had already drawn most of its local overdraft facility.
The exporting country attached importance to maintaining coffee shipment even during times of political unrest.	The exporting country was regarded by bankers as politically risky.
The world price was rising and coffee was much in demand.	
There was a large difference between the local cost of raw coffee and international market price for processed coffee.	

STRUCTURE

International Trade Bank (ITB) in London had decided early on that the principal strength of the transaction lay in the coffee itself. It also recognised that there was a significant benefit in the difference between the local buying price of raw coffee and that at which processed coffee could be sold in the international market. The structure which was eventually approved by the ITB's credit committee involved the following elements (see Figure 37.1):

1 The coffee which Africof bought from the growers would be inspected locally by an international inspection firm when it entered the processing works. The inspectors would certify its quality and quantity, supervise it throughout processing and insure it against damage by fire, pilferage and other local perils (but not political risk).
2 ITB insisted that Africof took out a political risk insurance policy. In the event of a claim, 90 per cent of the value of the raw, unprocessed coffee would be payable. ITB was listed in the policy as the party to whom claim proceeds would be made.

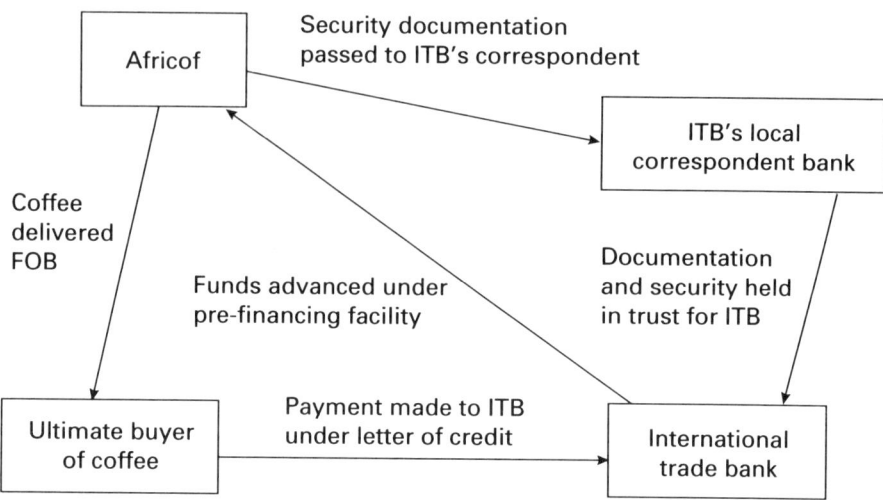

Figure 37.1: Coffee pre-financing facility

3 Inspection documents were passed to ITB's local correspondent bank, which would confirm to ITB that the inspectors were holding the coffee as security for an advance to be made by ITB. This was documented by agreements between the correspondent, the inspectors and Africof, and between ITB and the correspondent.

4 ITB would receive evidence of a confirmed order placed on Africof by an international buyer. The buyer's irrevocable letter of credit (L/C or credit) in favour of Africof would be opened and confirmed through ITB prior to any funds being advanced. The proceeds of the L/C would be assigned to the bank.

5 ITB established a US$1,500,000 facility under which it would advance 85 per cent of the value of the raw coffee on receipt by its correspondent of the inspection documents.

6 Once the coffee had been processed a further advance would be made to bring the total of the funding up to 85 per cent of the international market price of the coffee excluding freight charges and insurance costs.

Insurance certificates would be presented to the correspondent or ITB that the cargo had been insured, up to its high processed value. In the event of a claim being made 90 per cent of this value would now be payable.

7 The cargo would be sold Free On Board(FOB) Mainport. Meanwhile it would be transported by rail from the rail head in Africof's town, which was 300 miles from Mainport.

The coffee would be loaded onto the train in sealed containers and booked through to a secure warehouse at Mainport. The coffee would remain containerised and be loaded onto the vessel in the same sealed containers. Until loading it would remain as security for the advance and cargo and political risk insurances would stay in place.

8   As the terms of sale were FOB port, the buyer would take responsibility for the cargo, insurance and freight costs once the containerised coffee had crossed the ship's rail.

Shipping documents would be received by ITB under the incoming L/C (see 4 above) which would inspect them in line with the L/Cs terms. If the documents were in order ITB would receive the assigned proceeds which would repay its advances. ITB would debit its commissions before paying the balance to Africof's instruction.

9   The facility would revolve and be available for further drawings up to US$1,500,000.

10 ITB charged:

   a   a structuring fee of 2 per cent flat calculated on the US$1,500,000 value of the facility, payable as a condition precedent to effectiveness;

   b   commitment commission of 0.5 per cent p.a. calculated on the US$1,500,000 amount of the facility in arrears and debited to the L/C proceeds at the next utilisation;

   c   interest on the advance calculated at LIBOR plus 0.5 per cent p.a. payable from the L/C proceeds;

   d   all legal and other expenses up to US$10,000 were to be borne by Africof and payable as a condition precedent to effectiveness of the facility.

BENEFIT OF THE FACILITY

The first shipment was made successfully. The price of coffee was rising throughout this period and this made ITB more comfortable as the value of its security was also therefore rising.

Shipments were made every two weeks with an FOB value of about US$500,000. After the first couple of shipments the profit from the coffee trades allowed Africof to set funds aside to pay cash to growers on delivery and thereby receive an additional discount. Cash payment also attracted other growers to supply Africof which was therefore in a position to obtain, process and ship coffee more quickly. Its use of the line was therefore at full stretch most of the time and within ten weeks it asked ITB to increase the line to US$2,000,000.

The facility had enabled Africof to cover most of the 'credit gap' between making payment to local coffee growers and receiving payment from international buyers. The facility which was initially granted for one year was subsequently renewed for a further year.

38: Trading Spices for Bicycles – a Simple Countertrade Operation

A far eastern trading company, Fetrade, was able to obtain quantities of cloves for international sale. In a separate transaction Fetrade had found a local buyer for a quantity of bicycles. Because Fetrade did not have sufficient substance it could not open a letter of credit with which to pay for the bicycles and so a simple countertrade structure was arranged through CT Bank (CTB), London which linked the two trading operations in order to provide a means of payment (see Figure 38.1).

STRUCTURE

1 Fetrade arranged contracts for the sale of the cloves which were to be delivered FOB Localport.
2 Payment was to be made by irrevocable letter of credit (L/C or credit) opened in Fetrade's favour through the buyer's bank and confirmed by CTB in London.

   Among the documents required to be presented under the L/C was an inspection certificate issued by an internationally recognised inspection agency. The certificate was issued immediately prior to loading at Localport and testified to the quantity and the specifications of the cloves.
3 Upon presentation of documents which agreed with the terms of the credit funds would be payable to Fetrade. Under standing instructions the funds would be placed in an escrow account held by CTB. A deposit and pledge agreement was made between Fetrade and CTB on how to utilise these funds.
4 The terms of the agreement were that the funds were to be used to secure the issuance of L/Cs in favour of Bikeco, a French bicycle manufacturer. L/Cs could only be opened up to the value of the funds held in the escrow account for which CTB held irrevocable instructions from Fetrade as a term of the agreement.

   Upon presentation of correct documents to CTB under the L/C Bikeco

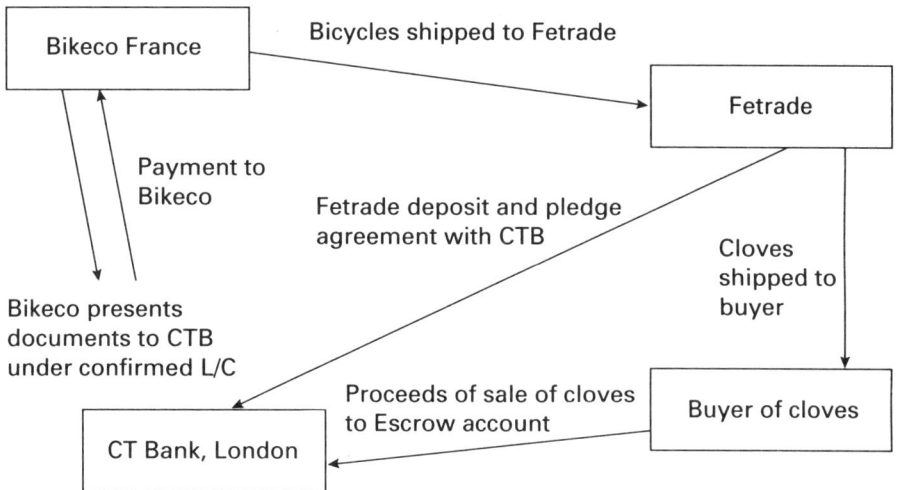

Figure 38.1: Cloves and bicycles

could obtain full payment for bicycles sold to Fetrade and to be delivered CIF Localport.
5   It was a term of CTB's involvement that a structuring fee of US$50,000
     would be payable. Of this, US$10,000 would be payable before effective-
     ness of the arrangements and the balance from the escrow account before
     any L/Cs in favour of Bikeco were issued.

     In addition a confirmation commission of 0.5 per cent flat would be
     payable by Bikeco on all L/Cs issued in its favour, deductible from the
     proceeds of their L/C presentations.

     All legal and other out-of-pocket expenses would be payable by
     Fetrade from the escrow account before any L/Cs were opened in favour
     of Bikeco.

TIMING

It was vital for the success of this financing structure that a shipment of
cloves was made at an early stage. The first shipment, worth US$250,000,
was made and the funds credited to the escrow account. This enabled Fetrade
to settle all outstanding fees and expenses owing to CTB and open an L/C
for US$50,000 in favour of Bikeco.

The balance remaining in the account was retained in US Dollars
and deposited with CTB earning interest which was credited to the escrow
account weekly. Fetrade paid for the cloves in local currency which it earned

from its other operations as well as from the sale of the bicycles imported from Bikeco.

Other shipments of cloves were made and the proceeds handled in the same way. More bicycles were purchased. Once the season for the export of cloves had finished there were still sufficient funds in the escrow account to fund Fetrade's purchase of several more shipments of bicycles.

The mechanism worked extremely well from all points of view. Fetrade and CTB developed a rapport and it was decided to expand the facility to allow for the inflow of funds from sales of other agricultural raw materials to secure L/Cs used to pay for imports of more manufactured products.

39: Forfaiting – Commercial Vehicle Sales

A European manufacturer, Busbuild, sells buses and coaches to its distributor, Coachco, in Israel on an ongoing basis. It takes some time for the distributor to sell or lease them and it needs to hold a stock of vehicles for demonstration purposes. The supplier therefore grants credit to assist the distributor's cash flow. (The process is illustrated in Figure 39.1.)

STRUCTURE

Each consignment of vehicles is covered by an overall distributorship agreement and a purchase order. When a purchase order with a value of US$750,000 is agreed Coachco pays a 15 per cent downpayment of US$112,500 to Busbuild. The balance of 85 per cent of the purchase price, US$637,500, is paid against four semi-annual bills of exchange which fall due 6, 12, 18 and 24 months after shipment. The bills of exchange carry interest at a fixed rate of 10 per cent per annum which is calculated on the basis of a year of 360 days and interest on each bill runs from the date of shipment.

The bills of exchange have been guaranteed by means of an aval issued by a prime Israeli bank. The aval is written on the bills of exchange. Prior to shipment the bills, pre-signed, accepted and avalised are lodged in trust with a bank in the exporter's country.

When the shipment has taken place the due date is added to each bill and they are released to Busbuild against presentation of shipping documents. The documents include:

- a full set of on board bills of lading;
- commercial invoice showing full description of the vehicles, their value, CIF Haifa with freight and insurance charges itemised and that 15 per cent downpayment has been made;
- packing lists.

Table 39.1: Schedule of payments due to be made by Coachco

Due date months	Principal US$	Interest US$ 10%	Total US$
6	159,375.00	7,968.75	167,343.75
12	159,375.00	15,937.50	175,312.50
18	159,375.00	23,906.25	183,281.25
24	159,375.00	31,875.00	191,250.00
Total	637,500.00	79,687.50	717,187.50

Busbuild has already agreed with a Forfait Bank (FB) that it will discount the bills when they are available. FB has committed to purchase them at a discount rate of LIBOR plus 1.5 per cent p.a. discount to yield compounded semi-annually with five days of grace. The rate will be fixed two days before discount. The offer is subject to final documentation which will include:

● the bills of exchange;
● copy bill of lading;

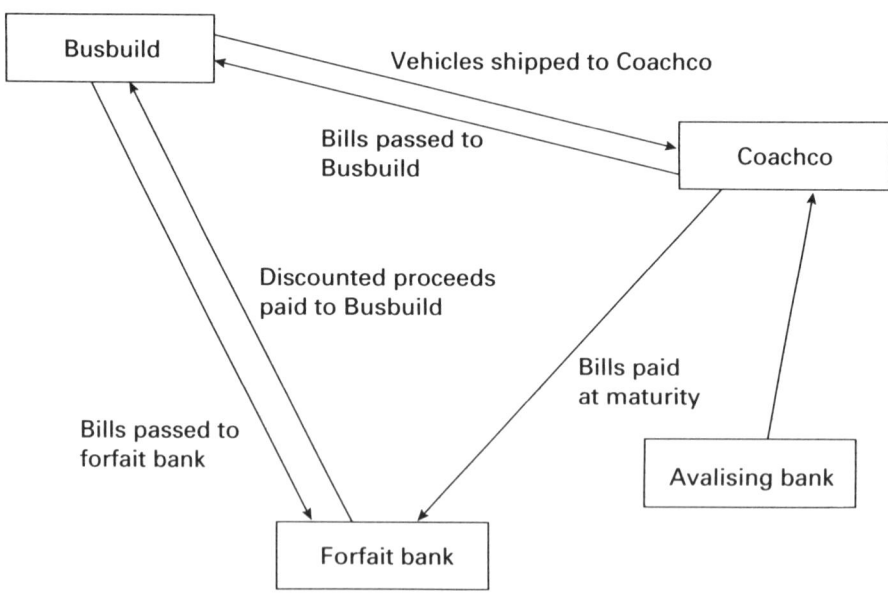

Figure 39.1: Forfaiting – Commercial vehicle sales

- copy commercial invoice showing full description of the vehicles, their value, CIF Haifa with freight and insurance charges itemised and that 15 per cent downpayment has been made;
- copy packing lists;
- written undertaking from the trustee bank for the bills that the signatures of Busbuild, Coachco and the Israeli avalising bank have been verified and are correct;
- specimen signatures and signature protocol of the trustee bank.

In addition, at the insistence of Busbuild, FB has agreed to issue its waiver letter in favour of Busbuild. This states that:

- FB will not take recourse to Busbuild if Coachco and/or the avalising bank fail to honour their obligations under the bills;
- FB will obtain a similar undertaking from any party to whom it endorses the bills;
- future purchasers of the bills will also waive their right of recourse to and through previous endorsers.

DISCOUNT

Two weeks after shipment the bills were released to Busbuild which agreed the date of discount with Forfait Bank. At 11 o'clock, two days before discount date, the discount rate of 7.5 per cent is fixed based on a LIBOR rate of 6 per cent. This is done by reference to a Reuter Screen page put up by a large bank, active in the US Dollar interbank market, previously agreed between Busbuild and FB. They had agreed to use the rate quoted for deposits of US Dollars at 12 months' duration, that being roughly the average life of the transaction.

BENEFITS FROM THE TRANSACTION

All documentation was found to be in order and the discount took place successfully with the following results:

- Busbuild has no further risk of non-payment by Coachco.
- Busbuild has the benefit of receiving the discounted cash flow from the transaction within a couple of weeks of shipment.
- Busbuild avoids all foreign exchange risk, having covered forward its sale of US Dollars.
- Busbuild has been able to offer credit to its distributor while not having

to fund the operation over the credit term of two years.

- Coachco has a cash flow benefit in that it has time to sell or lease the vehicles prior to having to pay for them in full.
- Although Coachco retains an exchange risk the prospects at the time of the transaction are for the Israeli currency to appreciate against the dollar. The 10 per cent interest rate borne by the bills is attractive to Coachco because it is much lower than local costs of borrowing.
- FB is content to take the two-year risk on the Israeli avalising bank for the 1.5 per cent return it makes.
- FB has the option of reselling the paper which it will do as soon as possible to clear its lines for further transactions.

40: Longer Term Forfaiting – Oil Industry Equipment to Latin America

BACKGROUND

Oilco, the hydrocarbon agency of a Latin American country, invited bids from international manufacturers to supply oil drilling and pipeline equipment. As part of its bid each manufacturer was required to submit a financial proposal.

The equipment, which was valued at roughly US$20 million, was fairly sophisticated but not proprietary and several major firms were able to meet its technical specifications to the standard required. Winning the bid therefore hinged largely on the price of the equipment and the most attractive credit terms offered.

At the time the contract was put out to tender, the Latin American country in question was in early emergence phase. The maximum terms to which its internationally offered bonds had extended was three years. No syndicated loans had been made to the country for five years, neither as a sovereign borrower nor to any private concern in the country.

Bankers had a poor opinion of its political risk because the debt crisis had left them with provisionable debt on their books. However, the country had never defaulted on its trade debt and Oilco, which had a number of repaying eurocurrency loans still running, had always made its debt service payments on time. Furthermore, Oilco was well-known in the trade finance market as an oil trader. It regularly arranged finance for its purchases and sales of oil. Some more adventurous participants in the forfaiting market were prepared to handle paper of up to two years' duration for the country risk involved.

STRUCTURE

PMC was the manufacturer which eventually won the contract. In putting in its bid it had pursued a two-pronged financial strategy. Either it would use:

A   A buyer's credit structure supported by its export credit agency (ECA)
This would involve a downpayment of 15 per cent of contract value. Some 85 per cent would be financed under a loan agreement where Oilco would

be the borrower with the support of its government's guarantee. The terms of the loan agreement would be a one-year drawdown period and repayment over 8½ years by 17 equal semi-annual instalments commencing 18 months after effectiveness of the loan. Interest would be payable at the fixed consensus rate ruling at the time of contract signature. The country was considered as Group 3 by the ECA, meaning that the lowest subsidised interest rate could be used.

The ECA would provide a guarantee for the principal and interest due under the loan agreement. It would also subsidise the interest rate to allow the lending banks to earn a margin of 0.75 per cent per annum. A bank had agreed to arrange the transaction and to lead a club of five lending banks to fund the operation.

B   Extension of supplier's credit to be arranged as a series of forfaiting operations

In this case promissory notes would be issued for each drawdown. These would be unconditional payment instruments. There would be 17 six-monthly maturities each comprising principal and interest, the first falling six months after shipment. The interest borne by the notes would be fixed at the same consensus rate as for the buyer's credit structure.

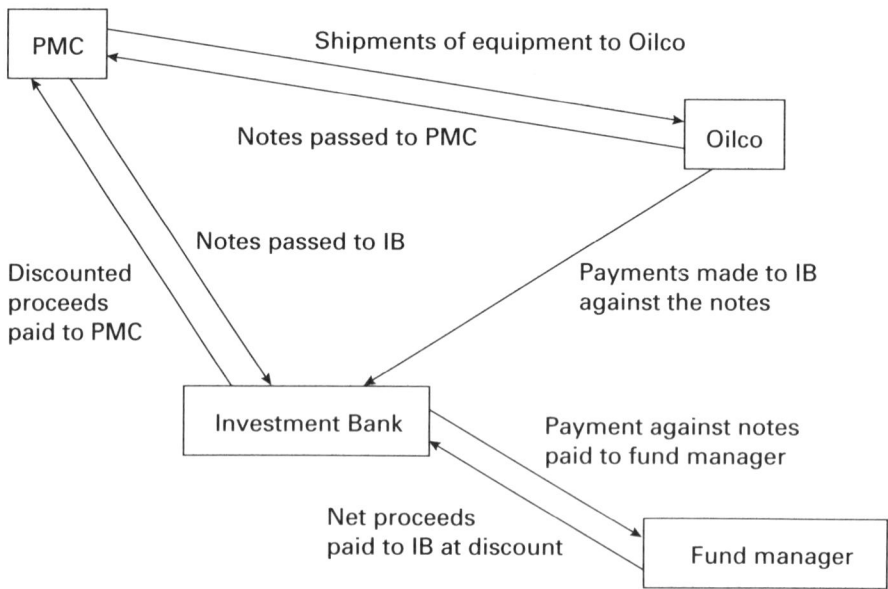

Figure 40.1: Structure of Oilco's longer term forfait transaction

After much discussion the forfaiting option was agreed between Oilco and PMC for the following reasons:

- it was less cumbersome and time-consuming to document and make effective;
- there was no up-front insurance premium to be paid to the ECA;
- legal and other expenses would be very much lower;
- the level of fees to be paid to the banks for carrying out the operation was much less; and
- It was possible to obtain an interest subsidy from the ECA.

The structure of the longer term forfait transaction is shown in Figure 39.1.

ADDITIONAL FEATURES

Oilco recognised that it would have to shoulder some of the discount and accepted that the price of its equipment would have to be raised accordingly. This was of some advantage to Oilco which was highly profitable and could depreciate the cost of its capital equipment, sheltering profits by means of capital allowances.

The transaction was arranged by Investment Bank (IB) which agreed a number of additional details with the exporter in order to carry out the deal successfully:

- The promissory notes would carry the aval of the Ministry of Finance. Oilco was state-owned and the largest foreign exchange earner in the country, so obtaining Ministerial support was straightforward. This would enable the paper to carry the full faith and credit of the Latin American country involved in addition to the internationally recognised name of Oilco itself.
- The notes were to be denominated in US Dollars. This was a suitable currency for both Oilco and PMC. It allowed Oilco to service the debt in the currency in which it sold its oil internationally, thus providing a natural hedge against currency risk. From IB's point of view this removed any additional complication which might arise from paper denominated in a currency other than dollars.
- The notes were payable at the counters of IB's New York branch. This removed any political or bank administration risk which might be perceived by potential buyers of the notes, from paper payable at a bank in Oilco's country.
- The notes would be issued for principal amounts of between US$2 million and US$5 million. This would ensure that the paper was available in large

enough amounts for the bank to fund in the interbank market. At the same time the values would not be too great for other forfaiters or investors to digest – if they could be found. If necessary, smaller shipments would be aggregated to produce notes of above US$2 million. Larger shipments would be split into packages of US$5 million or less.
- Pre-signed and avalised notes would be held in trust by PMC's bank. They would be completed once shipment details were known and released to PMC against shipping documents.

INVESTMENT BANK'S STRATEGY

IB had agreed an internal underwriting credit limit for the purchase of the paper of up to US$7 million. This authorised a commitment to buy paper up to a face value (principal and interest) of US$7 million. Paper could be bought and held for six months during which IB's trade finance department would have to sell it. If the line was full then no further commitments to buy the paper could be issued.

PMC's credit control office also agreed it would be prepared to hold up to US$7 million of paper for up to one year as its experience in supplying equipment to Oilco over many years had shown that Oilco had always been paid on due date.

IB had been closely following the pricing of emerging markets debt instruments in which it also dealt. It had noticed that pricing for Oilco's country's secondary market's rescheduled debt had been rising steadily for some time. In addition US Dollar interest rates were falling. IB's view was that it could buy the notes at a discount rate of 15 per cent per annum made up of a funding cost of LIBOR at 8 per cent plus a margin of 7 per cent. Within a couple of months it would be able to sell them for 13 per cent per annum equal to LIBOR of 7 per cent plus a margin of 6 per cent. This would provide a profit of 2 per cent.

In any case IB had calculated that purchasing at so deep a discount meant that it paid very little for the later maturities of the paper. If it sold the earlier ones separately to trade finance banks prepared to take risk up to one year it could immediately recoup some of its outlay.

IB's commitment to purchase paper was conditional upon it having space in its US$7 million line. IB also committed on the basis that there was no material adverse change in Oilco or its country's credit standing during the period of its commitment. This was sufficiently wide to ensure that IB could escape having to buy the paper if there was the slightest chance of another debt crisis occurring.

However, IB predicted that Oilco's country would be likely to announce new rescheduling and debt forgiveness arrangements and that a trade pact was imminent. This would be bound to improve its credit standing and encourage interest among the banks in purchasing trade debt.

PLACEMENT AND DISCOUNT

Having committed to buy the paper from PMC well before date of discount, IB had talks with an emerging markets investment fund (EMIF) which was interested in purchasing the paper.

EMIF was suspicious of the paper as it was not familiar with trade-related promissory notes – it was more accustomed to impaired debt, bonds and equities. IB agreed to assist EMIF by holding the paper on its behalf and collecting payments when due. Its obligation to make payments to EMIF was dependent on its own receipt of funds. IB also agreed to place the paper on a 'best efforts' basis if EMIF wanted to sell it in due course. IB made no undertakings to buy the paper itself nor to achieve any particular price on EMIF's behalf.

Following the first shipment IB discounted the notes paying PMC the net proceeds of a transaction with a principal value of US\$3 million. The rate of discount was 15 per cent per annum, discount to yield compounded semi-annually with seven days of grace. The documentation which IB wished to see included:

* the notes;
* copy bill of lading;
* copy commercial invoice showing full description of the equipment and that 15 per cent downpayment has been made;
* copy packing lists;
* written undertaking from the trustee bank for the bills that the signatures of Oilco, PMC and the Ministry of Finance had been verified and were correct;
* specimen signatures and signature protocol of the trustee bank;
* opinions from legal advisors in Oilco's country that: (i) the notes were regarded under local law as unconditional promises to pay; (ii) that those signing on behalf of Oilco and the Ministry were empowered to commit their employers to such payment obligations; and (iii) in the event of contractual dispute concerning the underlying goods, the obligation to pay would not be affected in any way.

All documentation was found to be in order and the discount took place without difficulty.

Simultaneously, that is with value the same day, EMIF purchased the paper from IB at 13 per cent discount to yield compounded semi-annually. IB at no stage held the paper on its own books.

BENEFITS

PMC

PMC was pleased to have sold Oilco's payment risk to IB. It set about arranging the next shipments of equipment to Oilco. This and other sets of notes relating to further shipments were similarly discounted until the full US$20 million had been supplied. Shipments took six months to complete.

Oilco

Oilco meanwhile had achieved long-term financing for its equipment purchases at good rates of interest. Borrowing locally would have cost in excess of 20 per cent per annum. It had no significant exchange risk, and furthermore had the advantage of off-setting its capital cost against profits.

Oilco had also achieved long-term financing in the international financial markets which enhanced its credibility for future capital markets operations. It publicised the transaction in the financial press in the form of 'tombstones' to draw attention to this.

IB

IB earned trading income from the transaction of the difference between the buying and selling price of the paper. It earned a commitment commission of 0.5 per cent per annum for the period of time during which is was committed to buy PMC's paper. This was deducted from the net proceeds of the discount paid to PMC.

EMIF

EMIF achieved above average returns for taking the country risk and that of Oilco associated with investing in the notes. It had been underweight in both of these risks prior to purchase. Interest rates fell and the country risk improved which enhanced the risk considerably over the following two or three years. It also preserved an adequate level of liquidity considering the return on its investment, and later sold the paper prior to final maturity making a windfall profit for the fund.

41: General Purpose Line of Credit

BACKGROUND

The following transaction will be explained as an export credit agency (ECA) supported line of credit based upon the Italian export credit system. The basic transaction did take place but has been altered in certain respects for the sake of illustration and discretion.

This example is used purely for the purposes of describing the structure of such an operation because it is relatively transparent and the Italian system allows the use of an interest subsidy without having to make use of the credit guarantee aspect. This is not necessarily the case with other ECAs.

The intention is not to describe the workings of the Italian system in detail. That ECA like all of the others is in a constant state of evolution with new forms of support becoming available and old ones being superseded. Although none of the ECAs work in exactly the same way as explained in Chapter 7 on export credits, the line of credit facility holds good for all of them as a common type of financing tool.

SALE OF EQUIPMENT TO TELECOMMUNICATIONS UTILITY

Fetel, the public telecommunications utility of Ringring, a poor though emerging country, needed to buy a variety of plant and equipment. This included cabling, pylons, vehicles and plant for cable laying, compressors and a host of other items. Because there was such a variety of relatively low-priced items on the shopping list a general purpose line was an appropriate structure by which to provide credit financing. Another reason that this structure was chosen was that interest rates were high both locally in Ringring and in the US Dollar eurocurrency market while the available consensus rate offered a fixed 6 per cent. Thirdly, by agreeing to support the project the export credit authority could provide its exporters with a useful credit tool with which to help sell their products.

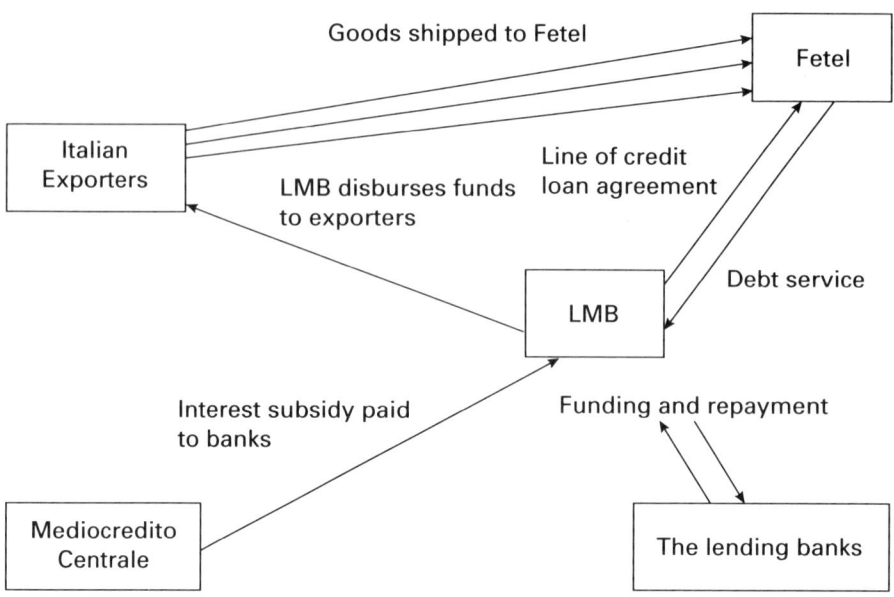

Figure 41.1: Structure of Fetel's general purpose line of credit

The initiative for the financing came from a London-based merchant bank LMB with representation in Ringring. It became aware of Fetel's procurement needs and had the expertise in its London export finance department to put the deal together. The transaction was negotiated over several months in London, Rome and Ringring resulting in a structure which had the following features:

- A loan of US$150 million arranged as a general purpose line of credit (GPLOC) was established.
- The borrower would be Fetel.
- The loan would be guaranteed by the Republic of Ringring.
- The loan could be drawn over a period of one year from its date of effectiveness.
- Drawings could be made in minimum amounts of US$2 million. There was no maximum drawing amount provided there were sufficient undrawn funds available.
- The loan would bear interest at a fixed rate of 6 per cent per annum.
- Interest on the loan would be payable six-monthly in arrears on 30 April and 30 October each year.
- LMB would receive an interest subsidy from Mediocredito Centrale, the interest-paying arm of the Italian export credit system.

- Repayments would be made in ten equal, consecutive, semi-annual instalments on 30 April and 30 October each year, to coincide with the interest payments, commencing six months after the end of the draw-down period, that is 18 months from effectiveness.

SYNDICATION AND OPERATION

LMB formed a syndicate of 16 lending banks to fund the operation. They were largely Japanese and German banks. The largest lenders would contribute US$20 million each while the smaller participants would lend up to US$5 million each. LMB itself lent US$10 million. The make up of the syndicate of lenders was as follows:

Table 41.1: Syndicate of lenders

Size of participation	Number of lenders	Total (US$ millions)
US$ 20 million	3	60
US$ 10 million	5	50
US$ 5 million	8	40
Total	16	150

As agent for the loan LMB was responsible for arranging for the loan agreement to be prepared, negotiating the interest make up agreement, managing drawdowns, collecting fees, commissions, interest and principal on behalf of itself and the lending banks and liaising on all issues with the lenders, borrower, guarantor and exporters. LMB's duties to the lenders were documented by an agency agreement to which the lenders were parties.

Following signature of the loan agreement the following conditions needed to be met before the loan could be declared effective and available for drawings:

- the interest make up agreement to be signed by Mediocredito Centrale and LMB on behalf of the lenders;
- a management fee of 1 per cent to be paid by Fetel to LMB;
- all legal expenses to be paid to LMB by Fetel;
- legal opinions from lawyers in Ringring to be received confirming the status of the borrower and the guarantor, that they were entitled to take on obligations of this nature and that those committing them to do so were so entitled.

For drawings to be made the procedure was as follows:

- Fetel would advise LMB that it had entered into a purchase contract with a supplier and wished to make a drawing. Fetel would outline the contract value, the specification of the goods and date of expected delivery. It would also authorise LMB to disburse 85 per cent of the contract value to the supplier under the line of credit.
- The supplier's bank would, in due course, confirm to LMB that it had received a payment of 15 per cent of the contract value for the account of the supplier.
- Following shipment, the supplier would present a payment request to LMB in a form set out in the loan agreement supported by original documents. These would include a clean on board bill of lading, certificate of marine insurance, commercial invoice, packing list and certificate of origin.
- Assuming documents were in order LMB would inform the syndicate of lenders of their participation amount in the drawing and the fact that they should pay the funds to LMB's US Dollar clearing account in New York on the drawdown date.
- At 11:00 am London time two days before drawdown a rate of interest would be fixed by reference to three of the lending banks including LMB, as set out in the loan agreement. The rate would be advised to all of the lenders. This would form the basis of an interest subsidy claim on Mediocredito Centrale to be paid on interest payment date.

ADMINISTRATION, INTEREST AND REPAYMENT

The interest period for all drawings would be fixed to the next interest payment date provided that that was not less than 30 days, in which case they would be fixed to the next of the six-monthly interest payment dates. This was in order to allow the Italian authorities 30 days, in which to process claims for interest make up.

On each interest payment date LMB would receive interest, or principal and interest once repayments had begun. It would also receive an interest subsidy payment from Mediocredito Centrale. The total of these cash inflows would be divided pro-rata to each bank's proportion of the loan and distributed accordingly.

During the one year drawdown period, commitment commission would be charged to Fetel at 0.625 per cent p.a. of the undrawn balance of the loan and this would also be payable in arrears on interest payment dates.

Any amounts not drawn at the end of the drawdown period would have been cancelled. However, in this case the loan was fully drawn and continued to pay on due dates according to the terms of the loan agreement.

BENEFITS AND BENEFICIARIES

Fetel

The borrower obtained medium-term credit with which to purchase its plant and equipment. It did so at an interest rate which was much cheaper than it could have achieved either locally or internationally (for example by taking out a commercial loan or issuing bonds).

Fetel had the additional advantage of effectively having a central administration at LMB to handle payments to all of it suppliers. It did, incidentally, have a natural hedge against foreign exchange risk between its local currency and US Dollars payable under the loan by virtue of its large dollar revenue from international telephone call tariffs.

Suppliers

Having received 15 per cent downpayment on or shortly after contract signature, the balance was paid through a first class bank (LMB) following shipment. This removed the risk of non-payment by Fetel. Considering that they were effectively selling on five-year credit terms which gave them a commercial advantage over their competitors, the line of credit had the effect of providing speedy payment as well. The line of credit was an attractive payment arrangement for the suppliers.

LMB

In addition to its lending margin, LMB received a larger management fee than the other lenders. This was achieved because the lenders were unaware of the full amount of the fee which was paid by Fetel and agreed to participate in the loan on the basis of the fees offered to them by LMB. LMB received its commitment commission in line with its participation. It also negotiated an annual agency from Fetel of US$10,000 to pay for administrating the loan throughout its life.

A collateral advantage which LMB had as agent for the facility was good profile with the borrower with whom it dealt on an almost daily basis throughout the life of the loan. This enabled them to develop a close relationship with the borrower and to arrange other transactions for them in the future.

Over the one year drawdown period LMB had contact with a range of suppliers. This gave them contacts and information which enabled them to market other of their capabilities, particularly their export finance activities.

215

The Lenders

The lenders received their proportion of the lending margin, commitment commission and management fee. Their administration was minimal. It was carried out by LMB on their behalf and they only had to do what LMB asked them to do. Once the repayment phase had begun it was necessary merely to roll over the loan every six months and monitor the risk of Fetel – assuming LMB performed its role properly.

It is important to note that the lenders did take Fetel's risk. If Fetel were to have defaulted they would have had to have suffered the consequences and acted through LMB to recover the loss.

Glossary

Agency fee	An annual fee payable to an agent or lead bank in a loan transaction for managing the loan and its lenders throughout the life of the transaction.
Amortising loan	A loan repaid by a series of repayments, often monthly, quarterly, six-monthly or annually.
Anticipatory credit	A type of pre-finance/pre-shipment finance of which a red clause letter of credit is a variety.
Applicant	The party who applies to a bank to open a letter of credit.
Arrival or ex-ship	See Chapter 15 on shipment risk.
Assignment of proceeds	Instructions given to a bank or other payer by a beneficiary to pay another beneficiary. For assignment of letter of credit proceeds see Chapter 3 on transferable letters of credit and assignment of proceeds.
Back-to-back letter of credit	Simultaneously issued letters of credit where the credit standing of the ultimate buyer is used as security for issuing further credits in favour of other beneficiaries in the supply chain.
Barter	The exchange of goods for goods without the use of a unit of exchange such as currency.
Berne union	The International Union of Credit and Investment Insurers. Plays a central role in defining and governing the activities of the ECAs.
Bilateral trading accounts	Reciprocal arrangements between two countries to trade together, maintaining records at their respective central banks of the exchange of goods and the values attaching to them in hard currency.

217

BOOT	Build, Own, Operate and Transfer. A structure used to finance revenue-driven projects.
BOT	Build, Own and Transfer. A structure used to finance revenue-driven projects.
Bullet repayment	Repayment of a loan or other financing by one instalment at the end of its life.
Buy-back	Form of countertrade where payment for capital plant and equipment is made, in whole or in part, from the proceeds of using the plant or equipment.
Buyer's credit	A loan to a buyer of goods to enable him or her to purchase imports on extended credit terms.
C & F	Cost and freight. See Chapter 15 on shipment risk.
CIF	Cost, insurance and freight. See Chapter 15 on shipment risk.
CIRR	Commercial interest reference rate, a concessionary interest rate applied to ECA-supported export credit loans.
Club loan	A loan made by a small group of banks a mini-syndication.
COMECON	The trading bloc formerly made up of the communist countries of eastern and central Europe.
Commitment fee	A fee payable to a bank, forfaiting house or export finance house for committing itself to providing finance. Usually charged at percentage per annum of the funding committed, it is payable whether or not the finance is utilised.
The consensus	Proper name: Guidelines for Officially Supported Export Credits. An agreement between ECAs governing the terms of their support of export credit guarantees and interest rate subsidies.
Countertrade	The use of goods to trade with in the place of currency.
Currency swap	A financial instrument which enables one or a series of payments or cash flows to be exchanged for payments or cash flows in another currency.

DACON	Data on Consulting Firms. A database complied by the World Bank.
Delivered	See Chapter 15 on shipment risk.
Disaggio	A subsidy used to balance the prices in an exchange of goods. Often used in countertrade transactions.
ECA	Export credit agency. A state-supported export finance corporation which guarantees overseas debtors payment obligations in respect of export credit loans. It may also subsidise the interest payable on such loans.
Escrow account	Funds held in a designated account for a specific purpose which can be disbursed once certain conditions have been met.
Eurocurrency	Funds deposited in centres outside the normal territory for their currency. Eurodollars, for example, are deposited with banks outside the USA. Such funds re-lent by banks are termed 'eurocurrency loans'.
Ex quay	See Chapter 15 on shipment risk.
Ex ship	See Chapter 15 on shipment risk.
Ex works, ex warehouse or ex store	See Chapter 15 on shipment risk.
FAS	Free alongside ship. See Chapter 15 on shipment risk.
FOB	Free on board. See Chapter 15 on shipment risk.
FOR	Free on rail. See Chapter 15 on shipment risk.
FOT	Free on truck. See Chapter 15 on shipment risk.
Factoring	Discounting of short-term trade receivables, usually with recourse.
Forfaiting	The discounting of trade-related bills of exchange or promissory notes denoting future cash flows under a supplier's credit.
Forward cover	To buy or sell a foreign currency in advance of its receipt or payment. Usually used to control foreign currency risk.

Franco domicile	See Chapter 15 on shipment risk.
Free delivery	See Chapter 15 on shipment risk.
Front end fee	A fee paid to bankers for setting up a transaction, usually payable before or shortly after funds are drawn.
Grace period	A period of time following an advance under a loan or other financing during which no principal is repaid.
Grant aid	Gifts of aid by wealthier countries to developing ones, not expected to be repaid.
Green clause letter of credit	A mechanism by which funds may be advanced to an exporter under a letter of credit in advance of goods being shipped (see Chapter 3).
IBRD	International Bank for Reconstruction and Development, often referred to as the World Bank.
ICB	International Competitive Bidding: method used to select bidders to World Bank and other aid-funded projects.
IDA	The International Development Association. The long-term lending arm of the World Bank.
IFC	International Finance Corporation. The commercial lending arm of the World Bank group.
Interest subsidy/interest make up	A subsidy paid to banks in relation to ECA-supported export credit loans enabling the borrower to receive a cheaper, fixed rate of interest.
LCB	Local Competitive Bidding. A procedure used in bidding for World Bank funded projects.
LIB	Limited International Bidding. A procedure used in bidding for World Bank funded projects.
Lien	Claim of a creditor over property.
Limited recourse	Where, in the context of an export financing operation, the financier is able to look to another party to cover only part of the risk of non-payment.

Line of credit	A loan to a buyer to enable him or her to pay for a variety of imported goods on extended credit terms.
Management fee or commission	Payable to a bank for arranging a loan facility or structuring a transaction. It is usually payable before or shortly after funds are drawn.
MIGA	The Multilateral Investment Guarantee Agency: a division of the World Bank which provides guarantees to support foreign investment in developing countries.
Mixed credit	A credit package, typically assembled in support of exports from a wealthy country to a less developed one, which may incorporate elements of export credits, soft loans, grant aid and so on.
OECD	The Organisation for Economic Co-operation and Development.
Packing credits	A type of pre-finance/pre-shipment finance of which a red clause letter of credit is a variety.
Performance bond	Often issued by banks or insurance companies on behalf of suppliers or contractors providing surety to the recipient that contractual terms will be performed. The recipient can call the guarantee if they are not.
Praecipium	A type of front-end fee payable to the lead bank in a loan transaction.
Pre-finance/pre-shipment finance	A method of advancing funds to an exporter prior to shipment of goods (see Chapter 3).
Recourse/limited recourse	Where an exporter or project sponsor provides whole or partial guarantee for future payment.
Red clause letter of credit	A mechanism by which funds may be advanced to an exporter under a letter of credit in advance of goods being shipped (see Chapter 3).
Revenue-driven	A financing structure which is developed based upon the cash flows of the project being financed.
Revolving letter of credit	A letter of credit which provides for automatic reinstatement of funds available for drawing once a drawing has been made from it.

Rohirst Forfait Management System　　Commonly referred to as 'Rohirst', this is the principal software application used in the forfaiting market.

Silent confirmation of letters or credit　　A bank or other party confirms to the beneficiary that it will pay if conforming documents are presented under a letter of credit to which it is not a party.

Soft loan　　Loan made to developing countries at low rates of interest which is part of a government's aid budget.

Sovereign borrower/ guarantor　　Government borrower or guarantor.

Standby letter of credit　　A form of demand guarantee.

Supplier's credit　　A credit arrangement made by a supplier to enable his or her buyer to pay for the goods purchased over extended terms.

SWIFT　　Society for Worldwide Interbank Financial Telecommunications. An electronic method of transferring funds between banks which subscribe to the SWIFT system.

Switch trading　　Using outstanding credit balances in bilateral trading accounts between two countries to finance imports from third parties.

Syndication　　A loan made by a group of banks.

Tied aid　　Aid funding, guarantees, loans or export credits which can only be utilised in relation to exports of goods, equipment or services purchased from the country providing the aid.

Tombstone　　A form of publicity, usually shown in the financial press which sets out the highlights of financings arranged in the capital markets. Tombstones usually show the clients, the arranger or agent bank and the lenders or funding providers which were involved in the transaction.

Tranche　　A discrete sum of money, perhaps a part of a loan or payment.

Transferable letter of credit	A letter of credit where the beneficiary transfers to a second beneficiary its right to perform under the credit's terms. (See transferable letters of credit and assignment of proceeds in Chapter 3.)
UCP	*Uniform Customs and Practice for Documentary Credits* published by the International Chamber of Commerce, Paris. The principal rule book governing letters of credit.
Value date	The date on which a payment is received and on which the holder of the funds is able to make use of them.
Value dating	Adjusting or backdating the value date of a payment made between banks to allow for delays in payment.
Without recourse/non-recourse	Where, in the context of an export financing operation, the financier takes on the risk of non-payment.

Useful Names and Addresses

African Development Bank
BP V 316
Abidjan 01
Cote d'Ivoire
Tel: + 225 20 40 23

Asian Development Bank
PO Box 789
1099 Manila
Philippines
Tel: + 632 632 6079

Bureau Veritas
International Trade Division
92077 Paris La Defense
France
Tel: + 33 1 91 5468

COFACE
Compagnie Francaise d'Assurance
   pour le Commerce Exterieur
10 Cours Michelet
92065 Paris La Defense
France
Tel: + 33 1 49 02 20 00

Colburn French & Kneen Ltd
   London
19/21 Great Tower Street
London EC3R 5AQ
UK
Tel: + 44 171 626 5644

Cotecna Inspection SA
58 Rue de la Terrassière
BP 6155
1211 Geneva 6
Switzerland
Tel: + 41 22 849 6900

ECGD
Export Credit Guarantee
   Department
PO Box 2200
2 Exchange Tower
Harbour Exchange Square
London E14 9GS
UK
Tel: + 44 171 512 7000

EDC
Export Development
   Corporation
151 O'Connor Street
Ottawa
K1A 1K3
Canada
Tel: + 1 613 598 2739

European Bank For Reconstruction
   and Development
One Exchange Square
London EC2A 2EH
UK
Tel: + 44 0171 338 6499

European Investment Bank
100 Boulvard Konrad Adenaur
L–2950
Luxembourg
Tel: + 352 4379-1

EXIM
Export-Import Bank of the United
  States
811 Vermont Avenue NW
Washington DC 20571
USA
Tel: + 1 202 565 3200

HERMES A G
Friedensallee 254
Postfach 50 07 40
D 22763 Hamburg
Germany
Tel: +49 40 8870

Inter-American Development Bank
1300 New York Avenue NW
Washington DC
USA
Tel: + 1 202 623 1055

International Finance Corporation
1850 I Street NW
Washington DC
USA
Tel: + 1 202 473 9331

International Chamber of
  Commerce
38 Cours Albert 1er
75008 Paris
France
Tel: +33 1 261 8597

Islamic Development Bank
PO Box 5925
Jeddah 21432
Saudi Arabia
Tel: + 966 2 6361400

JEXIM
Export-Import Bank of Japan
1-4-1 Ohtemachi
Chiyoda-ku
Tokyo 100
Japan
Tel: + 81 3 3287 9101

OPEC Fund for International
  Development
A–1010,
Parkring 8
Vienna
Austria
Tel: + 43 1 513 92 38

SACE
Sezione Speciale per
  l'Assicurazione del Credito all'
  Esportazione
Piazza Poli 37
00100 Rome
Italy
Tel: + 39 6 67 36 213

Sedgwick Europe
Political & Financial Risks Division
Sedgwick House
The Sedgwick Centre
London E1 8DX
UK
Tel: + 44 171 377 3456

SGC – Société Generale de
  Surveillance SA
1 Place des Alpes
BP 2152
1211 Geneva
Switzerland
Tel: + 44 22 7399111

SITPRO
The Simpler Trade Prodecures
  Board
29 Glasshouse Street
London W1R 5RG
UK
Tel: + 44 171 287 3525

SWIFT
Society for Worldwide Interbank
  Financial Telecommunications
Avenue Adele 1
B 1310 La Hulpe
Belgium
Tel: + 32 2 655 3111

Trade Indemnity PLC
12-34 Great Eastern Street
London EC2A 3AX
UK
Tel: + 44 171 739 4311

United Nations Department for
  Economics and Social
  Information
PO Box 5850
Grand Central Station
New York
NY 10163 - 5850
USA
Tel: + 1 212 963 4116

World Bank (International Bank
  for Reconstruction and
  Development)
1818 H Street NW
Washington DC
USA
Tel: + 1 202 458 4090

Bibliography

Bank of England, Dec. 1990: *Notice to Institutions Authorised under the Banking Act 1987*. Banking Supervision Division.

Baum, Warren C., 1982, 7th edition, June 1994: *The Project Cycle*. World Bank.

Bond, Gary and Carter, Laurence, 1994: *Financing Private Infrastructure Projects – Emerging Trends from IFC's Experience*. International Finance Corporation.

Griffiths, Ian, 1990: *Creative Accounting*. Unwin Paperbacks.

International Chamber of Commerce, 1978: *ICC Uniform Rules for Contract Guarantees*. ICC Publications No. 325.

International Chamber of Commerce, 1990: *Incoterms 1990*. ICC Publication No. 460.

International Chamber of Commerce, 1993: *Uniform Customs for Documentary Credits*. Publication No. 500 (revision in force as at 1 January 1994).

International Chamber of Commerce, 1992: *Guide to the ICC Uniform Rules for Demand Guarantees*. ICC Publication No. 510.

International Chamber of Commerce, 1993: *Documentary Credit; UCP 500 & 400 Compared*. ICC Publication No. 511.

Pierce, Anthony, Risk Control Ltd, 22 May 1995: 'How to find and Use Innovative Techniques to Finance your Exports'. Paper given at a meeting of the Institute of Export, London and Home Counties branch at the Royal Society of Arts.

Schmitthoff, Professor Clive M., 9th edition, 1990: *Schmitthoff's Export Trade*. Stevens & Sons.

SITPRO, 1995: *Top Form 2 – The A to Z of Export Documents*. London: The Simpler Trade Procedures Board.

Smith, Terry, 1992: *Accounting for Growth*. Century Business.

Swiss Bank Corporation, 1994: *Documentary Credits: A Practical Guide*. Swiss Bank Corporation.

Watson, Farley and Williams, 1994: *A Guide to Trade Finance*. London: Watson, Farley and Williams (lawyers).

Willsher, Richard D., 1993: *Introduction to Forfaiting*. Couble Notes.

Willsher, Richard D., 1994: *Introduction to Trade Finance*. Couble Notes.
Willsher, Richard D., 1994: *Secure Payment for Overseas Sales*. Self Published.

Index